THE PIPING TRADITIONS
OF THE OUTER ISLES

The Piping Traditions
of the Outer Isles

of the West Coast of Scotland

BRIDGET MACKENZIE

This one is for Jeannie Campbell, in gratitude for her help and friendship, and her generosity in sharing the fruits of her scholarship. She keeps me right.

First published in Great Britain in 2013 by
John Donald, an imprint of Birlinn Ltd
West Newington House
10 Newington Road
Edinburgh
EH9 1QS

www.birlinn.co.uk

ISBN: 978 1 906566 71 5

British Library Cataloguing-in-Publication Data
A catalogue record for this book is available
on request from the British Library

Typeset by Carnegie Book Production, Lancaster
Printed and bound in Britain by Bell and Bain Ltd, Glasgow

Contents

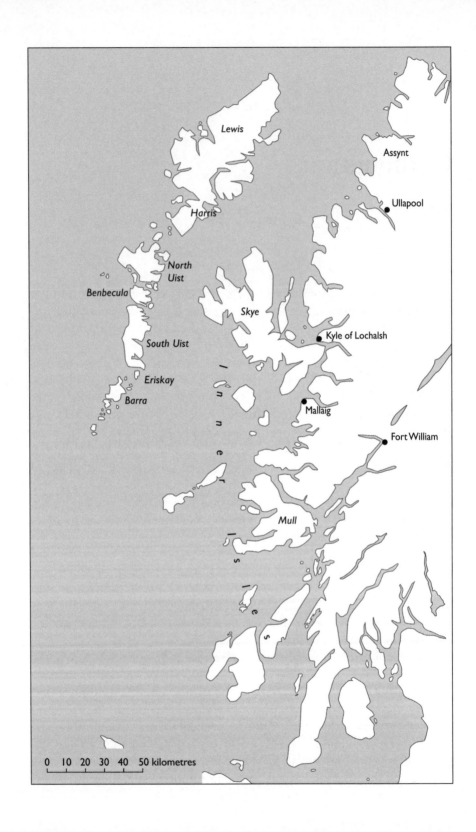

Lewis

Assynt

Ullapool

Harris

North
Uist

Benbecula

Skye

Kyle of Lochalsh

South Uist

Eriskay

Mallaig

Barra

Fort William

Inner Isles

Mull

0 10 20 30 40 50 kilometres

Introduction

Most of this book was written in the early years of the 21st century, but publication was delayed by illness. 2012 saw the appearance of its predecessors, *Piping Traditions of the Inner Isles* and *Piping Traditions of the Isle of Skye*, the third and fourth in the series which began with the North of Scotland and Argyll. This fifth volume will be the last – unless someone else will take on the Central Belt and the East of Scotland.

Anyone with little or no Gaelic is going to feel alien in the Outer Isles, however kind and welcoming the folk there, and it is not always easy to collect piping lore from those who really know. Islanders are naturally cautious about talking freely to a stranger from the mainland, though mention of piping does help. Written sources are not plentiful and usually not much use, though there are some exceptions, such as *Tales from Barra Told By the Coddy* (1959), and the delvings into the Dunvegan muniments by Alick Morrison, published by the Gaelic Society of Inverness in their Transactions.

Tape recordings made by Willie MacLean, Calum Johnstone and others for the School of Scottish Studies give us a taste of the real thing. Valuable information came from Barry Shears and Scott Williams in Nova Scotia, and the work of Josh Dickson in South Uist and Benbecula enriches our knowledge of those islands. By and large, however, evidence about the Outer Isles is scrappy and scattered.

It is encouraging to see the eager response in Lewis to the provision of piping instruction in the schools. Lewis in particular is benefitting from the work of Iain Morrison, assisted by Nicky Gordon, and some first-class players have come to the fore, as a result. Where good instruction is available, the response is phenomenal, from young and old. If only it could be extended to all the islands, which are a huge reservoir of inherited talent, most of it going to waste, there would really be grounds for optimism. Cuts in local authority spending, however, mean that fees for piping instruction in schools have had to be greatly increased, so that many children will be deprived of their chance (unless they have parents both affluent and pipe-loving).

Even before the spending cuts took hold, we were unable to find a piper in Barra, which was amazing – and sad. In South Uist, stalwarts such as Calum Beaton and Louis Morrison keep the tradition going, and piping is still alive in Benbecula and North Uist. In Harris there is continuing conflict on religious grounds; piping in the Long Island is largely confined to Lewis.

I offer the usual warning here, that I have not discussed currently competing pipers here, for fear of jeopardising their chances before the bench. This has led to the absurd situation where I have mentioned Emily MacDonald in the section on Harris, but not her husband Dr Angus (he will doubtless be grateful for that).

A note to Gaelic speakers: as in the first four books of this series, the term piobaireachd is used as the pipers use it, to mean the classical music of the bagpipe. To Gaelic speakers it means simply 'piping' in general, and they have Ceol Mor for the classical works. There is evidence that piobaireachd in this specialised sense was used in the piping world long before the term Ceol Mor was coined, probably in the late 19th century – Ceol Mor seems to have been invented as a partner for Ceol Beag, the light music which had come to the fore when army piping became dominant. A third term, Ceol Meadhonach 'Middle Music', appears to be the creation of Archibald Campbell of Kilberry, or Sheriff Grant of Rothiemurchus, or possibly General Thomason, none of whom was a native Gaelic speaker.

Many write piobaireachd in its anglicised form pibroch, which has the sole merit of distinguishing the two uses of the term. Both are often found in the plural form, piobaireachds and pibrochs, which must offend any Gaelic speaker: it is comparable to saying 'musics' in English. Piobaireachd is an abstract noun, with no plural when used in either sense. A possible compromise is the term 'piobaireachd works'.

The format of this book is much as before, here starting with Mingulay and the southern string of small isles, working northward through the Outer Islands, and ending with Lewis. I have tried to make each section complete in itself, and this, as before, leads to some repetition, but that is, I hope, kept to the minimum.

As a general policy I try to visit all the places I have written about – possible for all except St Kilda – and this has been pure pleasure with the islands. Everywhere, the mention of piping has opened doors, and we have been made to feel welcome by all who share our interest. I would like to thank all who helped, and in particular those named here – but there were many more, and my debt to them is as great as ever.

My sincere thanks go to the following for their generous help:

Malcolm Bangor Jones, Dundee
Calum Beaton, South Uist
Jeannie Campbell, Glasgow
Myles Campbell, Gairloch
Calum Ferguson, Stornoway, Lewis
Catriona Garbutt, Benbecula
Norman Johnston, North Uist
Rona Lightfoot, Inverness
Emily MacDonald, Skye
William MacDonald ('Benbecula'), Inverness
William M. MacDonald, Inverness
Neil Campbell MacGougan, Dingwall
John MacKay, South Uist
Colin Scott MacKenzie, Stornoway
Duncan MacLean, Ardrishaig
Angus J. MacLellan, Glasgow
John A. MacLellan, Benbecula
Neil MacMillan, South Uist
William Matheson, Edinburgh
Christina Morrison, Skye
Fred Morrison, South Uist
Ludovic Morrison, South Uist
Dr Barrie MacLachlan Orme, Australia
Barry Shears, Nova Scotia
Robert Wallace, Glasgow
Roy Wentworth, Gairloch
Scott Williams, Nova Scotia

Some of these friends have died since I spoke with them; I have kept their names in the list, as a token of my gratitude.

There are bound to be errors and omissions in this book, and I would appreciate being told of these. Please address them to me by post, via the publishers.

Abbreviations

In the lists of tunes, the following abbreviations are used:

J	Jig, preceded by the time signature and followed by the number of parts
GA	Gaelic Air, followed by the number of parts
H	Hornpipe, preceded by the time signature and followed by the number of parts
M	March, preceded by the time signature and followed by the number of parts
NoP	Notices of Pipers
P	Piobaireachd (Ceol Mor), followed by the number of variations, including the Ground (Urlar)
R	Reel, followed by the number of parts
RM	Retreat March, followed by the number of parts
S	Strathspey, followed by the number of parts
SA	Slow Air, followed by the number of parts
SM	Slow March, followed by the number of parts

In the text, sources and bibliography, the following abbreviations are used:

HLI	Highland Light Infantry
MSR	March, Strathspey and Reel
QOH	Queen's Own Highlanders
SPA	Scottish Pipers Association
TGSI	*Transactions of the Gaelic Society of Inverness*

Where names only are given in the lists of Sources in the text, the source was a personal interview or correspondence.

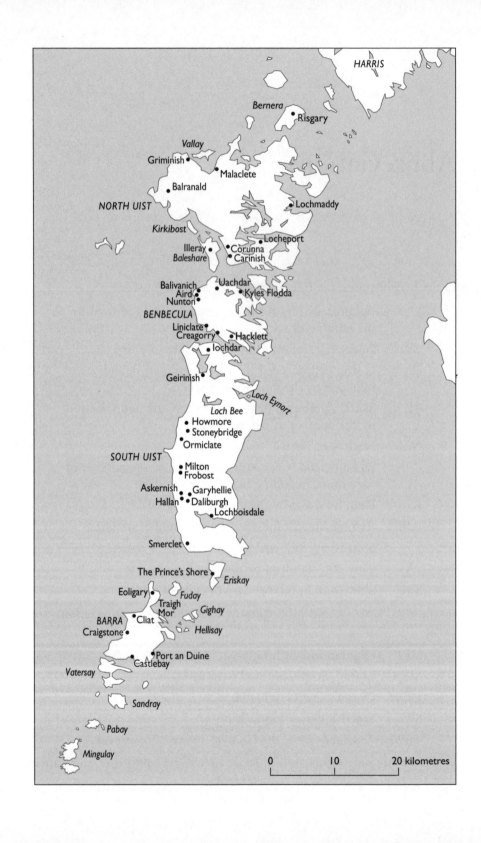

HARRIS

Bernera
● Risgary

Vallay
Griminish ●
● Malaclete
● Balranald

NORTH UIST

● Lochmaddy

Kirkibost

Illeray ● ● Corunna
Baleshare ● Carinish
● Locheport

Balivanich ● Uachdar
Aird ● ● Kyles Flodda
Nunton ●

BENBECULA

Liniclate ●
Creagorry ● ● Hacklett
● Iochdar

Geirinish ●

Loch Eynort

Loch Bee
● Howmore
● Stoneybridge
● Ormiclate

SOUTH UIST

● Milton
● Frobost

Askernish ● ● Garyhellie
Hallan ● ● Daliburgh
● Lochboisdale

Smerclet ●

The Prince's Shore ●
Eriskay

Eoligary ● Fuday
Traigh
Mor ● Gighay
BARRA ● Cliat
Craigstone ● Hellisay

● Port an Duine
Castlebay

Vatersay

Sandray

● Pabay

● Mingulay

0   10   20 kilometres

Mingulay, Vatersay, Barra and Eriskay

Pipe Tunes Associated with Mingulay, Vatersay, Barra and Eriskay

Angus John MacNeil of Barra, by A.J. MacNeil 6/8 J 4
Castlebay R 4
The Claymore, by C. Hunter
Dan Rory MacDougall 2/4 M
Donald Johnston of Castle Bay, by George Johnstone 6/8 M 2
The Eriskay Love Lilt, or *An Eriskay Song* SA 1
The Fair Maid of Barra, by Donald J. Campbell 6/8 SA 2
Father MacMillan of Barra, or *John MacMillan of Barra*, by Norman
    MacDonald 2/4 M 4
Leaving Barra, by Michael MacKinnon 6/8 SM 1
Leaving Eriskay, by Donald McInnes 9/8 SA 2
MacNeill Is Lord There P 6
MacNeill of Barra's Lament P (in Gesto's Collection)
MacNeill of Barra's March P 7
MacNeill's March 2/4 M 4
MacNeill's Oran Mor 6/8 SA 1
Malcolm Johnston, by Roderick Campbell R 4 and 6/8 J 4
Marion My Wife Returns No More, arr. by Malcolm Johnstone 3/4 SA 2
Merrily Sailing, by Malcolm (Calum Mor) MacInnes 6/8 M 4
Michael Joseph MacKinnon, by Evan MacRae 2/4 M 2
The Mingulay Boat Song 3/4 SM 2
The Mingulay Love Song, by A.M. Cairns 9/8 SM 3
Mingulay Wedding R 2
Moireach bho Eirisgeidh, by Charles B. Stephen 6/8 SA 2
Murdo MacGillivray of Eoligarry, by Roderick MacDonald R 4
The Pride of Barra P 8
Ruairidh Barrach (Ruairidh of Barra's Reel) R 4
Vatersay Bay, by William M. MacDonald 6/8 SA 2

See also, below, lists of the compositions of Duncan Johnstone and Neil
Angus MacDonald.

Mingulay

Mingulay, now uninhabited, is at the southern tip of the island chain, with only Berneray lying south of it (the chain is Berneray, Mingulay, Pabay, Sandray, Vatersay, Barra, Fuday, Eriskay, South Uist, Benbecula, North Uist, Bernera, Harris, Lewis). It is reached by private arrangement for a boat from Barra or Vatersay.

Mingulay appears to be a Norse name, possibly a corrupt form of N *mikill-ey* 'big island'. These islands to the south of Vatersay were known as 'The Bishop's Isles', and Mingulay was the biggest of them; it has towering cliffs, six hundred feet high, on its west side. The Gaelic name is Miughlaigh.

The island was evacuated in 1912, at the request of the few remaining inhabitants, when they found they could no longer make a decent living there. A few years earlier some of the Mingulay crofters had joined the movement to squat illegally on the neighbouring islands of Sandray and Vatersay, which were much more fertile than Mingulay and, crucially, had adequate facilities for landing boats. Some of the squatters, known as the 'Vatersay Raiders' were put on trial in Edinburgh and given three months in prison (see also below, Vatersay and Barra).

In his book *Mingulay: An Island and Its People*, Ben Buxton wrote that singing songs was an important part of life there – as it was in St Kilda. These songs included love songs and many kinds of work songs, and local islanders would compose their own, as well as singing the traditional songs. Ben Buxton points out that these were all sung unaccompanied by any instrument. The only music they had was that of the pipe, but it was used exclusively for dancing. Pipers played for wedding dances, but there was no piper at the funerals.

The Mingulay Boat Song, made popular by Marjorie Kennedy Fraser, has been set as a 3/4 Slow March in two parts for the pipes. It is said that it was never sung in Mingulay, being a West Highland air to which Hugh Robertson, conductor of the Glasgow Orpheus Choir, wrote the words in 1938. He included a line about the womenfolk waiting at the pier-head for their men to come home from the fishing – but Mingulay never had a pier, and that lack of a safe landing place was one of the main reasons for the evacuation.

Ben Buxton writes that Hugh Robertson, born in Glasgow, was very fond of the melody of a Lochaber song called *Creag Ghuanach*, which celebrates a crag near Loch Treig (about 10 miles east of Ben Nevis). When he was looking for a suitable sea shanty, he adapted this tune, selected Mingulay as being a suitably romantic name, and wrote the words to go with the music. Ben Buxton adds: 'It is ironic that this song should be the only well-known song associated with the island, and, for many, the only reason they have heard the name Mingulay at all.'

Mr Buxton describes a typical Mingulay wedding in 1902: each wedding would last at least two days, as the couple had to go to Barra for the ceremony, and the celebrations that followed were held on Mingulay itself. When the bridal pair returned, they would go to the house next door to the bride's family's house where those who had travelled a distance could change their clothes. Meanwhile the dance started, with pipes played by two or three pipers in turn, depending on who was available – there was no fiddler on Mingulay, nor any tradition of one. Weddings were usually in autumn or winter, so as not to hinder the vital agricultural work of spring and summer, but this timing often meant delays if the weather turned bad on them.

Neil Angus MacDonald recalled his mother telling how his father had been over from Barra at a wedding in Mingulay, which lasted three days. 'In those days the piper sat on an up-turned creel and played away. If he thought he wasn't being suitably treated, the reed went missing. No music. No dancing. Everybody searching on the floor for the reed and when the piper thought that amends had been made, he found the reed in the upturn of his trousers, and proceeded as before' (BBC radio recording, 1972).

Sources
BBC radio recording, 1972
Keith Branigan, *Barra*
Ben Buxton, *Mingulay*
Queen's Own Highlanders,*The Cabar Feidh Collection*
Frederick Rea, *A School in South Uist*

Vatersay

Vatersay, pronounced VAA-ter-say, is a Norse name probably meaning 'Water-island'. It is reached nowadays by a causeway from Barra.

The history of the islands of Vatersay, Mingulay, Sandray and Barra is closely interwoven, especially in the early 1900s, when the 'Vatersay

Raiders' were imprisoned for seizing land-holdings in Sandray and Vatersay. The crofters on Mingulay had reached the end of their tether, recognising that they could no longer maintain their life on the island; cottars (landless tenants) in Barra were also restless, both parties wanting to settle in the comparatively fertile land of Vatersay. Sporadic raids had been made, and application sent to the land owner, Lady Cathcart, for allocation of plots – to which she did not respond. In February 1908, 30 families from Barra and Mingulay had moved to Vatersay, and two from Mingulay had settled in Sandray, which had no other inhabitants at that time.

Ten of the Vatersay raiders, of whom half were from Mingulay, were taken to court in Edinburgh and sentenced to three months' imprisonment, but they were released after six weeks, returning to a heroes' welcome in Castlebay. Lady Cathcart then sold both Vatersay and Sandray to the government, who created sixty crofts in Vatersay, with common grazing on Sandray – the Mingulay settlers from there moved to Vatersay, led by a piper. There were more applicants for the crofts than land available, and some of the original Raiders who had served prison sentences were excluded, which caused outrage locally.

MICHAEL MACKINNON, known as 'Bronni', was a seaman from Vatersay who came of a family widely talented in poetry and song. He based the pipe tune *Leaving Barra* on a song which tells of his voyage to Montreal, recalling his early days when he fished for his living. He seems to have composed both the music and the words of the song, but left it in one part as it was felt the air of the song could stand by itself.

The Slow Air *Vatersay Bay* was composed when Willie M. MacDonald was on a working trip to Barra (he was a water engineer with Highland Region). Father MacCormick invited Willie to accompany him by boat to the Isle of Vatersay, where he had his Sunday service. It was a beautiful sunny day, and as Willie was waiting for Father MacCormick, he lay on the beach 'and this was the result of that tranquility'.

Barra

Barra, now linked by causeway to Vatersay, is the most southerly of the larger islands in the chain known as the Western, or Outer, Isles. English speakers often call these the Hebrides, but the term is unknown in Gaelic. Hebrides is derived from a Greek word, probably based on an ancient, pre-Gaelic name picked up by Greek and Roman map-makers as Hebudes, and later mis-copied, so that not only is the term Hebrides probably not Gaelic, it is a copying error (as are the Grampians, and St Kilda). In Gaelic the Outer Isles are *Innse-Gall* 'The Isles of the Foreigners (or Norsemen)'.

The origins of the name Barra are equally obscure; the island is said by some to have been named for Saint Barr, but this may be zealous rationalisation by pious Catholics. Others associate the name with Gaelic words for 'corn' or 'the sea', or a Norse word meaning 'barley', but these are probably also merely attempts to explain a much older, obscure name.

To reach Barra, take the car ferry from Oban to Castlebay, a voyage of about three and a half hours, with superb scenery in clear weather. Or you may fly from Glasgow to Barra, where the landing is on the beach at Traigh Mor and possible only when the tide is out.

For a really enjoyable week, given favourable weather, try crossing from Ullapool to Stornoway on an 'Island Hopscotch' ferry ticket, and drive (or cycle) through the Long Island to Leverburgh, exploring Lewis and Harris as you go; cross by a small ferry from Harris to Bernera, explore that island and North Uist, drive across the causeway to Benbecula, then to South Uist, seeking out all the many places with piping connections, before crossing the bridge to Eriskay. Take the short ferry trip to Barra – then, after a visit to Vatersay, travel by steamer to Oban from Castlebay. Mention of an interest in piping will ensure you a welcome wherever you go in the islands (except in Harris on the Sabbath).

The name always associated with Barra piping is Johnston or Johnstone. The Barra Johnstones, who were Catholics, do not seem to be related to the Protestant Johnstons of Coll and Islay. The name Johnston may be spelled with or without the final *e*, at will – and sometimes without a *t*. These spelling variants have no significance at all.

Pipers in Barra

JOHN MACALLAN (this is probably a patronymic, that is, an indication that John's father's name was Allan, rather than a surname) was a piper in Barra. In 1613 a complaint was laid against him when he led twenty men in an invasion of the house of Rory MacNeill of Barra with dirks and drawn swords, putting violent hands on the inmates and robbing the house (Notices of Pipers).

Calum MacNeill and his Sons

Barry Shears, in his book *Dance to the Piper* (2008), in the section headed 'The Fraser Highlanders' (pp.134–7), gives an interesting account of the piping MacNeill family from Barra, descendants of CALUM (MALCOLM) MACNEILL who emigrated to Cape Breton, NS, probably in 1802.

Iain (or John) MacPherson, the well-known Barra story-teller whose by-name was 'The Coddy' (1876–1955), gave his account of the landing of Prince Charles Edward in Eriskay in 1745. His ship was the French vessel *Du Teillay,* and on arrival off the Scottish coast she was piloted into the Eriskay anchorage by a man called Calum the Piper (he was Calum MacNeill from the island of Gighay in the Sound of Barra, between Barra and Eriskay). The Prince's party landed at the beach now called Coilleag a' Phrionnsa, translated by John Lorne Campbell as 'the Prince's Shore', and, headed by Calum the Piper, the Prince was taken ashore by a man from Eriskay called John MacEachen. 'Then they opened up a big spread, which consisted of the famous liqueur Drambuie, and the piper played at the spread, and I know the place well' (translated from the Coddy's Gaelic by John Lorne Campbell).

The Notices of Pipers have a slightly different version: they say that the piper was DONALD MACNEILL, piper to MacNeill of Barra, and he was on Eriskay when the Prince's ship arrived and he was persuaded to pilot it into harbour. He was reputed to be a MacCrimmon pupil, and a 'finished performer'.

The Coddy added that several years later, Calum the Piper fought on the Heights of Abraham, Quebec, alongside his Chief, MacNeill of Barra. He was MacNeill's valet as well as his piper 'and when Mac-Neill was wounded by a French bullet it took Calum six long weeks, sucking and cleaning the wound, until one day he sucked the bullet out of the back of his ear.' (Barry Shears has a slightly different version of this story, ending with the comment made by Calum that if he had not earlier had the blood of the MacNeill chiefs in him, he had it now.)

After the war was over, Calum came back to Barra but he said he would not stay there any longer, and he left for the Island of Cape Breton with his seven sons. And seeing a little corner of Cape Breton, he called it 'Piper's Cove', because it was so like the little cove he left behind on the Island of Gighay.

This island may be seen from the ferry which links Eriskay to Barra, and the narrow strait between Gighay and its neighbouring isle of

Hellisay must be the 'little cove'. This Gighay should not be confused with the island of the same name off Kintyre, much further south.

The Coddy mentioned Calum the Piper in other stories, saying that Calum's descendants did very well in their new life, becoming important businessmen 'all over the States and Cape Breton'. Before they left, another story has it, Calum and his sons were going to the fishing, 'and they ordered a smack from the Island of Arran to come to supply them with salt. Calum went aboard with his seven sons to discharge the cargo. Now they set up planks and made stages to unload the boat, and they made the stages in a position that the one man could hand the other the barrel of salt, and so hand over hand until it was piled on the shore. The Arran man was so amazed at seeing the activity of the men discharging the boat that he did not tell the boys how much the salt cost. He said 'Good-bye, boys, we will call to see you again next year', and went off without his money.' They emigrated before he came back.

Barry Shears mentions DONALD MACNEILL, born around 1758 in Barra, a brother of the above Calum Piobaire. He emigrated to Cape Breton in 1817, and his petition to the governor for a grant of land gave his occupation as 'piper'. Several of his adult children settled with him at Rudha Dileas, on Bras d'Or Lake, which came to be known as the Lake of the Barra Men, so many piping MacNeills had settled there. They were still known as 'The Pipers' for generations after most of them had given up playing.

Scott Williams names a Nova Scotian piper, HECTOR MACNEILL, who was a son of Malcolm MacNeill of Barra – this Malcolm was Calum the Piper, from Gighay, who figures in the Coddy's stories. Hector emigrated in 1802, going to live at Piper's Cove, in Cape Breton. His brother RORY MACNEILL went with him – he was also a piper. According to the Coddy, Calum and all his seven sons went out together. The testimony of Scott Williams seems to tally generally with that of the Coddy, and the Notices of Pipers may have got the first name wrong, confusing Calum with his brother, or one of his sons.

Keith Branigan has an account of these emigrations from Barra in 1802 and 1817. There had been a big emigration of Barra families in 1801, apparently on the ships *Sarah* and *Dove* – but no Barra people are named on the passenger lists of these two vessels. It is thought that the captain took on many more than he acknowledged, and even then some applicants were left behind. They would have been taken on by two other ships in 1802, the names of which have not been recorded, and the first wave of piping MacNeills, the piper Calum and his seven piping sons, must have been among them. Possibly up to a thousand people left Barra in those two years, an exodus organised by two MacNeill tacksmen, Roderick Og of Breivig and James of Earsary.

One reason for this wave of emigration was conflict between the Catholic population of Barra and their Protestant chief, known as Roderick the Gentle. This conflict reached a peak in 1800, making the Barra folk uneasy. The years immediately before 1801 had seen poor harvests, and food was scarce. Emigration agents were active in the islands at this time, and there was a brief lull in the hostilities against France which made crossing the Atlantic both safer and cheaper. In 1803 the wars with Napoleon were renewed, and fares to Canada were trebled, so that emigration fell away after that, until 1816.

A certain Simon Fraser in 1816 was stirring up emigration fever once again, partly as a result of the defeat of Napoleon at Waterloo in 1815. The MacNeill chief offered his help with arrangements and fares, but his offer was flatly refused by his tenants, who did not trust him. Keith Branigan tells us that in May 1817, two ships, the *William Tell* and the *Hope,* sailed from Greenock with 382 emigrants on board, most of them from Barra, including Calum's brother, Donald, and his sons.

They landed at Cape Breton, Nova Scotia, to find that the agent, Simon Fraser, had let them down: he failed to supply the promised provisions and agricultural implements (rather to the glee of the chief whose offer had been turned down). It seems that the Cape Breton Authorities made good these deficiencies, sending food and tools and transport by boat to different parts of Cape Breton. Such help was most unusual, and documents of the time comment that it was given because of the 'particular circumstances' of the Barra people at this time. There is no record of these circumstances: no mention of famine or sickness, nor conflict between Catholic and Protestant.

The MacGillivrays of Eoligarry

A reel in four parts, *Murdo MacGillivray of Eoligarry*, was composed by Roderick MacDonald (Roddy Roidean from South Uist).

The MacGillivrays were a family of pipers living at the north end of Barra. In the 1880s they held 3,000 acres, about a third of the land in Barra, including most of the good arable areas. The tenant at that time was Dr MacGillivray, who imposed restrictions on the people living on his land: if they gathered shellfish on the foreshore, they had to pay him one day's labour on his estate, and for 'two small cart-loads' of bents (tough grass from the dunes, used for thatching roofs), the cost was twelve days' work for MacGillivray. Another bone of contention was that he insisted on bringing in Presbyterian families to settle in the Catholic island of Barra.

The Coddy had a story about the MacGillivrays:

On the field of Culloden Moor one time was found bagpipes, and a bonny set they were. They were taken to Greenock by the man who found them on the field. Now an uncle of the MacGillivrays of Eoligarry was one time out in Greenock. He was a piper and was very interested in the pipes, especially when he heard they were found on the battlefield of Culloden. He asked could he have a loan of the pipes – either that or could he buy them?

The man said, 'No, you are a piper and I am not, and I will have much pleasure in giving you the pipes, as you can play them.'

So he took them with him to Eoligarry and he left them in charge of MacGillivray's two boys who were then learning to be pipers – and I need not tell you that they were taken care of there – the boys were very fond of playing them, and they remained in that house for over a hundred years.

Well, William was the last surviving of the boys and it was always troubling him what would happen to the pipes when he would fade away. And he decided to give them as a present to the lady who was in charge of the West Highland Museum at Fort William. Her name is Mistress Ryan. I was on one occasion going to Inverness, and William asked me would I convey the pipes to Lochaber – that he was going to give them to Mistress Ryan of Spean Bridge, who was going to see that they would be well looked after. So a day before I left for Inverness I called and the pipes were made up in a beautiful parcel and sealed more than a few times – I believe it took him a fortnight to do it – and 'Here you are' he said, 'John, here are the pipes and give them to Mistress Ryan, and I sincerely hope they will be looked after as well as we did for the last hundred years.'

I took my very best care of them. I asked Captain Duncan Robertson if I could put the pipes in his cabin, to make sure nothing would happen to them, and he said 'Oh yes, certainly, Coddy.' Now I visited him again in his cabin to see if the pipes were in order and then he said 'What have you got in this wonderful parcel?'

'It is not a bottle, anyway, Captain', I said. And then I told him the story, and at that he took out a knife to cut the string and open the parcel.

'Oh no, Captain, you are not going to do any such like', I said. And so I arrived in Lochaber. I had an interview with Mistress Ryan and gave her the pipes.

The Coddy told how he suggested to Mistress Ryan that the pipes should be played at the Glasgow Exhibition of 1938, and she asked who should play them. The Coddy said 'Angus Campbell', and the whole story was announced in the *Radio Times*, and Angus was to play them on the wireless. When MacGillivray of Eoligarry was told about this, he got the minister to bring the Coddy down to Eoligarry so that they could listen together to Angus playing the old pipes. He played *MacIntyre's Lament*, 'a very pathetic pibroch'.

The Coddy said later: 'I was carefully watching the old man, and as Angus Campbell was going into the heart of the piping I saw poor MacGillivray's eyes getting very moist and I clearly understood what was inside. And when Angus was finished, William was leaning heavily on his stick, his eyes were soaking in tears. He could not for a while give us even a remark. Latterly he says, "I am very pleased to hear such an excellent player handling them tonight."'

This piper may have been Angus Campbell from South Uist, or possibly Angus Campbell from Ballachulish, who taught Duncan Johnstone. Neil Campbell of South Uist, the father of Angus Campbell, pupil of John MacDonald, is said to have learned his piping from the Mac-Gillivray pipers at Eoligarry, when he was living in Barra, as a young man. This connection suggests that the player in the above story was Angus from South Uist, a very fine piobaireachd player.

'Old Donald', a Barra Piper

In another story, the Coddy mentions a piper called OLD DONALD at North Bay in Barra, when a boat came in on a particularly stormy night. The skipper had been keeping up the crew's morale by promising them a dram when they reached land. They came to the inn at North Bay, and

> it happened that there was in the house an old piper called Donald. He loved a dram, did Donald. And he never refused a dram when he was at a wedding – when he was full himself he took the dram and blew it down the pipes. The skipper ordered a bottle – and a big one – but out of the hundred pounds they made at the fishing this was little enough. They started the bottle, and gave Donald a good share.
>
> Then the stories began and another bottle was called. Then the skipper felt inclined to have a dance for himself and told Donald to play the pipes. The four boys (the crew) stood up and danced a reel just as they were, in their oilskins and seaboots. When they were finished they put off their oilskins, and the old woman of the house gave them something to eat, and Donald played the pipes, and after the third bottle, the old woman says 'Well', she says, 'That is all you will get' and

she sent them to their beds and they were very comfortable. And the next day they saw their wives and children in very good order.

This Donald may have been DONALD MACAULAY, listed by Barry Shears among the earlier settlers in Nova Scotia. Born in Barra, he came to Washabuck, NS, in 1817.

The 1851 Census lists a piper named DONALD MACKINNON, aged 30, living at a place in Barra called Green (Gaelic Grian. The OS map spells it Greian, near Cliat). Interestingly, he was born in South Uist, but had married a Barra girl and had a son. Giving his occupation as 'Piper', presumably he had enough engagements to make a living.

Fairy Piping in Barra

The Coddy tells the familiar story of the man lured into a fairy mound, where he was kept for several generations; while walking up from the shore 'he heard music, pipe music of the finest order, and going closer he found a stone there, and when he turned the stone he saw there was a stairway going down, and he walked down. And there was the piper, dressed in kilts and playing the pipes – an old grey-headed man beautifully dressed in green, with silver-buckled shoes. As soon as the stranger came in, he was cordially invited to sit up at the fire, and this the man did. And then the music continued.' Usually in such stories the mortal is taught piping by the fairy folk, but not in this case – he merely enjoyed food and music before returning to his village, to find hundreds of years had passed. This is a familiar, and almost universal, folk-story element.

The Cave of Gold, in Barra

The Coddy told that story which crops up in connection with so many caves of the Highlands and Islands; this certainly suggests that it was Celtic in origin, whether Irish or Hebridean. In the Coddy's version, which he entitled *Uaimh an Oir, The Cave of Gold*, he says there was a tradition that it was possible to walk underground from the west coast of Barra to the east, from Cliat to Port an Duine, across the north of the island.

So a party set out, and there were two pipers and three dogs, to explore. And one of the pipers started to play the pipes at Cliat, and – very peculiar – those that were following above were hearing the pipes and keeping the course until they came to Port an Duine, and the pipes then faded away and none of the party were ever discovered. How they met their fate no one knows, but the dogs that came out, they came out bare, without a hair from their nose to their tail; and what was the cause of that no one could form an opinion. But it is believed they met some queer folk below the island who killed the two pipers. And as the dogs could not tell what happened, and they were showing no signs of recovery, the people decided to shoot them. Therefore there is no trace of what happened to the party.

There is no explanation of the name *The Cave of Gold*. Perhaps the doomed pipers were playing the tune of that name.

These traditional tales told by the Coddy show how much pipes and piping were part of island life. The pipe was the instrument they used for both celebration and mourning.

Sources

The Coddy (John MacPherson): see John Lorne Campbell, *Tales from Barra*
William M. MacDonald
Barry Shears, *Dance to the Piper*
Scott Williams, *Pipers of Nova Scotia*

More Pipers in Barra

Scott Williams said that LACHLAN MACLEAN (1728–1842), emigrated from Barra in 1817, at the age of 89. His wife was Annie MacPhee. He had fought at Culloden when he was eighteen, probably as a piper, and his two sons, Peter and Roderick, were pipers, too. On their way abroad from Barra – they emigrated as an entire family – they bought new pipes in Tobermory, and these remained in the family in Nova Scotia until 1897. Lachlan died at the age of 114.

Lachlan's son PETER MACLEAN was a piper, living at Washabuck, Victoria County, Cape Breton, NS. He was unmarried, and drowned in 1827. He and his brother RODERICK MACLEAN were both born in Barra, and both were 'ear' players, i.e. did not play from written music. Roderick married Ann MacIntyre, in NS. It is not clear whether JOHN MACLEAN, listed by Barry Shears as a piper from Barra who settled at Big Pond in 1831, was related to Lachlan's family. Barry's book has a photograph of Roderick MacLean, taken around 1870.

RORY MACDOUGALL (1848–1936) was a piper in Nova Scotia, living at Ingonish. He was the son of Donald MacDougall, of the family of Malcolm who ran the grist mill in Barra in the 18th century. Born in Nova Scotia, both Rory and his son DAN RORY MACDOUGALL were well known as pipers as well as playing the fiddle and becoming expert step-dancers. Barry Shears tells how Rory used to travel all over Cape Breton, playing at dances, and he was employed by a horse-trader to pipe up and down dusty roads to attract customers' attention. He was also piper to the 94th Regiment, Victoria Battalion, in the 1890s.

Rory's son, Dan Rory (1885–1957), was known for his versatility and his stamina. On one occasion he walked more than thirty miles to attend a wedding, at which he played all night and most of the day, alternating between pipes and violin. He was unable to read music, but had memorised an enormous number of tunes. Barry Shears has a photograph of him playing his pipe, seated, at a dance in Ingonish, around 1955. Tape recordings of his fiddle-playing demonstrate the richness of his musical tradition.

Dan Rory's sons MIKE (1928–1981) and GABRIEL MACDOUGALL (1925–1986) inherited the family's musical talents. Mike was a gifted violinist and composer, and Gabriel played both pipes and violin.

There is a 2/4 March *Dan Rory MacDougall* which appears in Barry Shears' *Gathering of the Clans Collection* (Nova Scotia 1986), and a version of this has been recorded, sung in canntaireachd by Mary Morrison in Barra. Allan MacDonald commented: 'If these tunes went over to Nova Scotia with the early settlers, then this is one of a relatively small number of 2/4 Marches which, at least from published evidence, were played during that period. The four-part 2/4 March is believed to have been a mid- to late-19th century development' (*Piping Times*, June 1992)

The Notices of Pipers name DONALD MACINNES who was born in Lochaber and became piper to Colonel MacNeill of Barra in 1832. He competed at Edinburgh in that year, gaining second prize, after trying unsuccessfully three times in the previous decade. He had another try in 1835 before eventually winning the Prize Pipe in 1841 – but his triumph was spoiled when the other players lodged an objection, asserting that Donald Cameron had played better. Donald MacInnes was related to John MacColl, whose mother was a MacInnes.

Donald may well have been the unnamed piper to Colonel MacNeill of Barra, mentioned in a report in the *Glasgow Herald* in 1836: he played at the anniversary dinner of the Ossianic Society, where the guest of honour was Ranald MacDonald, the Laird of Staffa, who by that time had left Staffa and was living in Stirling and Edinburgh. For the dinner, to accompany the serious drinking, the players were the Society's own (unnamed) piper, Colonel MacNeill's (also unnamed in the report) and 'a youth of extraordinary musical talents in the services

of Staffa'. This last was John MacDonald, grandson of Donald Mac-
Donald, the Edinburgh pipemaker who published his collection of
piobaireachd in 1820.

Father MacMillan of Barra

Father MacMillan of Barra, or *John MacMillan of Barra*, is a well
known tune, a 2/4 March in four parts, popular with fiddlers,
accordionists and dancers as well as with pipers.

FATHER JOHN MACMILLAN OF BARRA is commemorated in this
march by NORMAN MACDONALD. He was the subject of an article by
DAVID BOYLE, published in the *Piping Times* in November 1993, and
quoted here. (David was the composer of *The Sands of Barra* written
when he was living on the island. He moved to Muir of Ord, in Easter
Ross, but later returned to Barra.)

John MacMillan, known as Maighstir Iain, was born at Craigstone,
Barra, in 1880:

> He was well over six feet tall, generously proportioned, and although
> his bearing was one of massive dignity, he was quick to crack a joke
> with his friends, which he would conclude with uproarious laughter,
> while strangers were immediately captivated by his native kindness and
> ingenuousness.
>
> His presence at ceilidhs throughout the Western Isles ensured a
> large turn out, and his own composition *Cluic nan Caintean* and
> MacKinnon's *An Dubh Gleannach* were the songs he was most
> requested to sing. He had an exceptionally fine singing voice, and once
> sang in the Albert Hall in London in the presence of King George VI
> and Queen Elizabeth (then Duke and Duchess of York).
>
> Father MacMillan was also a prolific composer of Gaelic poetry and
> his renditions of these, sad and humorous, were enjoyed and appreciated
> by all who heard them.

In 1923, many of his parishioners left Barra for Alberta, Canada, where
they had been promised land and good housing. Father MacMillan
went with them, and found that the promises were empty. Conditions
were terrible, and he had to fight the Canadian and British governments
for two years before he won any improvement for his people. Once they
were established, he returned to Barra. David Boyle said he had heard
that the priest was deported as a trouble-maker and an embarrassment
to the Canadian authorities.

Back in Barra, he gained a wide reputation as a Gaelic scholar,
and in 1933, John Lorne Campbell of Canna included him in a list of

the leading Gaelicists of his day, describing John MacMillan as 'the doyen of all these ... a native of Barra, great in heart and in body, a wonderful preacher in Gaelic, and a true poet'.

When crofters from Mingulay left their island to take land on Vatersay, in the early 1900s, they were prosecuted and served prison sentences. On their release, a large crowd of well-wishers met them in Castlebay, and they were greeted with applause and song after being piped ashore. It is said that Father MacMillan gave his blessing to the assembled crowd.

He was a friend of Compton MacKenzie, another resident of Barra, who wrote the book *Whisky Galore*, basing the character of Father MacAllister on the real-life Father MacMillan.

John MacMillan's sister was the mother of Duncan Johnstone, who went to live in Glasgow. She married a man from Benbecula. Duncan lost the gift of speaking Gaelic, for which his uncle used to reproach him gently.

Father John MacMillan died in Castlebay, Barra, in 1951, and was buried close to the sea at Borve Point, on the west coast of the island.

Sources

David Boyle
Glasgow Herald 1836
Piping Times
Scott Williams, *Pipers of Nova Scotia*

The Johnstones

CALUM JOHNSTONE (1891–1972) in Barra was a 'prominent exponent' of singing pipe music in canntaireachd, and was himself a piper. He and his sister Annie were known as Clann Aonghais Chaluim (the Children of Angus Calum), and became famous as tradition-bearers who gave information, stories and songs to collectors such as Marjorie Kennedy Fraser and Calum MacLean. The Folklore Institute of Scotland and the School of Scottish Studies had the benefit of receiving some of their material, much of it being songs inherited from their mother, Catriona MacNeill. Annie used to sing the words to *Lament for Red Hector of the Battles*.

Calum sang *port-a-beul* (music sung unaccompanied, for dancing) which he learned from other singers in Barra as a boy, but he probably later developed his singing of canntaireachd along with his own skill as a piper. Described as 'highly literate and highly intelligent' (Morag

MacLeod), he was not only a piper and singer but also a story-teller, proverb-collector and true tradition bearer. The origin of his canntaireachd is not known, but it differs from what we know of the Nether Lorn system, and from the MacCrimmon canntaireachd as recorded on paper by Gesto and Simon Fraser. Calum was emphatic that the note C was not represented by *o* in the canntaireachd.

In 1965, the pilot of the air ambulance to the islands, Captain David Barclay, retired at the age of 60, having logged over a million air-miles, all of them in Scotland. A farewell ceremony was held at the beach air-strip in north Barra, where many islanders had gathered, and as Captain Barclay flew in on his last mission, he was welcomed by Calum Johnstone playing him a salute and leading the crowd to the aircraft to cheer the pilot as he stepped down. The *Stornoway Gazette*'s account said: 'There were speeches, presentations, pats on the back, reminiscences, but above all the noise could be heard the skirling of the pipes, the gallantry of the Scottish music having a counter melody of sadness on this occasion.'

The Captain and the British European Airways representative were then piped along the beach, back to the plane, and Calum played as the aircraft vanished over the horizon.

We are left peevishly wondering why journalists, even on the *Stornoway Gazette,* which should know better, always refer to the 'skirling' of the pipes, as if that was a compliment.

Calum, born and brought up in Barra, lived for many years in Edinburgh, where he was Secretary to the Highland Pipers' Society. He died on 4 December 1972, after piping the coffin of his friend, Sir Compton MacKenzie, to his grave in Eoligarry, Barra.

Barra had a number of excellent canntaireachd singers, notably MARY MORRISON and FLORA BOYD, but Morag MacLeod says that the canntaireachd used for singing piobaireachd was not the same as that used for waulking songs (sung by women shrinking tweed).

MALCOLM JOHNSTONE was born in Barra but lived in Edinburgh. He was a good all-round player, taught by Willie Ross in the Castle. He is described in the Notices of Pipers as 'a frequent prize-winner in the early 20th century'. D.R. MacLennan said he loved to play in the train travelling north to catch the boat to Barra. On one occasion, he was playing John A. MacLellan's tune, *The Bens of Jura* when he was heard by fellow-passengers Marjorie Kennedy Fraser and the Rev. Kenneth MacLeod, who declared it was an old traditional Gaelic tune which they had 'discovered' – and they turned it into *The Road To The Isles.* It was remarked at the time that this could hardly be blamed on

Malcolm Johnstone. The tune had many titles given to it by different army regiments: *The Highland Brigade's March to Heilbron* in the South African War, and later, *The 71st's Farewell to Dover, The Burning Sands of Egypt* and *The Sands of Cairo*. The composer had to take Mrs Fraser and Mr MacLeod to court before he received any royalties for this very popular tune.

Sources
Morag MacLeod
D.R. MacLennan
Piping Times
Stornoway Gazette

Duncan Johnstone (1925–1999)

In 1996, the Balvenie Medal was awarded to DUNCAN JOHNSTONE for services to piping 'in recognition of more than fifty years as a first-rate teacher, composer and performer', as Robert Wallace put it, in his interview for the *West Highland Free Press*, published later in the *Piping World*. And Robert added 'No one deserved it more'. Duncan's comment was 'It's nice to have a bit of recognition'.

There followed a most interesting and entertaining interview, in which Robert brought out the essential Hebridean quality of Duncan's character. Among other things, Duncan said: 'When I visited Father John MacMillan during my holidays, I used to go to see this old man with him, he was bed-ridden, but he used to sit up when I took the practice chanter to him. He couldn't read music and his fingering was as false as hell, but if you didn't look at the fingers and just listened, the music was brilliant. I got a feeling for that type of music' – and he memorised hundreds of old tunes and old styles in Barra.

In the *Piping Times*, in January 2000, Robert wrote of Duncan: 'Everyone knew his ability as a top-class piper, his rock-steady, though round, style, the crispest of finger work and an expressive form so west-coast that you could almost hear the Atlantic swell crashing onto the machair strand with every off beat. His tunes, too, were deeply rooted in that culture, and are all the better for it.'

Deeply Hebridean though he was, Duncan spent most of his life away from the islands. His home was in the south side of Glasgow; he had lived as a boy just off the Paisley Road, in Glasgow. He spent the war years at sea, in the Royal Navy, serving mainly in submarines and minesweepers in the Mediterranean, work he described as 'dodgy,

I suppose'. He learned all his piping in Glasgow rather than in Barra, because 'there was no one there except Neil Angus MacDonald and Calum Johnstone who played piobaireachd [and they both left the island in the war years]. Going to Roddy [MacDonald, from South Uist] was the next best thing to being taught by someone from Barra. Barra was the poor relation in piping compared to South Uist. In South Uist, for instance, they could play from music, but in Barra it was all learned by ear' – which many might think accounted for the exceptionally musical quality of Barra piping.

Duncan's first piping lessons were when he was nine years old. A friend was learning, and Duncan's father, from Benbecula, was keen for his son to learn too, he himself being a very poor player. Duncan and his friend went to Angus Campbell, a Glasgow policeman who came from Ballachulish, in Argyll (not the South Uist Angus Campbell, pupil of John MacDonald, Inverness). This Angus had been taught by John MacColl and Willie Lawrie, and was known for his clean, crisp fingering.

As soon as he was on the full pipe, Duncan joined the St Francis Boys' Guild pipe band, 'and that was good fun'. On leaving school, he served his time as a cabinet maker, an apprenticeship cut short by the war. He told Robert how he had been offered a place as a piper in the Black Watch, towards the end of the war, but preferred to go home and complete his time as an apprentice. He was then 21, and plunged back into the piping world, still going to Angus, who by that time had retired from the police. Soon Angus said he could teach Duncan no more, 'you'll have to go to someone above me', and he suggested Roderick MacDonald (Roddy Roidean) from South Uist, who was then in the band of the City of Glasgow Police. Duncan also went to 'Wee Donald' MacLean for a while.

He felt an empathy with Roddy MacDonald, who encouraged him to develop his own island style of playing piobaireachd. 'It was just the way it happened. I didn't set out to do that, it just came to me, it was a natural thing.'

He had done a little competing in his teens, and recalled a practice chanter competition in 1938 – 'Calum Johnstone from Barra was the judge, so I won the prize! I've still got it to this day. Do you know what it was? . . . bear in mind I was only a boy of 13 . . . a whisky flask! It must have been an investment for when I was older.'

Duncan was never a major competitor, being temperamentally unsuited to competition, and it has to be admitted that his love of a good dram interfered with a focused competing career. He did not attempt Oban or Inverness, though he attended the Uist Games. He used to learn the set tunes every year, presumably for teaching purposes, but 'I was just not interested enough in competing, in whether I could beat Tom, Dick or Harry. I liked to play well, right enough'. He did compete at Braemar, and at Taynuilt and Luss. 'I once played at Cowal. It was old George MacDonald who was judging, and the tune he gave me was *Grain in Hides and Corn in Sacks*. It was a bad day, so we were playing inside a hall. I was going great guns, but in the crunluath a mach I went into *Praise of Morag*. I finished the tune and turned round, and MacDonald was laughing his head off. But I won the strathspey and reel that day.'

He was a good friend of many of the major players of his time, naming in particular the two Roidean brothers and Donald MacLeod ('I got on well with the wee man. He had returned from the army and came down to run Grainger's shop and I used to visit him regularly when I was a joiner on the Clan Line').

This friendship led to the composition of a tune. Rory Sinclair told how he was visiting Duncan, who asked him if he knew how the tune *Duncan Johnstone* was written. 'Well, we were going on the radio live, and I always knew when the wee man (Donald MacLeod) was writing a new tune because he had a different look in his eye. I knew he was writing a new tune and I could hear him jigging around with something. I thought it was pretty good, but I didn't let on. When it was good I always would laugh, and this was a laughing tune.' Then the wee man said to him about an hour later 'What do you think of that tune I'm writing?' and Duncan said 'I think it's hellish', and Donald said 'That's why I'm calling it *Duncan Johnstone*.'

Duncan enjoyed playing in a pipe band, with experience in the Glasgow Shepherds' band and the Glasgow Corporation Transport band, under 'Big Donald' MacLean. He also liked playing for dancing, and at one time was playing at dances in the Cuba Hall, Paisley Road, on Monday nights, the Kingston Hall on Wednesdays and Fridays, and St Margaret's Hall on Saturdays. 'That's where I did all my practice and where I learned about rhythm. Angus Campbell used to say playing for an eightsome reel was a long blow and that you had to play a two-parted tune 29 times to complete the dance. Well, I used to play 29 different two-parted reels without any repeat. I used to go into all sorts of stuff. I always played sitting down. I loved playing for dancers, and the pipes were always singing'.

As a youngster he had no pipe, 'as the old man was only a labourer and couldn't afford to buy me a set'. But he managed to buy a set of ivory Hendersons going for only £15, and 'they did me for the rest of my playing career'.

Perhaps, for most of us, the climax of that career was the famous SPA Knock-Out competition of 1964, the first time it was held, and Duncan met his friend Donald MacLeod in the Final. Duncan had not been invited to enter, but he went along with John MacFadyen to watch the draw. Once there, it emerged that John M. MacKenzie had withdrawn, and Duncan was asked to take his place. Many suspected that John MacFadyen had engineered this, and were grateful.

He beat Hector MacFadyen in the first round (the result is decided by the audience), and worked his way through the next rounds, to come up against Donald in the Final. He gave the Cup he won that night to one of his pupils, Dr Myron Berwick of Brooklyn, New York, who later said 'I was never sure why he gave it to me, I think it may have been because I was his worst pupil, but his good friend'. Myron passed the cup on to the College, after Duncan's death. Duncan won the Knock-Out again in 1966.

Duncan began his teaching career in the 1970s; he was an instructor at the College of Piping (1974–78), before he started his own school in Robertson Street (1976–79). He also taught at home. 'I had a lot of good ones who stopped, and a lot of bad ones who didn't,' he said. He never felt it was difficult to put the message over. 'They had come to learn, and I could always find a way round a problem. Teaching is always a challenge because you never get two people playing the same. It is just as hard to teach a good player as it is a bad one . . . I enjoy every minute of it'.

Alex Mackenzie was a pupil at the College in the 1970s, and lucky enough to go to Duncan. Coming late in life to piobaireachd, and not wishing to waste Duncan's time, Alex said that he wanted just to get a feel for it and learn perhaps a few Grounds – but Duncan would have none of this. 'If you learn from me you learn it all,' he said, and he made him play complete works, opening Alex's eyes to the Great Music, a gift for which he will always be grateful.

Duncan was keen to instil a feeling for the music of piobaireachd, as he deplored the modern style. 'I listen to a lot of playing on the radio and I don't get any music out of it at all. There's some very good technical playing and good pipes, but it is all so mechanical it leaves you cold.' He said he could not play 'kitchen music', nor did he understand it. We are reminded of Seumas MacNeill's story of how he and Duncan used to argue about the merit of competing, Seumas maintaining that a piper always played his best on the platform, 'with the adrenalin running'. Duncan disagreed, saying 'No, no, when you're playing away in the kitchen, that's when you're at your best. No strain, no tension.' Seumas said 'Nonsense. Anyway you've never heard me playing in the kitchen', to which Duncan replied 'I've heard you on the platform, and that's bad enough.'

Duncan was teaching the son of the BBC's Iain Anderson. The boy was a keen Rangers fan, but Duncan, being from Barra, supported Celtic. One day after Celtic had scored a notable win, Duncan started young Anderson on a new tune he had written, saying it was called *Linowt*. The boy liked it, learning it diligently, and asked what the title meant. Duncan laughed, and said 'Read it backwards.'

Among his best pupils was Roddy MacLeod, now Director of Piping at the Piping Centre in Glasgow, a former Pipe Major of the Scottish Power band, and a leading competitor. Roddy admits that at first Duncan used to frighten the living daylights out of him, 'but I stuck with him until ill-health made him take a year out. Later I sort of drifted back to him, going to his house for tuition'. Many feel they can hear Duncan's influence in Roddy's music.

Duncan used to tell how his uncle, Father John MacMillan of Barra (for whom the well-known March was made by Norman MacDonald), one day asked him how his Gaelic was getting on: living in Glasgow he was largely English-speaking. Looking sheepish, Duncan said 'Oh, I can't speak it, Father, but I can understand it'. His uncle looked at him, smiled, and said 'My dog can do that, Duncan'.

For many their most vivid memory of Duncan was a radio broadcast of conversation between him and Neil Angus MacDonald, with Duncan playing and Neil Angus recalling far-off piping days in Barra.

Duncan Johnstone was a prolific composer. His first composition was a Slow March he made as a young boy in the St Francis boy band. He never wrote it down, but kept it in his memory all his life. His masterpiece is held by many to be his march *Farewell to Nigg*. His son Neil, a professional cellist, played it at Duncan's funeral at St Helen's Church, Glasgow; Duncan's pupil, John MacInnes of Strathclyde Police, was the piper at the graveside.

His poignant piobaireachd work *Lament for Alan My Son*, composed when Alan died from leukaemia, was played at the Memorial Service for the little children killed at Dunblane, and was included in the Book of Remembrance. Of its composition, Robert Wallace wrote 'the story of how the tune came to Duncan as he listened to his dying son's laboured breathing (the long high Gs were the intake of breath and the following E with high A gracenote the exhalation) is almost too heart-rending to repeat'.

This work has been taken by his son Neil and worked into an orchestral piece named *Suite for Alan*. It incorporates not only the playing of the lament on the pipes, but also many of Duncan's light music compositions, woven into movements played by the full orchestra. Pipers Allan MacDonald, Iain MacDonald and Roddy MacLeod took part in the recording of this work, which is on sale as a CD entitled *Pipes and Strings – Suite for Alan*.

Duncan's total of 70 works includes:

Alex MacLean of Lurebost 4/4 M 4
Andrew Bain of Kytra 6/8 J 4
Barbara's Jig (parts 3 & 4) 6/8 J 4
Bonnie (Isle of) Coll 3/4 SA 2
Cabar Feidh (sett.) 6/8 J 4
Cameron MacFadyen 6/8 M 4
Catherine Lenkas 6/8 M 4
Charlie's Welcome (arr.) R 8
Chrissie Smith's Jig 6/8 J 4
Cutting Bracken (arr.) 6/8 J 4
Donald of the Sun 6/8 J 4
Dr Myron Berrick's March 2/4 M 4 [Duncan's own spelling of Berwick]
The Drover Lads (sett.) 6/8 J 4
An Eriskay Song (sett.) SA 1
An Exercise 3/4 in 3 parts
Farewell to Barra 4/4 M 4
Farewell to Nigg 6/4 M 4 or 3/4 M 4
Father Colin's Dedication S 4 (formerly SA 4)
Finlay MacDonald 6/8 J 4
Finlay Murchie's Birthday 6/8 J 4
The Geese In The Bog (arr.) 6/8 J 4
Guido Margiotta 6/8 J 4
Harvest Home (arr. with parts 3&4 added) 2/4 HP 4
The Herring Wife (arr.) 6/8 J 4
I Hae A Wife O' My Ain (sett.) 6/8 J 4
Invercharron Highland Gathering (sett.) 6/8 M 4
Isabelle MacLean 2/4 HP 4
Isa Johnstone S 4
The Isle of Barra March 2/4 M 4
James MacLellan's Favourite 6/8 J 4
Janet's Jig 6/8 J 4
Jimmy Anderson's Welcome to Arran 6/8 M 4

Jock Anderson of the Glen 6/8 J 4
The Kilt is my Delight (sett.) R 4
Lament for Alan My Son P
The Last Dance 6/8 J 4
Lt. McGuire's Jig (parts 3&4) 6/8 J 4
Linowt
Margaret's Wedding 6/8 J 4
Meg MacRae 6/8 M 4
Michael Brady's Jig 6/8 J 4
Mrs Alex Johnstone 2/4 M 4
Mrs Mary Anderson of Lochranza 2/4 M 4
Paddy's Leather Breeches (arr.) 6/8 J 4
Ray Anderson 6/8 J 4
The Reel of Tulloch (sett.) R 7
The Rest 6/8 J 2
Roddy's Ticket 6/8 J 4
Romany 6/8 J 4
Rona MacDonald 6/8 J 4
Seonaid R 4
The Shepherd's Crook (arr.) R 4
The Skyeman's Jig (arr.) 6/8 J 4
The Smith's a Jolly Fireman (sett.) S 4
The South Uist Emigrants (parts 3&4) 6/8 M 4
Staggering 6/8 J 4
The Streaker 2/4 HP 4
Whinrigg 6/8 M 4
Willie Cumming's Rant (arr.) R 4

Duncan composed three tunes for a piper who had lost the use of his bottom hand. They are published in Book I of Willie M. MacDonald's Glencoe Collection (1993). Willie said he wondered if Duncan could do the same for a bottom hand player, but Duncan said it was not feasible.

The top-hand tunes are:

AGFED's March
DEFGA's Strathspey
The FAGED Reel

Note also:

Duncan Johnston, by Willie Lawrie 2/4 M 4
Duncan Johnstone, by Donald MacLeod 2/4 HP 4

Duncan Johstone, by Roderick MacDonald 2/4 M 4
Duncan Johnstone's Strathspey, by Robert Wallace S 4

When Duncan died in 1999, one of his pupils, Stuart Finlayson from Aukland, New Zealand, composed a 2/4 march in four parts, *Duncan Johnstone's Final Journey.* He said that Duncan 'was like a father to me during my time in Scotland', and hoped the tune was worthy of his name.

Duncan produced two books of pipe music, and made three commercial recordings. A book and CD of his complete works is to be published by his family.

In his memory a competition was started in 2000, the Duncan Johnstone Memorial Solo Piping Competition for B and C graded members of the Competing Pipers Association. The first winner was Decker Forrest of San Diego, California, who now lives in South Uist.

When Duncan died in 1999, Angus J. MacLellan, a fellow-instructor at the College, said: 'He was a very humorous man, with a sharp wit, always ready for a laugh and a joke. It was a great joy to be in his company. I doubt if there was a man with greater knowledge of pipers and piping during the golden post war years in Glasgow.'

Robert Wallace added: 'Duncan held his ability lightly. He never seemed burdened by it. It was as natural to him as sleep. As a consequence he was utterly without pretension and able to do everything with endearing humour. After coming out of hospital, and obviously ill, he met someone who said 'Were you in again for the usual trouble, Duncan?'

'Aye, that's right,' he said, 'Trying to sort out my crunluaths.'

Sources

Myron Berwick
Jeannie Campbell, *Highland Bagpipe Makers*
Morag MacLeod
Alex Mackenzie
Angus J. MacLellan
Derick Thomson, *Companion to Gaelic Scotland*
Robert Wallace

Neil Angus MacDonald

NEIL ANGUS MACDONALD was born in Barra in 1910, and was educated at St Mungo's Academy in Glasgow, and at Glasgow University.

He obtained his teaching qualification at Jordanhill College of Education, Glasgow. His first appointment was in Barra, where he became headmaster of Eoligarry School.

Neil Angus recalled his mother, on church holidays, trying to get into the room in her own house, with a teapot in one hand and a plate of scones in the other, unable to push in through the throng of pipers, which included Calum Johnstone. 'I often marvelled at her patience,' said Neil Angus. 'Of course she was very fond of pipe music.'

His teaching career was interrupted in 1939 when he served with the RAF in India, but after the war he returned to Barra, as headmaster in Castlebay. In 1953 he became head of St Joseph's School in Inverness, living at Longford Villa, 5 Kenneth Street. He soon established himself as a leading figure in the piping and Gaelic worlds of the north.

He came of a long line of pipers in Barra, and was first taught by his father, who was well known as a piper and reed maker. Later, as a pupil of John MacDonald, Inverness, Neil Angus won many prizes. His playing was known for its exceptional musical quality, and it was remarked that he made Ceol Mor sound like Gaelic song.

He took an active part in the Gaelic Society of Inverness, to whom he was the official piper; he was also Gaelic tutor to the Inverness Gaelic Choir, and became President of the Inverness Piping Society, and a member of the Piobaireachd Society.

David Murray in 2003 wrote of the days when he was stationed in Inverness and used to attend meetings of the Inverness Piping Society held in the Castle, and he would pick up 'all manner of traditional and Hebridean tunes from Neil Angus of Barra'.

Neil Angus was in office as President when the Inverness Piping Society was put out of Inverness Castle, at the instigation of the legal fraternity, against whom he fought a magnificent rearguard action: he was not successful in winning re-admission for the Society, but he managed to heap ridicule on the lawyers by making their attitude to piping a laughing stock throughout the country, in a memorable broadcast of biting wit and humour – and at the same time gave welcome publicity to the society.

He made a number of broadcasts for the BBC (the wireless, in those days), a classic being an unforgettable exchange between himself and Duncan Johnstone, recalling far-off piping days in Barra, with Duncan playing the illustrations.

Neil Angus was held in deep affection in the piping world, and was greatly respected as a composer, teacher, judge and player. In 1961 the Vatican awarded him the Benemerenti Medal.

He died in 1994 in Inverness Royal Infirmary, at the age of 84. He is recalled with great fondness, for his good-natured wit and humour as well as his wisdom and knowledge of the traditions of piping. As the *Piping Times* put it, 'he will always be remembered with an affectionate smile'.

Sadly, his son RUAIRIDH MACDONALD, who succeeded him in 1979 as piper to the Gaelic Society of Inverness, fell ill soon after Neil Angus' death, and followed his father to the grave in 1995. Ruairidh was born in Barra in 1940, and became a teacher of mathematics, first in Inverness, then in Vancouver, before returning to Inverness. He was an excellent piper who as a boy had won the Junior Silver Chanter at the Northern Meeting for three consecutive years. He was also known as a keen cricketer (unusual for a piper), and a good bridge player. Ill health had compelled him to retire in 1992, and he died from cancer three years later.

Neil Angus MacDonald published a book of pipe music called *A New Bagpipe Collection of Old and Traditional Settings*. It contains a number of unusual compositions, both his own and those of others, often based on Gaelic songs. He made two piobaireachd works: *Lament for Dr John MacInnes of Glenelg,* with six variations, and *The Clan Rose Piobaireachd*, with seven variations. Donald MacLeod made in his honour *Neil Angus MacDonald's Salute*, a piobaireachd work with five variations.

Neil Angus' works include:

> *Angus Ramsay's Lullaby* 6/8 SA 2
> *Ann Fionnghal MacDonald* (1971) 6/8 M 4
> *Dr Ronald MacLean of Applecross* 6/8 SA 2
> *Eilean Fraoich* (or *Eilean an Fhraoich*) (Isle of Heather) arr. 6/8 SM 2
> *General Sir Philip Christison* 6/8 M 4
> *John Rennie* 2/4 M 4
> *Leaving Port St Jude* 4/4 SA 2 (1975)
> *Mary Kiely* 6/8 M 4
> *Murdo Morrison* 2/4 M 4
> *Murdo Morrison of Lewis's Centenary* 6/8 SA 2
> *Nan MacDonald* 6/8 M 4
> *Neil MacMillan* 6/8 J 4
> *Tuning Prelude* 2/4 SA 2

The Fair Maid of Barra

The Slow March *The Fair Maid of Barra* is based on a popular Gaelic song, the words of which were made by Donald A. MacDonald, South Uist, who won the Gaelic Bardic Crown at the National Mod in Stirling. The composer of the music was Donald J. Campbell, the schoolmaster in Castlebay, Barra, and the Fair Maid was Morag MacAulay, Castlebay, whom Donald A. MacDonald met at a dance in Lochboisdale. He was instantly captivated by her beauty and charm.

She was born in 1911, and died in 1998. David Craig described her in 1990 as:

> an elegant woman in her eighties, wearing a plum organdie dress with a high ruffled collar, a long sleeveless tunic of mallard green, and her white hair prettily curled . . . She rejoiced in having been the subject of 'The Fair Maid of Barra', and sings it herself with a skilled shaping of the phrases and the power still to hold the long poignant notes –

> > Young maid of the fair hair,
> > Listen to the poetry from my lips,
> > Give me your promise, my love,
> > And for your sake I'll return.
> > Although I have been fond of many girls
> > From various countries and races,
> > Oh please consent.
> > When I ask so earnestly . . .

Angus J. MacLellan said 'she was a very well loved and respected lady who seldom left her native isle, and led a very happy and contented life, just like the beautiful song and tune that is such a fitting memorial to her'.

Other Pipers in Barrra

The tune called *The Claymore* refers to the SS *Claymore*, the ferry for Barra and South Uist from Oban. Charles Hunter was a fiddler who was the wireless operator on the *Claymore*, and he and Willie M. MacDonald had many musical sessions in his office on board. He gave Willie some of the fiddle tunes he had composed; Willie transposed this one into pipe music, and published it in Book I of his *Glencoe Collection* (1993).

RORY CAMPBELL comes of a Barra family, and learned his piping from his father RODDY CAMPBELL, who was well known as a singer of *port-a-beul* (mouth music for dancing). Rory produced a solo album *Magaid a Phibir*, but is probably best known for his part in the folk band Deaf Shepherd, in which he plays the Highland pipes and the big whistle. He is also a player of the Border and small pipes. The *Piping World* published a photograph of him with his car, licence plate PI PES.

MALCOLM MACINNES, known as Calum Mor, composed a 6/8 March in four parts, *Merrily Sailing*.

Evan MacRae commemorated the Barra clarsach maker in his 2/4 March in 2 parts, *Michael Joseph MacKinnon*. Michael was in the Merchant Navy during World War II, and while captaining his ship in the Indian Ocean was taken prisoner, to spend the rest of the war as a prisoner of war in Germany. His two grandsons are pipers, both pupils of Evan MacRae.

Sources

David Craig, *On the Crofters' Trail*
Allan MacDonald
David Murray
Piping Times
Piping World

Eriskay

There is now a causeway across to Eriskay from the south end of South Uist, and a ferry link from Barra, so that it is possible to travel the length of the Outer Islands by road, with only two short sea crossings (Barra–Eriskay and Bernera–South Harris), both memorable for beautiful scenery.

Eriskay is a Norse name, probably meaning Eric's Island. Eriskay is known to many as the first landing-place of Prince Charles Edward Stuart on his arrival from France in 1745. He was guided ashore by a piper, Calum MacNeill (see above, Barra).

The well-known *Eriskay Love Lilt* has two versions, the tune as rendered by Marjorie Kennedy Fraser, and the much more subtle 'original' island version. It was set for the pipes by Duncan Johnstone, as *An Eriskay Song*, a Slow Air in 1 part.

The Notices of Pipers say that well into the 19th century, the congregation of the Roman Catholic church in Eriskay were summoned to service on Sunday by the strains of the pipes, which the writer considered very unusual (there was an instance of this practice in Caithness, but the Protestant church frowned on it). It is not said who played the pipe – was it perhaps the priest himself? And was it done by more than one incumbent? Presumably there was no church bell.

Roger Hutchinson, in his biography of Father Allan MacDonald, describes a funeral on Eriskay during an epidemic of typhus in the 1890s. He says the funeral of a man of 37 years old was attended by a huge crowd of mourners, and the procession was led across the island by a piper. It is clear that pipes were used not only to accompany dancing, but were part of any big community occasion as well.

The book *A School in South Uist,* by Frederick Rea, has a photograph of EWEN MACLENNAN playing his pipes in Eriskay in 1899. Rea described Ewen as the shop-keeper on Eriskay from 1890 to 1900, and said that the entire population of Eriskay at that time was Roman Catholic, with the exception of Ewen, 'a very pleasant, affable young fellow, intelligent, fairly well educated, speaking good English'. He was not so much a shopkeeper as an agent or manager of the store, acting for a businessman living elsewhere, who owned a number of stores throughout the islands. Part of Ewen's job was to buy fish and shellfish from local catchers, paying them in cash or goods. Every second Friday, the fishermen donated their entire day's catch to the church, the proceeds going to the upkeep of church buildings, and Ewen was constantly surprised to find that that Friday's catch was always a bumper one. He lived on Eriskay with his pretty young sister Marion, aged seventeen.

DONALD MACINNES from Eriskay was a well known teacher of piping in Glasgow. He composed *Leaving Eriskay,* a 9/8 Slow March in two parts.

RODDY MACLEOD, Director of Piping at the Piping Centre in Glasgow, and a leading solo piper as well as ex-Pipe Major of the Scottish Power band, is of Hebridean ancestry, and his mother came from Benbecula. It is said that his grandmother was from Eriskay. He is directly descended from MacLeods in Balallan, Lewis (see below).

Eriskay Graffiti

In 2003, Professor William Gillies was at a dinner, giving his farewell address as Chief of the Gaelic Society of Inverness. His theme was how greatly life in the islands had changed during his tenure, while at the same time some aspects never change. He said the first time he went to Eriskay and wanted to see the beach where Prince Charles Edward landed, he had to walk across rough moorland, knee-deep in thick heather, to reach it. On returning recently, he found there is now a 'broad highway' (a single-track but tarred road) passing the beach, with motor traffic roaring along, heading for the ferry to Barra. In the car-park of the new ferry terminal, he saw a Portaloo (toilet hut), with its walls covered in graffiti left by those who feel the need to record their presence. Beside 'Jimmy from Falkirk 2002' was scribbled 'Charlie E. Stuart 1745'.

Sources

William Gillies, *TGSI* LVI
Notices of Pipers
Piping Times
Frederick Rea, *A School in South Uist*

South Uist

To reach South Uist, take the car ferry from Oban to Lochboisdale. The crossing takes about five hours. For a shorter sailing time, go to Uig in Skye and cross by car ferry to Lochmaddy, in North Uist. The three islands, North Uist, Benbecula and South Uist are now linked by causeways. It is also possible to fly to Benbecula from Glasgow or Inverness, and cross by the causeway into South Uist.

Uist, Gaelic Uibhist, pronounced (approximately) YOU-ist or OO-ist, is another obscure name. It is probably related to Gaelic *uidh*, a ford or tidal crossing, as both North and South Uist were linked to Benbecula by tidal fords before the causeways were built. Some Gaelic speakers call South Uist *Tir a' Mhurain*, Land of the Sea-bent (grass on the machair). Much of the island is either machair or mountain (or water).

Pipe tunes associated with South Uist:

Adam Scott, by J. McInnes 6/8 J 4
Angus J. MacLellan, by James Wark R 4
Angus MacPhee, by Yahya Abdelsamad 6/8 M
Archie MacPhail, by Adam Scott R 4
Archie MacPhail's Tuning Phrase, by Adam Scott 6/4 SA 1
Boisdale's Salute P 8
The Cameronian Rant, (sett.) by Willie Morrison 6/8 J 8
Captain Alec Fraser, by John Scott R 4

Clan Ranald's Gathering P 8
Clan Ranald's Salute P 12
Dolina MacKay, by John Scott R 4
Donald MacMillan, Daliburgh, South Uist, by John W. Scott 2/4 M 4
Donella Beaton, by George Johnstone 6/8 J 4
The Eye Peninsula, by John W. Scott 6/8 J 4
The Fairy's Hornpipe, (parts 3 & 4) by Rona Lightfoot HP 4
Finlay MacKenzie, by J. Wilson 6/8 J 6
Finlay MacKenzie, by Neil MacLennan 6/8 J 4
The Gathering of the MacDonalds of Clanranald P 8
Glasgow Police March Past (or *The Sands of Loch Bee*), by John
    MacDonald 4/4 M 2
The Hills of South Uist, by John Steele 2/4 M 4
Hugh Ferguson, by John Scott 6/8 M
Hugh MacNeill, by John W. Scott 9/8 SA 2
John MacDonald's Welcome to South Uist, by D. (or S.?) MacMillan,
    Daliburgh 2/4 M 4
John M. Walker, by John W. Scott 6/8 M 4
Katy MacDonald of Croydon, by John Scott SA
Leaving Lochboisdale, by J. Wilson 6/8 SM 2
Leaving Uist, by Fred Morrison SA
Lindsay's Lament, by Archie Lindsay 6/8 SM 2
The Little Nuance, by John W. Scott 2/4 M 4
Loch Boisdale, arr. by Roderick MacDonald S 2
Lochcarnan Bay, by J. Johnston 2/4 M 4
Lonely Loch nan Eun, by Bert Barron 6/8 SA 4
MacLeod's Taxi, by John W. Scott 6/8 M 4
Pipe Major Jimmy MacGregor, by John Scott 6/8 M
Pipe Major John MacDonald's Exercise J 4
Over to Uist, by Donald MacLeod 6/8 J 4
The Queen's Own Highlanders' Polka, by Archie Lindsay 2/4 M 4
Reel, by L. MacCormick, South Uist R 2
The Rev. John MacLeod, Oban, by John W. Scott 2/4 HP 4
The Road to Geirinish, by George Milton 4/4 M 4
Robert Thompson of South Uist, by Iain MacCrimmon 6/8 J 4
Roderick MacDonald (Glasgow Police) 2/4 M 4
Rona MacDonald, by Duncan Johnstone 6/8 J 4
Sheshader, by John W. Scott 6/8 J 4
The Skylark's Ascension, by Archie Lindsay 6/8 J 4
The South Uist Emigrants, or *Mrs Dugald Matheson,* SA 4
South Uist Golf Club, by Lachlan MacCormick S 2

A South Uist Melody 6/8 SM 2
The Three Peaks of South Uist, by John W. Scott R 4
Tommy Grant, by Adam Scott 6/8 J 4
Tony Lightfoot, by Rona MacDonald 6/8 J 4
The Uist Milking Song 12/8 SA 2
The Wee Man from Uist, by Angus J. MacMillan 2/4 M 2

The South Uist Emigrants is a traditional Slow Air, also known as *Mrs Dugald Matheson* 6/8 SA 2, to which Duncan Johnstone added Parts 3 and 4. Dugald Matheson, from Kyle of Lochalsh, served in the Queen's Own Cameron Highlanders from 1899 to 1920, before becoming Pipe Major of the 2nd Camerons 1908–1916. He was severely wounded at Salonika when in charge of the battalion snipers.

To the above may be added the compositions of Donald Morrison and those of Ronald I. MacLean, George Johnstone and Fred Morrison (see below).

Joshua Dickson

Since this section was written, Joshua Dickson's excellent book *When Piping Was Strong* has been published (2006). Clearly much of the material gathered by him in South Uist overlaps with what I have included here, but I have left mine in its original form, as my approach to the material is different from his, and mine is part of a series covering the Isles and areas of mainland Scotland. I defer to his scholarship, however, and recommend his book to those who want a deeper and more scholarly study of a more restricted aspect of the subject.

Piping in South Uist

Pipers in South Uist seem faintly surprised to hear of the respect in which their piping tradition is held on the mainland – where there is admittedly a tendency to explain aberrations, somewhat hastily, with 'Oh well, that was the South Uist setting, you see.'

Piobaireachd players on the island maintain that their tradition derives from the teaching of John MacDonald, Inverness, who in the years before the First World War, was in Uist on business, and was asked by Simon MacKenzie and Canon MacDougall to take on the teaching of piobaireachd to island players; this tuition was continued by Willie Ross and Robert Nicol, between the wars, and Willie Gray in 1947.

Islanders say that piobaireachd in South Uist had virtually died out before that, and that John MacDonald resurrected it, saving it from extinction. This makes it difficult to find evidence of the tradition before 1900, but it is certain that piobaireachd had been played there for centuries, and that the MacIntyres, pipers to Clanranald, carried much of the tradition. The MacDonald family, the Campbells, and the two families of Morrisons, all owe much to John MacDonald's tuition, but their playing, full of melody and musical interpretation, is so distinctive that it is clear there really is a South Uist style, even when it is underlying the teaching of John MacDonald. John himself said that he found the South Uist players ready pupils and easy to teach, as they had the idiom in their blood.

Neil MacMillan says that John MacDonald first came to South Uist in 1910, at the behest of Canon Alexander MacDougall and the hotelier Simon MacKenzie (see below). Later an agreement was reached with the Piobaireachd Society, but the initial invitation came from the island, asking John to teach island pipers during his bi-annual two-week visits on business – John was a travelling salesman for a brewery, coming over once in winter, once in summer.

The response was instant, and John's first class was held in Daliburgh School, with more than sixty pupils, aged between 6 and 60. Many of the youngsters were barefoot. There is said to be a photograph extant of the first class of youngsters, all of whom except one were barefoot: the one wearing boots had borrowed them from his granny. This big class was held in the evenings, after both tutor and pupils had finished their day's work. There was a thirst for learning, and Neil says that every house had at least one piper, mainly playing for dancing. This is borne out by the account given in *A School in South Uist*, in which Frederick Rea describes life on the island in the 1890s, before John MacDonald arrived. Rea also mentioned the playing of piobaireachd in South Uist in his time.

Rea described a small wedding party in Uist, not long after his arrival in the early 1890s: after the church ceremony, the piper led the newlyweds to the priest's house, and it is interesting to note that although there were only four present – the couple, their best man and bridesmaid – they still had a piper. He downed his full glass of fiery whisky, and began to play for dancing in the priest's kitchen. Rea, an Englishman, wrote: 'the swirl of the air seemed to grip me up and whirl me around with its rousing rhythm; and as the ripple of notes rose and fell they made my toes ache to dance'. After two reels, the wedding party was fetched by their friends, the piper leading the way playing a march, with others firing occasional guns in salutation. Neil Mac-Millan says that no music other than that of the pipes was ever played for dancing at that time, and on into the early 20th century, probably up to the First World War. When Frederick Rea described a dance in Eriskay, he did not mention the instrument to which everyone was dancing, but it would have been the pipes.

Neil MacMillan says that in those days chanter reeds were some-times made from barley straw – it had to be barley, no other straw would do. This would have been bere barley, an old type of barley, full of flavour, which has a tough stem. It is on record that young pipers in Skye used barley-straw reeds, too. They have an exceptionally sweet tone, but have to be replaced frequently. Although the North Uist bard John MacCodrum, in the 18th century, describing one of the previous owners of the inferior pipe played by the poor piper, Donald Ban, said he used so much straw for his reeds that he could have fed cattle with it, the use of barley straw for pipe reeds was by no means confined to the islands. It was probably a widespread practice among pipers who could not afford cane, or to whom no alternative was available.

In spite of the tuition from all those experts from the mainland, South Uist pipers retained the idiom of their forebears. Ludovic (Louis) Morrison, for example, plays the *Lament for Mary MacLeod* in a way which he says is all his own, self-taught, beautiful, and very much South Uist in its flavour, based on what he heard his father and other family members play. Angus Campbell, who died in 2002 at the age of 102, was a pupil of John MacDonald, but all who heard him play agreed that his piobaireachd had a 'tang' not found in the music of many of John's other pupils, with the exception of Neil Angus MacDonald, from Barra. The playing of Rona Lightfoot, daughter of Archie MacDonald, has this special flavour, too, and the Morrisons all have (or had) that magic island touch, full of Gaelic song.

Peter Cooke said that there was a piper in South Uist who was asked if he had ever heard *Mary MacLeod* played with the opening a long first A. 'Oh yes', he said, 'My uncle used to play it that way until John MacDonald came out and told him it was wrong.' General Thomason said this tradition of the long first A survived in Skye until about 1905, and longer in South Uist.

Joshua Dickson, in an article about the early traditions in South Uist, said that some pipers were remembered as having played Ceol Mor before John MacDonald came over, and they included Lachlan Ban MacCormick, Neil Campbell (father of Angus Campbell of Frobost), and Willie MacLean – but Willie was not a South Uist man; although he lived at Creagorry in Benbecula for a time, he had learned his piping elsewhere, partly from his father, who was from Raasay. He had his piobaireachd from Calum Piobaire MacPherson at Laggan. Lachlan MacCormick, too, was not from South Uist, but from Benbecula, and Dickson said that reports in the *Oban Times* show that Ceol Mor was not played in competitions in South Uist before 1908. Claims of piobaireachd before that are based largely on oral tradition – including a claim that MacCormick played settings which conflicted with those of the Piobaireachd Society (who didn't?), and that he had learned them in Uist.

Dickson went on to say that Neil Campbell was taught his piobaireachd by the MacGillivray family in Eoligarry, Barra, in the 1880s (see above, Barra).

Frederick Rea made it clear that piping was part of the social life of the island, and this was presumably light music, with only a little Ceol Mor. In his account of a school picnic, a piper was brought along to lead the children in procession to the bay where they would have tea, and the schoolmaster found that the pupils organised the dancing of reels while the piper played. Later it was the piper who selected a few boys and girls to dance the Highland Fling, before several of the boys took out their chanters, and took part in a competition run by the piper (whose name we never learn). 'It was amazing to me', wrote Rea, 'to see and hear how well these lads played, and as I watched their easy but rapid fingering of the notes and listened to the variety of tunes, I felt that they were natural players. The (other) teachers seemed to take it as a matter of course, and when I expressed surprise they told me that the families to which these boys belonged had been noted as great pipers for many generations; indeed, there was scarcely a house on the island where you would not get one or more pipers in the family.' If only he had named the families – and he spoils his most interesting account by saying they marched home to the skirling of the pipes, that word which the English inevitably apply to the instrument, unaware that it is an insult to the player.

In Chapter 12 of Rea's book we have a description of a specific player of what Rea calls pibroch: he is unnamed in the narrative but has been identified as Lachie Ban MacCormick (see below, Benbecula). Rea tells how much pibroch meant to the priest, Father Allan (MacDonald), whose face 'became suffused with colour . . . at its warlike strains'. Yet Rea says 'it was supposed to be a musical poem telling of the beauty of hill and dale, of gentle love, joys, wars, of battles, victory, defeat, and sorrow. The Highlander to whom the airs are familiar is naturally stirred by the music of the pibroch' – but he himself found it left him cold.

There has been a wealth of piping in South Uist over the years, and in recent times Calum Beaton and Louis Morrison have been teaching the youngsters, putting back into piping all that they themselves drew from it.

In South Uist there are many renowned piping families, and they are linked by marriage to form a network of piping genes: Rona Lightfoot, for example, is a MacDonald who is a cousin of Johnny Roidean, the Glasgow Police Pipe Major; her uncle was Angus Campell ('Angus Frobost'), and his cousin was Calum Campbell of the family in Benbecula and South Uist. Angus Campbell was married to Belle Morrison, of the piping Morrisons, who were married into the MacKillops and the Steeles, not to mention the MacDonalds of Glenuig, . . . and so it goes on. Small wonder that John MacDonald, Inverness, remarked how easy it was to teach in South Uist, where the learners all had piping in their blood. Perhaps piping shops should market Uist genes as a sideline.

Sources

Peter Cooke, *Proceedings of the Piobaireachd Society Conference*
Joshua Dickson, *When Piping Was Strong*
Neil MacMillan
Frederick Rea, *A School in South Uist*

Pipers in South Uist

JOHN MACDONALD in the 17th century was piper to the Captain of Clanranald. In 1636 a complaint was laid that he and others had seized and plundered the ship *Susanna* when she was wrecked in the Western Isles, two years earlier. It was alleged that the Uist men had struck and stripped the marines (sailors) of their clothes and left them nude and destitute. No wonder there was a complaint – it was the middle of December. There is no suggestion that the Uistmen caused the shipwreck, merely that they took advantage once it had happened.

DONALD and JOHN MACARTHUR were tuning their pipes at the bedside of the North Uist bard, Niall MacMhuraich, when he had smallpox. This incensed him so much that he was roused from his illness, and composed a satirical poem deriding the bagpipe. He died in 1726.

Another bard, Gilleasbuig na Ceapaich (Archibald of Keppoch, who was the chief of the MacDonalds of Keppoch from 1670 until he died in 1682) was inspired by Niall's satire to make a poem in defence of the pipes, preferring pipe music to poetry such as that made by Niall. He spoke of

Mor phiob leis an duisgear gach minneach,
a torman moid is misde beum

The great pipe that inspires all courage,
Her noise the more terrifying for its beat

and declared:

B'fhearr leam spealtach dhith ri h-uair
Na na bhuil go tuaim de duan

Better a blast from the pipe for an hour
Than all the poetry between here and the grave

He saw the pipes simply as instruments of war, and made no reference to the kind of music played.

This exchange of poems seems to have given rise to two more, both MacLean songs, one for the pipes, one against.

IAIN RUADH MACCUITHEN (MacQueen) was a player in South Uist in the early 18th century, and 'allowed [considered] to be a good piper'. Archibald MacDonald, the North Uist bard, had composed two poems about him, as well as a satirical poem *Tha Biodag air Mac Thomais* (Thompson Has a Dirk). This is also the name of a pipe tune, presumably based on a song. It is usually associated with the Frasers of Lovat.

The two Gaelic poems or songs about Iain Ruadh were a Marbhrann (Elegy) on Iain's reported death, and a 'Resurrection' on finding he was still living. The poet Archibald Macdonald was known as Gille na Ciotaig, 'Lad of the Left Hand', because his arm and hand were deformed. The young Sir James MacDonald (subject of *Sir James Mac-Donald's Lament* after he died as a young man in Rome) had given money to Archibald's mother for his education, and he became a clerk. He composed a number of poems and decided to have them published, so set off for Inverness to arrange this. At Fort Augustus, however, he fell ill, and died there. His best known works concern the Uist piper Iain Ruadh MacCuithen 'Red-headed John MacQueen'; both the Elegy and the Resurrection are clever, witty works, which amused Iain so much that he paid the poet a sum of money for them. It is clear that Archibald was well aware that Iain was not dead when he wrote the first poem.

The *Marbhrann* starts:

Fhuair mi sgeula bho'n ghobha'	I got news from the blacksmith,
Cha'n aobhar meoghail ach gruaim;	The subject was not joyful but sad;
E fein fo mhi-ghean 's fo thrioblaid	He himself was sorrowing and distressed,
Ri iarunn cist' do dh'Iain Rudh.	With Iain Ruadh in an iron coffin.

It goes on:

Tha'n gaothair air stopadh,	The pipe's mouth-piece has stopped,
Tha'n da dhos 'n an trom shuain,	The two drones are in a heavy sleep,
Chaill an seannsair a chlaisteachd;	The chanter has lost its sound;
Tha'n gleus air a ghrad leigei suas,	Its tune is suddenly broken up,
Bho'n tric a thainig ceol taitneach,	From it often came delightful music,
Rogha caismeachd mo chluais.	The best of marches to my ears.
Ceol bu bhlaisd' 'us bu bhinne,	How tasteful his music, and how sweet,
Dhuisgeadh spiorad do 'n t-sluagh;	It would arouse the spirit of the people;
Ceol bu tartaraich 'siubhal'	Such resounding music, and ever changing,
Thionndadh tioma gu cruas.	Turning delicacy into strength.
Ceol mar smeorach a'ghlinne,	Music like the thrush in the glen,
Ceol a's binne na cuach;	Music that is sweeter than the cuckoo;
Meoir gun bhraise, gun ghiorradh,	Fingers not rushing, not cutting,
Dionach, ruith-leumnach, luath.	Supple, leaping, swift.
Bu sgiolta seallach do sheannsair,	Your chanter was neat to see,
Air port 's air crunn-luath 's air cuairt,	With a tune, or a crunluath, or a set of tunes,
Pronnadh cnaparra, lughmhor,	Playing powerfully, vigorously,
Caismeachd shunntach 's an ruaig.	Marching cheerily and fiercely.

The rest of the poem laments the loss of a good friend and drinking companion, as well as the loss of his music: the poet says he much pre-ferred Iain's pipe to the fiddler's music ('like rain dripping on the bog'), and goes on to praise Iain as a dancer, a swimmer and an athlete. He was missed, says the poet, by his tobacco pouch, his glass in the inn, as well as the jug, bottle and flask which used to fill it – they all spoke up, remembering him, and he would be buried with a bottle of rum at his feet and a roll of tobacco at his head.

Then comes the Resurrection, *Aiseirigh Iain Ruaidh,* by the same author, 'Horo, what joy I have on hearing that you have risen, what gladness I feel at that report that Death's grip on you has gone'. He tells how Iain's wife is happy not to be a widow, and the inn-keepers are rejoicing.

> *Cha'n'eil m'intinn gearanach,*   I have no intention of complaining
> *O'n chuir thu dhiot an galair ud,* That you put from you that disease,
> *'S ann tha do phiob 'na deannal* And that your battle-pipe
> *A'toirt caithream air ceol dannsa.*   Is giving joyful dance-music.

And he looks forward to seeing Iain back in the inn once more. It is interesting that he is specific about Iain's two-drone pipe: this must have been in the middle or early 18th century.

A South Uist piper in Nova Scotia in the 19th century was ALEXANDER MACLEOD, who, as Barry Shears tells us, settled at French Road, where many of the MacIntyres from Uist were living, as was JOHN MACPHEE (1790–1870) from South Uist, who arrived around 1828. John's father was a piper, EVAN MACPHEE, who served with the 84th Regiment, Royal Highland Emigrants; and John's son ALEXANDER MACPHEE (1827–1912) was a piper, too (see Barry Shears, *Dance to the Piper*).

MacIntyre Pipers

Traditionally the MacIntyres were the pipers to the Chief of Clanranald, whose stronghold for a short time was Ormiclett Castle, before it burned down in 1715. It is now a picturesque ruin. Subsequent chiefs went to live in Nunton, Benbecula. The MacIntyre pipers lived south of Ormiclett, at Smerclett (sometimes spelled Smerclate); it is said in South Uist that some of them married MacCrimmon girls from Skye, and this greatly influenced their playing. This tradition could be symbolic, that is, the marriages may be merely a concrete image for an abstract idea, the introduction of MacCrimmon teaching into Uist piping.

Dr MacVicar, a direct descendant of MacDonald of Kinlochmoidart, was said by Seton Gordon to have a pipe given to his family in 1790 by a MacIntyre of Uldary, the last of the hereditary pipers to Clanranald.

He gave away his pipe before emigrating to the New World (this seems unlikely, unless he had several pipes). The pipe he gave away was very old, and said to have been played at Bannockburn. It had an extra hole below the low G hole, made on the advice of a fairy being, and it had a four-sided mouthpiece. This pipe, or one very like it, is now in the museum of the MacDonald Clan Centre, at Armadale, in the south of Skye.

In 1723, the MacDonald chief at Armadale had a piper called MALCOLM MACINTYRE, who had a holding of land at Tarskavaig Mor, in the south of Skye, on the west coast of Sleat. Malcolm may have been from the MacIntyre pipers of South Uist.

A Gaelic poem addressed to ROBERT MACDONALD MACINTYRE (1769–1833), piper to Clanranald, was composed at Nunton in the late 18th century by a North Uist bard, Blind Alexander MacDonald, known as An Dall Mor 'The Big Blind One'. He described Robert as 'son of Donald Ban of Rannoch', thus linking the island's piping MacIntyres to those at Rannoch (see below, Benbecula).

Barry Shears gives an account of him: he won the Prize Pipe at Edinburgh in 1790, and moved to Nova Scotia around 1813. Before this he had served a few years with MacNeill of Barra, and later went to MacDonald of Kinlochmoidart. Robert's descendants were pipers, scattered widely in Canada.

Many of the family of piping MacIntyres emigrated around 1820. DONALD MACINTYRE (Domhnull mac Thormoid), of Boisdale, Nova Scotia, was born in South Uist around 1748, and seems to have been the first of the family to emigrate, in 1820, with his son and two grandsons, all pipers. Donald was a good piping teacher. Another DONALD MACINTYRE went out to Nova Scotia in 1826, and settled at French Road. According to Nova Scotian tradition, one of these two Donalds had seven sons, most of whom were pipers. One of them may have been 'BIG JIM' MACINTYRE, born at French Road in 1833, a celebrated piper and step-dancer, who became a coal miner at Glace Bay. Barry Shears tells us that of his eleven children, four sons were pipers and dancers, and founder members of the MacIntyre Pipe Band. Barry's book has a photograph of Big Jim.

Yet another DONALD MACINTYRE, probably a nephew of Domhnull mac Thormoid, was known as Domhnull Mor, and was born in Scotland in 1799. His mother was Mairi MacPhee.

With a party who left in 1826 was DUNCAN L. MACINTYRE, who also belonged to the piping MacIntyres. His mother, Catherine Mac-Donald, emigrated with him from South Uist. There were many pipers and fiddlers in that family. Barry Shears says they were all descended from Clanranald's piper in 1759, DUNCAN MACINTYRE. It is thought that these were the MacIntyres related to the MacIntyre pipers of Rannoch.

Barry gives a family tree of the Rannoch MacIntyre line, based on work done by himself and Keith Sanger. It covers more than 200 years, taking in seven generations.

Barry lists among the early piping settlers in Nova Scotia LAUCHLIN MACINTYRE and his son DUNCAN MACINTYRE, both from South Uist. They settled in Beechmont around 1844.

Frederick Rea's *A School in South Uist,* has an account of one of the MacIntyre pipers, from Smerclett. His name was DONALD MAC-INTYRE, and he was probably a descendant of a piper known as DOMHNALL RUADH PIOBAIRE. He was evidently much in demand in the islands, and Rea has left us a good account of the man and his playing. Rea was organising a dance in the school, and he engaged 'a special piper who came from a distance but who was very popular at all weddings and parties – he was said to be the best player of reels on the island'. On his arrival by pony and trap, Donald said he had not been to bed for three nights, as he had been playing at three weddings and had just come from the last one, on a neighbouring island. 'On my suggesting a rest, he laughed and said: 'Ach! That's ahreet, Mr Rea; I shall do fine!', at the same time wiping his mouth. I took this as a hint, so poured him out a small dram of whisky and was going to add water when he said: 'Never mind that. I like it dry', and he tossed off the neat spirit.

Rea goes on:

> When he had put his pipes in order he started to play, stood up,
> marched out of the room, through the hall, out at the front door, and
> round to the school door which some hand opened for him, the pipes,
> with ribbons flying, blaring a march. Still playing, he advanced into the
> school, followed by a motley crowd who had been waiting outside. Up
> and down the middle of the floor of the main room he marched, playing
> away, while the young people filled the benches, men on one side of the
> room, the girls on the other. When all seemed there, the piper halted
> at one end, still playing the march he had commenced in my house and
> had continued playing without pause till now.

The piper then played 'a kind of wail' while the young men paired up with their partners, whereupon the piper 'immediately changed to a rousing reel tune.' When the tempo increased, the young men all danced in pairs, until Donald slowed his tune – 'it died away and the dancers were glad to rest – Donald knew his work!'

The dancing lasted for hour after hour, reel following reel, the piper apparently as fresh as ever. After about fifteen reels non-stop, Rea stopped him for refreshments, but after half an hour, he re-tuned, and the reels continued until the early hours of the morning. Then Donald suddenly ceased playing, stood up and said something in Gaelic which was the signal for everyone to go home. Evidently Donald played sitting down throughout the dancing.

After this night of playing, Donald went off to have some real drams, returning to Rea's house at dawn, considerably under the weather. He fell into his pony-trap, and the horse took off with Donald lying comatose behind him. When Rea met him two days later, he asked Donald how he had managed to get home. 'Oh! Fine!' said Donald 'You see, I met three good companions on the road and they saw me right'. And when Rea asked who they were, the reply was: 'Father, Son and Holy Ghost'.

(Rea's representation of the South Uist men's dialect of English is a little eccentric at times.)

Barry Shears gives an account of a descendant of the French Road MacIntyres, DUNCAN MACINTYRE, who served with the North Nova Scotia Highlanders in the Second World War. While overseas he took the army Pipe Major's course at Edinburgh Castle, under Pipe Major Willie Ross. Duncan was a traditional fiddle player as well as a piper, and Willie Ross was interested in his style of playing. Willie's daughter Cecily used to accompany Duncan's fiddle-playing on the piano. On his return after the war, Duncan became a piping instructor at Amherst, Nova Scotia, and his son BEN MACINTYRE followed in his father's footsteps as a piper.

There were descendants of the Clanranald pipers living in Uist until recently, the MacIntyres of Kildonan, in the middle of the island; they were not related to Donald John MacIntyre, the army piper, but were connected to DONALD MACINTYRE, known as 'The Paisley Bard', who was not only a first-class Gaelic poet but also an excellent piper. Born in 1889 and brought up in South Uist, he became a piper in the Cameron Highlanders and fought in France in the First World War. On his return he had to move to the mainland to find work, but returned to Uist every year. He died in 1964, and his direct piping line died out around 1970: there were three brothers, all good players, but none of them married. There is some connection with Duncan Ban MacIntyre in Glenorchy, the

Gaelic poet who made a well-known piobaireachd poem, in the 18th century.

In the 19th century, Clanranald had DONALD MACKAY, eldest son of John MacKay, Raasay, and brother of the famous Angus, as his piper from 1822 to 1834, before Donald went into Royal service. It was as Clanranald's piper that he won the Prize Pipe in 1822. By that time, Clanranald was no longer living in the islands.

MacIntyre pipers were for long the hereditary pipers to the Menzies chief, and also to the Campbells of Glenorchy and of Breadalbane. Fionn (Henry Whyte) said they originated at Cladich, Loch Awe, where they were renowned for the weaving of hose and garters in every clan tartan. According to Fionn, they made the Quickstep which became the 2/4 March *We Will Take the High Road (Gabhaidh sinn an rathad mor)*, also known as *The MacIntyres' March*, which 'was early appropriated by the Stewarts of Appin, with whom the Mac-Intyres were frequently associated in offensive and defensive warfare'. Fionn gave the Gaelic words of the song, saying that the first verse is a declaration of independence, the second has a jeering reference to the Campbells who would resent this independence, and the third indicates the author's pride in being a MacIntyre of Cladich. 'This tune became very popular.'

Another MacIntyre tune was *The MacIntyres' Salute* P 9, and works attributed to the MacIntyre pipers of Rannoch include *The Menzies' Salute, My King Has Landed in Moidart, The Prince's Salute, The Battle of Sheriffmuir* and *The Bells of Perth*. The Coddy (John MacPherson) in Barra spoke of a 'very pathetic pibroch' called *MacIntyres' Lament* (see above).

These were the Argyll MacIntyres, and Keith Sanger has shown us that they were pipers to Campbell of Glenorchy in the 17th century; in 1697 one of them at least was sent by Glenorchy to both the Rankins in Mull and the MacCrimmons in Skye, for his tuition. It is not certain, but probable, that these were the same MacIntyres as were pipers to Clanranald in South Uist. They were the pipers to the Menzies clan chief, after the Glenorchy Campbells became the Breadalbane noble family at Taymouth Castle.

DONALD JOHN MACINTYRE, known as 'DJ', formerly of the Queen's Own Highlanders, later Pipe Major in the Argyll and Sutherland Highlanders and latterly, in civilian life, working in Gaelic media, is the son of a Uist piper, also called DONALD JOHN MACINTYRE. An excellent player, he served as a Pipe Major in the Camerons in World War II. This family is not the same as the Clanranald pipers.

The Morrisons

The Morrison family is connected to the MacDonalds of Glenuig, in Morar. The mother of Angus, Allan and Iain MacDonald in Glenuig was a MacKay whose sister married one of the Morrisons from the south end of South Uist, related to Alfred, Ronald and Bell.

There are two families of piping Morrisons in South Uist, not immediately related to each other. One is that of Alfred, Ronald, Young Fred and Bell (who married Angus Campbell, Frobost). They belong to the south end of the island. The other is the family of Angus Morrison, Locheynort, his son Ludovic (Louis) and Willie, as well as Donald Morrison of the Aberdeen Police. This latter Morrison branch came originally from Lewis, and is related to Pipe Major Iain Morrison (see below).

ALFRED ('OLD FRED') MORRISON was familiar to many as the long-standing piping correspondent of the *Oban Times*. He was born and brought up in South Uist, one of a large family, and graduated from Glasgow University in the 1930s. He returned to the islands as a teacher, later taking a teaching post in Aberdeenshire, where he had piping tuition from both of the 'two Bobs', Robert Nicol and Robert Brown. Latterly he was a headmaster in Paisley. He was an excitable man, outspoken, dogmatic and easily roused – perhaps not temperamentally suited to teaching unruly adolescents – but his enthusiasm for piping, and his humour and friendliness, made him well-liked.

Angus Morrison sent a letter to the *Piping Times* in 1998, recalling an occasion at a concert in Balivanich (Benbecula) 'many years ago', when Fred was going about asking people to subscribe to a piping magazine recently started in Glasgow (the *Piping Times*). 'A MUST for every PIPER' said Fred, and talked Angus into laying out ten shillings and sixpence (10/6) for twelve copies, post free. Angus rather grudged the money at the time, but Fred assured him he would not regret it, and he was right; Angus wrote 'had it not been for that, I would have lost interest in piping long ago', and he told Fred so, years later. Fred said 'I don't think you were too pleased parting with all that money in Benbecula that night. But there was no way out for you. Thou met me in an evil hour.'

Fred and his family lived in Bishopton, Renfrewshire, and his sons attended St Aloysius school in Glasgow. Of his three sons, only Young Fred took up piping seriously, but he went on to make it his livelihood. Old Fred was Vice President of the SPA for many years and took an active part in piping life in and around Glasgow. He taught at the College of Piping in the evenings during his working life, and during the day once he had retired. He especially enjoyed teaching piobaireachd.

Old Fred's obituary in the *Piping Times* describes him as 'one of the most interesting characters to come around the College. For some reason he never lost his strong Hebridean accent, and his slow emphatic words, with sometimes surprising syntax, were always a delight to hear' (he thought in Gaelic and translated mentally). 'He was a man of no compromise, which did not endear him to many as a critic and a judge'.

My family has memories of Old Fred in the bows of the Uist ferry on a rough day, crossing to Oban, expounding a complex piping theory, the light of fanaticism in his eye, as the waves threw spray over us, the wind howled in the rigging, and we all plunged violently up and down. He took our minds off our stomachs, anyway.

RONALD MORRISON, brother of Old Fred, was born in Geirinish, the youngest of the family of ten. They were known as Clann Sheonaidh Aonghais Ruaidh (children of Johnny, son of Red Angus). He was taught his piping by John MacDonald, Inverness, at the summer schools held in Lochboisdale in the 1930s, but at the outbreak of war in 1939 he joined the Lovat Scouts. Stationed in Beauly for that first year of his service, he visited John MacDonald in Inverness for twice-weekly lessons, before the Scouts were sent abroad. He fought in Italy and Greece, and was demobbed in 1946.

He then trained as a primary teacher, later becoming headmaster of a primary school in Glasgow. He married a Glasgow girl, Margaret Findlay, and they had four sons.

He succeeded his brother Fred as piping correspondent of the *Oban Times*, and wrote a number of articles on piping history in the *Piping World* in the 1990s. After his retirement, and not in the first flush of youth, he entered Glasgow University to take an MA degree in Celtic Studies, as a Mature Student. This he completed in his sixties, to the relief of the staff of the Gaelic department ('The old bustard, he just won't be told, don't know what he came for, he knows it all'). In the piping world, possibly his greatest claim to fame was the success of his pupils in Ceol Mor, notably that of Angus MacColl. Clearly his type of Hebridean teaching suited Angus, who went from strength to strength. Ronald's pupils were devoted to him, and often said how much they owed to his tuition and understanding of the music. Ann Sinclair, from Tiree, paid tribute to him as her teacher: 'Ronnie had a great knowledge of Piobaireachd, which he freely shared in a way which was most understandable, and I had many years of pleasure in studying with him – a true gentleman, with the expertise of a giant in piping terms.'

Ronald was known in the north of mainland Scotland as 'Mad Ronnie' because he was given to making outrageously inaccurate statements: once he declared, in a radio broadcast, that there is nobody north of Inverness who has more than three piobaireachd. This was not well received in an area where quite a few eleven-year-olds have more than three piobaireachd, not to mention John Burgess, the two MacGillivray Gold Medallists, George Stewart, James Mather, Gordon MacKay, Charlie O'Brien, Carol Anne MacKay, Yvonne MacKenzie, Andrew Hill, Colin Innes, A.J. Innes, Fiona MacKay and countless other fine players.

Soon after he had made this unwise statement, the National Mod was held in Golspie and Ronald kept bursting into the hall where piobaireachd for the Gold Medal was in progress, and interrupting the playing with announcements. By the time of the evening ceilidh, he had lost any remaining popularity he might have had with the pipers, and when he was acting as Fear an Tighe at the ceilidh, he was given a rough ride. Whenever he stood up to speak, a hissing broke out in the audience, and of course anyone can hiss without obviously opening his mouth, so that poor Ronald was unable to tell who was doing it. He resorted to the schoolnmaster's expedient of selecting a victim to be expelled from the hall – who soon returned, his hands full of brimming glasses – and the hissing continued unabated.

Ronald died in January 2004, and after a memorial service in Glasgow, his funeral was held in South Uist, where his pupil Graham Roy was the piper. His obituary in the *Piping Times* said 'Whilst his heart was in Glasgow, his soul never left South Uist. He loved the island, its culture, its people and the Gaelic language'.

ANGUS MORRISON who was an old man in the 1990s was a tradition-bearer and very knowledgeable about piping. He sent many interesting letters to the *Piping Times*.

DONALD MORRISON was born at Locheynort in South Uist, an uncle of Willie Morrison. He had been taught first by his father, then as a boy he attended John MacDonald's classes, and later went to Robert B. Nicol at summer schools in Uist. In the late 1940s and early 1950s he was in the Merchant Navy before joining the Aberdeen City Police, on the advice of John MacDonald, Inverness, so that he could go to Robert U. Brown and Robert Nicol (the 'Two Bobs') for tuition. He shared his lessons with Neville MacKay, who was then also a policeman.

Duncan Watson (yet another Aberdeen policeman) wrote in the *Piping Times* in December 2004 about a discussion between Donald Morrison and Robert Reid, who were interested in the differences, and the similarities, of their styles of playing, Reid being a product of the Cameron 'school', Morrison a pupil of a pupil of John MacDonald, Inverness.

Donald won the Gold Medal at Inverness in 1961. He also won the Bratach Gorm in London, and the Silver Chanter at Dunvegan. In his memory an annual recital is held at Loretto School, featuring a leading piper of the day.

Donald was a fine composer, whose works include:

Donald MacLean 6/8 J 4
Donald Ross of Vancouver 6/8 SA 2
Donald Willie and his Dog (also sometimes called *Donald Hugh and his Dog*) 9/8 J 4
Donna's Fling 9/8 J 2
Lady Diana Spencer's Welcome to Deeside 6/8 M 4
The Lost Drum 6/8 M 4
Mrs Amy MacDonald's Birthday 6/8 J 4
Mrs Jean Morrison S 4
Peter and Lorna 6/8 SA 2
The Red Speckled Hen 6/8 J 4
Spogan HP 4

LUDOVIC MORRISON (Louis) is the son of a piper who came to South Uist from Benbecula. His grandfather was a strong piper, and so were his grandfather's brothers. Louis, however, was self-taught, although his father had some piobaireachd from John MacDonald. Louis married ANDREWINA MACKILLOP, herself a player, and their son JOHN ANGUS MORRISON is a piper, as are their daughters ANGUSINA MORRISON and FIONA MORRISON. Andrewina's two uncles, Andrew and Willie MacKillop, were army pipers (her uncle Willie married Louis's sister).

Louis is a composer of light music, some of which has been published by the Uist and Benbecula Fiddle and Accordion Club. He enjoys composing jigs in particular. His piping pupils include KEVIN MACDONALD and ISHBEL MACKENZIE, two promising young players. He named a jig for Ishbel, and another for his wife.

In 1978, Louis played the *Lament for Mary MacLeod* at the North Uist Games, clad in a brown suit jacket and dark blue trousers, garb which aroused no comment even when he had been preceded by John

MacDougall in full and splendid Highland dress. (As Josh Dickson once put it, writing of another South Uist piper, 'He is not the only one on record in South Uist to have disassociated the pomp of the kilt from the act of piping'.) The first prize that day went to John, apparently because it was felt he had come a long way and gone to a lot of trouble with his gear, but it is the playing of Louis Morrison which stays in the memory. He played it in his own island style, and it was beautiful.

One of Louis's sisters married Willie MacKillop, an uncle of the piper Calum Beaton, and another married the son of piper Johnny Steele, Lochboisdale, thus linking three of the piping families of South Uist.

WILLIE MORRISON is Ludovic's nephew, living in Glasgow. He grew up in South Uist, where he learned his piping from his grandfather, DONALD JOHN MORRISON, who had been a pupil of Willie Lawrie when serving in the 2nd Cameron Highlanders.

In his early twenties, Willie moved to Kilmarnock to work for the Johnnie Walker distillery, playing for their pipe band which toured the world in the 1970s. He then moved to Glasgow, where he played with the Glasgow Skye Association band, the Glasgow Transport band, and then moved to the Scottish Power (Grade I) band. He teaches at the Piping Centre in Glasgow,

An exceptionally musical player, he has won the MSR at the Glenfiddich Championship, the Former Winners MSR at Oban, Inverness and London, as well as three times at the National Mod. His piobaireachd gained him first prize at Cowal and in the Uist and Barra competition. He has made several recordings, including a video in the *Hebridean Pipers* series.

Willie is not renowned for his punctuality, and in 1998 when going to Skye to play in the MacDonald Quaich competition, he arrived in Mallaig to see the ferry halfway across the Sound on its way to Armadale. Nothing daunted, Willie negotiated a ride in a fishing boat, and made it in time for the start. Playing in competition with Duncan MacGillivray, Wilson Brown and Stuart Samson, Willie won the Quaich, with *The Rout of Glenfruin* played in the Donald MacDonald setting.

When the Inverness Piping Society was arranging its winter schedule of recitals, Willie Morrison was approached one November, and asked if he would come, perhaps in the following March. 'March did you say?' he said, 'Well, I don't know, it's kind of soon after the New Year.'

In 1997, the Piping Centre in Glasgow issued No 3 in their Recital Series, and this one was the playing of Willie Morrison and Dr Angus MacDonald, who, according to the *Piper Press* in January 1998, 'are among the most exciting players on the recital circuit. Willie's performance combined interesting settings with his own innovative compositions and some great fingerwork. Willie's final track is the best – his legendary *Boneshaker* and *The (Cameronian) Rant*. Many's the time I've sat on the bus back from Cowal, listening with awe to Willie playing these tunes. This is even better than I remember, worth the price of the CD for this alone.'

Willie Morrison's compositions include:

> *Jan Alexander's Fancy* R 4. Made around 1990 for the wife of Greg Sharpe of Kintail (Bagpipe Makers) Ltd, this reel has been recorded by Fred Morrison on his CD *Broken Chanter* and by Willie himself in the *Hebridean Pipers* video.

LISA MORRISON, daughter of Willie, won the Highland Cup for piobaireachd in London in 1999.

FRED MORRISON ('Young Fred') when teaching piping in the schools of Glasgow was employed with full status as a teacher, rather than a mere instructor, because he was fully qualified, with a Teacher's Certificate. This meant he was paid more than an instructor, but the down-side was that he was less likely to be employed by an Education Authority who could take on an instructor for a smaller outlay. He did not enjoy teaching in Glasgow, where pupils seemed uninterested, and he gave it up, to live in Uist and earn his living by his playing and composing. He says he married and went on honeymoon to South Uist – and the honeymoon lasted six years. His wife Deirdre is related to John A. MacLellan, a piper in Benbecula. Fred and Deirdre lived near Ormiclett, in the centre of South Uist, but eventually moved back to Glasgow when Fred was so much in demand for recitals and 'gigs'. South Uist is not the most central place from which to organise tours, though a piper there hastened to point out that it is still the hub of the universe.

Fred is reputed to be able to play virtually any instrument in the world, and can make real music on them all. He has published several CDs and tapes, notably *The Broken Chanter*. In 1999 he brought out *Sound of the Sun*, a CD in which he was in ceilidh mood. Willie Gilmour, reviewing it in the *Piping Times*, said:

> He invariably repeats each tune with the repeat differing from the original rendering. Indeed, I suspect that Fred is enjoying this 'playing off the cuff' and this feeling is conveyed to the listener throughout the CD. Although my purist sensibilities were shaken on first hearing his treatment of *John MacColl's March to Kilbowie Cottage* and *Donald*

MacLean's Farewell to Oban, I soon began to appreciate what Fred was doing with the music. He slows things down and rounds out the tunes, even inventing his own embellishments and, in my book, scores a musical success. Fred, however, does point out that this is not the only way he would play the tunes – it was just how he was feeling on the day.

... The track from which the CD title is taken allows Fred to demonstrate his undoubted composing skill and his amazing breath control. *The Sound of the Sun* is a beautiful piece of music by any standard.

Another highlight for me was the treatment of the traditional strathspeys and reels, in particular an unusual setting of *Cabar Feidh* (S&R), all taken at a fair pace and transmitting a genuine sense of fun and enjoyment.

Fred resembles Allan MacDonald and Duncan MacGillivray in his enjoyment of experiment and innovation, while at the same time all three are accomplished pipers in the conventional style – and all have Gold Medals to prove it. Fred holds both the Gold Medals for piobaireachd, at Oban and at Inverness. In more recent times he rarely competes, to the disappointment of admirers of his very musical piobaireachd, but he gives his time to extensive recital tours and the playing of gigs with his band. He has the knack of holding huge audiences of young people enthralled by his wonderfully accurate flying fingers – and by his own obvious enjoyment of his music, his eyes gleaming through the shaggy mop of chestnut hair falling over his face.

In 2003 he was playing with the group Ceolas at the Celtic Connections festival in Glasgow, where he played the Border pipes. In her review of the festival, Jeannie Campbell said: 'Although the pipe was border, the music was mainly Highland. Fred was in great form as with head down and foot pounding, he launched into set after set of jigs and reels which had the audience demanding encore after encore until the band finally left the stage after 11 p.m., when the Concert Hall was closing for the night.'

When Fred played a barrage of super-fast jigs at a recital in Dingwall, an elderly piobaireachd aficianado was heard to remark that he would really prefer to hear Fred play *Maol Donn*, rather than all this Morse Code music – but the young folk do love it. In Fred's hands it may be super-fast, but it is always musical. As Jeannie put it: 'Fred can play faster than most but his tunes always have a fine melody, unlike many others who go for rhythm and speed and forget about melody.' In her account of Piping Highlights at the 2012 Celtic Connections, she added: 'As Fred has often been described as "on fire", the smoke effects behind the musicians during their last set were very appropriate.'

Among the many albums of pipe music that he has published, his *Outlands* in 2010 stands out for the sheer originality of the compositions which seem to stretch the range of the pipe and its music.

The MacDonalds of South Uist

Boyds

(See also North Uist)

Professor William Matheson said that there was a family of Mac-Donalds in North Uist, and around 1630 or a little earlier, one of them, Donald, sent his son, John, to be fostered in Bute. On his return, he became known as Boid ('of Bute'), which became the family by-name, Boyd. Their descendants were found, not only in North Uist, but also in Barra and South Uist. Another source of the name Boyd in the Uists was a corruption of the by-name Buidhe ('yellow, yellow-haired'). Both lines of Boyds, not related to each other, were later found in South Uist, the Bute family buried at Kilmuir, the Buidhe ones at Clachan Sands.

It seems that Boyd the King's piper, although he may have been at court before the time of the Bute fostering, could possibly have been of Hebridean origin.

A later Boyd piper from South Uist was ALASDAIR BOYD (1889–1970), who may have been one of the family of the King's piper. He was born in Iochdar, at the north end of South Uist, and served in the First World War with the 5th Cameron Highlanders. He was known more for his vast knowledge of Gaelic songs than for his piping, though accomplished as a player for dancing. Although not much of a player of piobaireachd, he had a piobaireachd song to the tune of the *Lament for the Children*, which he could also sing in canntaireachd vocables: he learned this from his mother and his aunt. We are reminded of Simon Fraser, in Australia, who learned the work from the singing of his mother, though it is not clear whether she sang it in Gaelic or canntaireachd, or both.

Alasdair Boyd had a note about a South Uist piper called DONALD MACPHEE: 'Donald MacPhee from Iochdar was a good piper and he was in a regiment called the 93rd [later the Argylls]. And he frequently played at the funerals and old people used to tell me that he had this piece of music 'Going to the Everlasting Home', and any time he played at a funeral this is the first tune he would play.' Allan MacDonald played it on the smallpipes, on his CD *Fhuair Mi Pog,* in 1998, with Margaret Stewart singing the words. It is a short piece. Allan gives the words:

> Dol dhan taigh, dol dhan taigh,
> dol dhan taigh bhuan leat   (×3)
> Dol dhan taigh Geamhraidh,
> dol dhan taigh Samhraidh.

To this Allan adds his comment: 'the song is short but evocative. The pibroch-like variations were added *ex tempore,* confirming my belief that such short songs easily developed into the pibroch genre.'

The Roidean Brothers

Any mention of South Uist piping has to include the two MacDonald brothers known as the Roideans (pronounced something like 'Rotch-ens'). The meaning of the by-name is obscure. Some spell it 'Roitean', deriving it from a word meaning 'a prodigious leap', referring to danc-ing ability; others say 'Roidean' was a diminuitive form of the name Ruairidh, or Roderick. The two brothers were John and Roderick, or Johnny and Roddy, in English, Seonaidh and Ruairidh in Gaelic. Both were pipers in the Glasgow Police Pipe Band in its glory days in the 1930s, indeed, they were part of the glory which made the band so successful. They were cousins of the piping MacDonalds at Garry-hellie, their father, DONALD BAN ROIDEAN, being a brother of Rona's grandfather.

JOHN MACDONALD, SOUTH UIST (1898–1988), known as Seonaidh (or Johnny) Roidean, began his piping career as an army bandsman. Taught initially by his father and then in Uist by John MacDonald, Inverness, he competed as a boy in local games, with great success. He then joined the 3rd (Special Reserve) Battalion of the Camerons as a boy piper aged 15. It is said that he gave his age incorrectly, being only 14 at the time, but keen to join up. This Battalion was made up largely of men and boys from the Outer Isles, and like the 3rd Seaforth it was a unit that was almost entirely Gaelic-speaking. The regimental history adds that its function was to keep the two Regular Army battalions up to strength in time of war. This must have given the pipers plenty of scope in peacetime.

John was then posted to the 6th, and later to the 7th Battalion of the Camerons, out in France. He was a pupil of John MacDonald, Inverness, in the army class, and began a highly successful career as a solo player. When asked about the influence of John MacDonald, Inverness, on his playing, he replied 'I always try to put something of myself into the tune'. One of his favourite sayings was 'There's only one sound, and that's the right one' – pipers will understand just what he meant.

After World War I he left the army and joined the City of Glasgow Police in 1920, later following Willie Gray as Pipe Major, in 1932. The band under his leadership won the World Championship in 1936, 1937, 1938, 1939, and after the war, in 1946 and 1949. He reached the rank of Inspector, as well as Pipe Major. He 'set a notable standard for pipe bands', at the same time pursuing his own career as a competitor, which made him one of the most successful prize winners of the period between the wars. He won the Gold Medal at Oban and at Inverness in the same year, 1926, as well as the Senior Open at Oban that same year, and was described as 'one of the best all-round players of his generation'.

In 1928, to the astonishment of the piping world, he was one of the pipers penalised by the judges at Oban for playing the G gracenote birl in his marches, this disqualification, mainly, it is said, at the instigation of Sheriff Grant of Rothiemurchus. Another of the three judges that day was Somerled MacDonald, from Skye, who dissociated himself angrily from the decision to disqualify G.S. MacLennan and Johnny Roidean – both considered to be outstanding players of Ceol Beag.

Not a prolific composer, John MacDonald made the 4/4 March *The Glasgow Police March Past* – which in the Camerons was known as *The Sands of Loch Bee*. He also made a setting of *The Pretty Apron*, a name which he got from Archie MacDonald in South Uist. The title probably refers to the apron worn over the kilt to keep it clean – but why 'Pretty'?

On his retirement from the police in 1960, he withdrew to South Uist, to live on the family croft near Daliburgh. He was one of the great characters of piping. About that time, an article appeared in the *Piper and Dancer Bulletin*, written in Gaelic by Finlay J. MacDonald and translated by Roderick MacDonald of Toronto, a native of South Uist. This article gives the *sloineadh* (family line) of John (Seonaidh Roidean), as John son of Donald, son of Roderick – was he the origin of the by-name Roidean? – son of Ranald Allan, son of Ewen, son of Donald, son of John. This last John was John MacDonald of Moidart, Chief of Clanranald, who fought bravely at the Battle of Inverlochy in 1645.

The article said also that Johnny Roidean was a great-grandson of Annie, daughter of Alexander MacEachain, uncle of Marshal Hector MacDonald, Duke of Tarentum. Hector was one of Napoleon's Marshals in the early 19th century. The piece adds that the nobility was not only in the blood but in the nature of the man. All who knew him agree that he was 'a thorough Highland gentleman'.

In South Uist, although the brothers were known as Seonaidh and Roddy Roidean, the name Roidean on its own is used always of their father, whose name was Donald – so Roidean in the names of Johnny and Roddy is a sort of patronymic. Roidean was remembered as an excellent Highland dancer, which might support the theory that the name should be Roitean, 'leaper' (also sometimes spelled Roidean).

When John MacDonald, Inverness, died in 1953, one of the pall-bearers at the funeral was Johnny Roidean. All six bearing the coffin were Pipe Majors who had been taught by the great man, who in 1938 had written to Kilberry, mentioning his piobaireachd class in Glasgow; it included five pipers from the Glasgow City Police, the two MacDonald brothers, Charlie Scott, Archie MacNab and John Johnstone. 'They are very keen' wrote John MacDonald, 'and are working hard'.

A great admirer of Johnny Roidean was an American called Frank, who worked for the FBI. He sent his son to Johnny Roidean in Uist, for a year's tuition. At great expense Frank had a full-length, life-size portrait of his hero painted by a well known American artist, from a photograph in which he was wearing his full uniform and all the trimmings. This he let Johnny have in his house in South Uist, having drawn up a legal agreement that when Johnny died, the painting would be returned to Frank. Unfortunately, when Johnny was an old man in the 1980s, the Roidean house near Daliburgh caught fire and burned to the ground, and the portrait was one of many treasured possessions destroyed in the fire. Mrs Chrissie Morrison, who worked in a solicitor's office in Portree and helped to compile the legal title to the painting, said that all contingencies were covered, including adequate insurance.

It is said that the remains of Johnny's ivory-mounted Henderson pipe were found on a windowsill, where they could have been rescued, had anyone known. Soon after this, he went into a care-home in South Uist, and died there in 1988.

Norman MacLean was a pupil and protégé of Seonaidh Roidean, and has described his experience of competing as a boy, under Seonaidh's wing. His account, in Norman's own distinctive style, appeared in the *Piping Times* in January 2005:

With Seonaidh five paces in front of me we'd glide into the assembly
hall of Glasgow High School, employing what in Uist is known as
ceum na mointich, the gait of the moors, a slow, long-striding march
accompanied by a kind of pimp-roll of the upper body. A massive oak,
alone in the garden of eyes, John would divest himself of his tightly
belted trench coat, soft hat, scarf and gloves, and lay them carefully
on the seat nearest the judges' table in the front row. Picking up the
massive wooden pipe-box which contained, among other things,
a handsome full-silver-mounted set of Henderson bagpipes, reeds,
hemp, a silver-mounted dirk and a searrag, flask, of whisky, Seonaidh,
with me in tow, would then march slowly in his confident, chin-out,
I'm-a-winner manner to the tuning room. There, he'd strike up his
magnificent instrument and let loose a volley of embellishments . . .
The effect of all this grandstanding on the other people in the room
was instantaneous. Fathers, uncles, tutors and competitors would make
a dash for the door . . .

Norman wrote that they used to attend many of the Games.

With the Great One behind me, footering with the drones, I'd blast
an endless series of birls. (Incidentally, John abhorred these birls. He'd
grimace as though his teeth hurt and described them as Edinburgh
tuning notes. He'd even sing 'Edin-boro-boro-boro' to discourage me).
Eventually, with the drones tuned to his satisfaction he'd step aside and
place an enormous paw on my shoulder. In a stage whisper that could
be heard in Inverness, he'd intone in a rich baritone: 'Siuthad, 'ill' oig, 's
ann dhuit fhein a rinneadh an saoghal' ('Proceed, young man, the world
was made for you') . . .

It is interesting that, at thirteen or fourteen, Norman did not tune
his own pipe, but depended entirely on his tutor to tune him for competitions. We have to wonder why Seonaidh did not teach him to do
it for himself. Many youngsters of that age today take pride in tuning
themselves – and in some cases they have to, as their tutors are not so
faithful as Seonaidh Roidean in accompanying their pupils to competitions. Times have changed, and some teachers have a large number of
competing pupils, so that they cannot go in support of them all – and
the teachers themselves may be competing on the same day.

One of Seonaidh Roidean's band players was NORMAN MACDONALD
from South Uist, who was killed in France in the First World War,
while serving as a piper with the Cameron Highlanders.

RODERICK MACDONALD, Roddy Roidean (1900–1981) was as well
known as his brother Seonaidh. He joined his brother in the City
of Glasgow Police in 1923, then under Pipe Major Willie Gray, and

competed successfully all through the 1920s and 1930s. He won the Gold Medal at Oban in 1938 and at Inverness in 1946 ('on either side of the War'), both times described as being of the 'Glasgow City Police'. His winning tune for both Medals was *Mary's Praise*. He was known most of all for his excellent teaching ability, and it was said that he had a natural affinity with beginners, something perhaps lacking in his brother. Among his distinguished pupils were the double Gold Medallist Kenny MacDonald from Tiree, Duncan Johnstone, Dr Angus MacDonald, Angus' brother Allan, and Iain MacFadyen.

David Murray recalled an occasion at South Uist when 'I listened, utterly entranced, as Roddy MacDonald, his back turned to the wind and the rain, played non-stop for the dancing. Out the music poured, tune after tune, strathspeys, reels, hornpipes, jigs and wee marches for the Hebridean dances, an unforgettable listening experience.'

Late in 1944, the Uist and Barra Association set up a sub-committee to study the feasibility of holding a professional piping competition the following year. On it were four worthies of Uist piping and athletics, Roddy MacDonald, D.J. MacLean (North Uist), Angus Morrison (South Uist) and A.J. MacDonald (North Uist). The first competition was held in the MacLellan Galleries in Glasgow in the winter of 1945, and it has now become an established part of the professional piper's year, the first competition of the season, usually held in March. It is now invitational.

In the 1970s, Roddy MacDonald of the Glasgow Police was 'the modern exponent' of the piobaireachd *Corrienessan's Lament* as reconstructed by Dr Bannatyne, apparently from an old Urlar, or perhaps an Urlar and 1st variation, reputedly composed by Iain Dall MacKay, the Blind Piper of Gairloch. The fact that Roddy Roidean played this reconstruction at an SPA meeting shows that he was open-minded and willing to accept new developments.

When Seumas MacNeill held his seminal evening classes on piobaireachd in the College of Piping in the 1970s, he used many well-known pipers to play his examples to illustrate the lectures. Roddy Roidean and Duncan MacFadyen were two who were prominent in these classes, and inspired many members by their beautiful playing.

ALEXANDER MACDONALD (1900–1992) – see under Benbecula, below.

ANGUS MACDONALD, Milton, was known as 'The King of Jigs'. He was said to play the piobaireachd *Cille Chriosd* 'very very fast'.

ARCHIBALD MACDONALD (Eairdsidh Raghnall) of Daliburgh, father of Rona, was described by Cailean MacLean as 'a piper and seanachaidh of renown'. David Murray said he was 'a man of many parts, a skilled fishing ghillie, and a highland historian. Archie had served in the Great War as a piper in the 5th Cameron Highlanders,' along with Neil MacLennan and Johnny Roidean. 'They were exceptional men. It seemed at times to me that they could recall every tune they had played together. On the morning after the Armistice on 11 November 1918, they set off to lead the 5th Camerons on the long road leading to the River Rhine and Germany. Archie reminisced "We started off playing *The 72nd's Farewell to Aberdeen*, and a right good job we made of it, too!"'

Col. Murray goes on to tell of Archie's skill as a raconteur, remembering a story of how Archie had been wounded in the war, and was sent to a barrack in Ireland to convalesce, and was subjected to some teasing by other soldiers there, because of his accent and background. The story tells of an inspection where all the others were 'booked' for minor misdemeanours, but when the inspecting officer heard that Archie was from South Uist and was the nephew of the officer's fishing ghillie, he was given seven days leave, with three days travelling time each way.

NEIL MACDONALD, son of Archie and brother of Rona, lived at Garryhellie, South Uist. He was a good piper, but did not compete much, and that only in local Games, as he went into the merchant navy and was away from home a lot. He retired to South Uist and took up teaching piping to local children. He died suddenly in 2001, aged 67.

Rona Lightfoot

RONA MACDONALD, daughter of Archie, and sister of Neil, cousin of the Roideans, niece of Angus Campbell, her genes brimming with piping, was an accomplished player at an early age, taught by her father; he presided over her competing career, anxious as a dancer's mother, as they say. She won many junior competitions. The *Piping Times* described her fingering at 13 as 'as good as Burgess at this age. Her Donald MacLean jig was a fitting climax to a fine day's playing. This is a young lass we will be hearing a lot about in the future'.

She married Tony Lightfoot, a merchant-seaman, for whom she composed a 6/8 Jig. They live in Inverness. Rona's Gaelic singing, whether solo or along with Margaret Stewart, is often the highlight of the ceilidh which follows the Donald MacLeod Memorial competition in Stornoway. At a recital in Dingwall in 2003, she sang the poignant Gaelic song *The Widow's Grief*, the tune of which is that of the piobaireachd work *Maol Donn* or *MacCrimmon's Sweetheart*, and immediately afterwards she played *Maol Donn* as a very sad lament, with great effect. She told the audience that the South Uist tradition concerned a poor widow lamenting because she had been unable to save her precious cow from a bog, so that now she could no longer feed her children. The South Uist tradition says the composer of the piobaireachd was one of the Clanranald pipers in the 17th century, presumably one of the MacIntyres. It was not associated with the MacCrimmons until well into the 19th century, when the title *Mac-Crimmon's Sweetheart* was introduced; before that, English speakers always called it *A Favourite Piece*. Because of the uncertainty about the English name, even non-Gaelic speakers often use the title *Maol Donn*.

Rona frequently judges the piping at Games in the north and in the islands, and features as a fine singer and teacher on Gaelic programmes on television.

Every April in the early 2000s she was prominent in organising a fund-raiser for the Donald MacLeod Memorial Competition. This is a big ceilidh held in the Legion Hall in Dingwall. The occasion is always a sell-out, with people standing at the back if no seats are available. Rona herself sings in the ceilidh, as well as looking after her fellow-artistes, and when the interval comes, there she is, serving teas to the whole audience, and then gathering up the cups and going off to do the washing-up. She breaks off from her duties at the sink, shedding her apron as she appears at the microphone to move the audience with her beautiful singing, and make us laugh with her comic songs. Then back to the dishes. An amazing woman, last seen taking a large packet of toilet rolls into the Gents.

In 2004, Rona's CD entitled *Eadarainn* ('Between us', or 'between you and me') appeared, an unusual collection of Gaelic songs and music, sung by Rona or played by her on the pipes. The word Ead-arainn 'perfectly reflects the intimacy and accessibility of the songs and music Rona performs on the CD'. In his introduction on the sleeve, Cailean MacLean describes Rona as 'a ceilidh personified', who inher-ited her talents and her repertoire from both her parents in South Uist, whose house at Gearraidh-shellidh (Garryhellie) was virtually 'a per-manent ceilidh, with music, amusement, and general diversion going on whenever folk called there'. Cailean goes on:

> She is a great piper – in fact with one or two others, Rona blazed a trail
> for women competing at the highest level and is credited with being
> the first of the fairer sex to win a major piping competition. She is also

a hugely talented singer and a veritable treasury of traditional Gaelic songs. What's more, Rona is a terrific raconteur with a great sense of humour and an infectious laugh.

Cailean described Rona's background:

> As the saying goes in Gaelic, she did not have to buy her talents – they came down to her through the many generations of celebrated pipers, singers and story-tellers which adorn her family tree. Rona's most immediate musical influences were her mother Kate, who was one of the most remarkable singers and tradition bearers of her age, and Eairdsidh Raghnall [Archie Ranald], her father, a piper and seanachaidh of renown . . . Theirs was a family and a household which cherished and fostered Gaelic traditional arts, and the CD is a distillation of the cultural legacy which she inherited, not only a delight but also an important part of the bequest which Rona is passing on to a new generation of singers and pipers.

Rona recalls the days when she would send in her application to enter various big competitions, enclosing her £1 entrance fee, only to have it all returned to her as women were not then permitted to compete. Similarly, she was refused membership of the Inverness Piping Society, although her husband, who comes from Kent and is not a piper, was admitted. Today Rona is the President of the Society, elected in 2010, the first woman to hold that office. She will fill the role admirably.

Rona was asked to give the Eulogy at the funeral of Alasdair Gillies in Ullapool, in 2011. Addressing a packed congregation of pipers from all over Scotland, she spoke movingly of her friend and colleague, with stories of his life, but managed to keep it light and affectionate, never over-playing the emotion. On a day of overwrought feeling, she hit exactly the right note – as she has always done as piper and singer.

Rona's niece is RONA MACDONALD, formerly at the College of Piping where she and Jeannie Capmbell made a formidable team. Rona, who is an excellent journalist, wrote a particularly memorable piece published in the *Piping Times*, about the state of the Ladies' lavatories at Cowal Games. She left the College to become Programme Director of the 'Year of the Artist' scheme.

A South Uist Piper in Japan

Another piping member of the MacDonald family of South Uist has his home far from the Western Isles. South Uist piping spreads its tentacles all round the world, but possibly the most unusual off-shoot is a piper who teaches Modern Japanese History at Kyoto University. YAHYA ABDELSAMAD is the son of a Sudanese diplomat who married Fiona MacDonald from Lochboisdale, whom he met when they were both at St Andrews University. Fiona was born in Rawalpindi, India, in 1931, when her father, a piper in the Camerons, was stationed there. Her grandfather, ALASDAIR MACDONALD, was also a piper in the Camerons, possibly the man named by Dr Angus MacDonald in his note on the tune *The Pipes of St Valery*. As a child she was sent home to Lochboisdale, to be raised by an aunt there, and during the summers, she had piping lessons from John MacDonald (Johnnie Roidean) of the Glasgow Police, who was a relative. She in turn taught her son (whose secondary name is Alasdair MacDonald) and her two daughters, but she died when they were still children.

Yahya, in Japan, is the only one of his immediate family who still plays. He bought the old pipes which belonged to Angus MacPhee, of Kessock, near Inverness. Made in 1880, they were ivory mounted, and had silver added in 1950. Yahya composed a 6/8 March and named it after Angus.

Although born in New York to a Sudanese father and now living in Japan, his South Uist genes seem to be dominant, and his piping clearly gives him great pleasure. He competes occasionally in this country. There is interest in piping in many parts of Japan, and piobaireachd seems to appeal to the Japanese mind. One day at the Games in Dornoch, a Japanese lady paused to listen at the piobaireachd platform, never having encountered the music before. She was held by it, and seventeen piobaireachd performances later was begging to be told where she could hear more. Many Japanese people have an instinct for patterns, and this lady was able to discern those of the structure in each tune, on first hearing.

Sources

Rona Lightfoot
Dr Angus MacDonald
John MacDonald, Inverness
Norman MacLean
D.R. MacLennan
Neil MacMillan
Finlay MacRae
William Matheson, *TGSI* LII
David Murray
Piper and Drummer Bulletin

Piping Times
Frederick Rea, *A School in South Uist*
Barry Shears, *Dance to the Piper*
Rev. A. MacDonald, *The Uist Collection*
Yahya Abdelsamad

Seton Gordon

Seton Gordon, in his book *Hebridean Memories*, wrote of an emigrant ship leaving South Uist in the spring of 1923, the *Marloch*, taking fifty families from the Outer Isles to St John, New Brunswick, heading for Alberta. Seton Gordon gave a moving description of the scene in Lochboisdale as three pipers played on the pier or on board the ship departing into the sunset.

This departure was in stark contrast to the emigrations from South Uist in the mid-1800s. The proprietor, Colonel Gordon of Cluny, wanting to be rid of as many of his tenants as possible, had persuaded some of them to sign an agreement that they would emigrate, the inducement being the offer of oatmeal at the time of the potato famines. When the time came, they did not want to go, and Cluny had them seized and tied up, and thrown into the emigrant ship. Another ploy was to take away a crofter's animals and boats, so that he had no means of supporting his family, and had to leave the country. Certainly there were no pipers playing on the quay at these departures.

In 1925, Seton Gordon was judging a competition at Grantown-on-Spey, 'where the top three pipers in pibroch were all from South Uist'.

The Campbells

ANGUS CAMPBELL, who went to Cape Breton in Nova Scotia in the early 19th century, from the Western Isles, probably South Uist, 'was strictly a piobaireachd player but did not pass it on' (Scott Williams). He was also a Gaelic bard, noted for his sarcastic wit.

ANGUS CAMPBELL who died in 2002 at the age of 102 was a pupil of John MacDonald, and was related by marriage to the Morrison piping family, his wife being Bell Morrison, a sister of Ronald and Old Fred. Angus came originally from Benbecula, and was a cousin of Calum Iain Campbell (see below, Benbecula). Angus was taught by his father NEIL CAMPBELL, who along with Archie MacDonald had been a pupil in Daliburgh of John MacDonald, Inverness, before and after the Great War. Neil, who was known in Uist for having made pipes using sheep's bones for drones, had a great liking for the tune *Arthur Bignold of Lochrosque*, by John MacColl. There is a detailed account of this Campbell family in Joshua Dickson's book *When Piping Was Strong* (2006).

Angus himself was also taught by John MacDonald 'and anything ever taught to him then never left him'. It is said that John MacDonald was his piping god, and he became very dogmatic about John's teachings: piping had to be John's way or it was worthless. His family said that piping was a way of life to Angus, and he played his chanter every night, as well as singing piobaireachd as John had taught him.

John MacPherson in Barra ('The Coddy') told how Angus played an old set of pipes at the Glasgow Exhibition in 1938, and how his performance of *MacIntyre's Lament* was broadcast on the wireless. A very old set of pipes found on the battlefield after Culloden, now in the West Highland Museum, was played on a BBC programme, and it was Angus Campbell who gave a performance of *My King Has Landed in Moidart* on it, finding the pitch very low compared to that of more modern pipes.

Angus was a devoted crofter, at Belleview, Frobost, South Uist, and he was known as a great raconteur of Gaelic stories. He was often shy with strangers, but, it was said, a good dram would usually thaw him.

His niece and pupil, Rona Lightfoot, says he went only once in his life to the mainland, when he competed at the Argyllshire Gathering and came second in the Gold Medal, losing to Pipe Major Charles Smith of the Black Watch. Angus played *The Blue Ribbon* on that occasion. He had to play the same tune shortly afterwards, in the Senior Open, and again came second, this time to Robert Reid. (At that time, in 1934, the Open was indeed an open competition and entrants did not have to be holders of either of the Gold Medals.)

Angus's favourite work was *Patrick Og*, and Young Fred Morrison played it at his funeral. Fred is a nephew of Angus's wife, Bell Morrison.

Rona has a photograph of Angus as a boy of about twelve, barefoot and playing his pipes, wearing a pair of trousers made by Rona's mother, Kate MacDonald – a noted Gaelic singer. Kate, then aged only thirteen, was given an old pair of trousers of her father's, and told by her mother to make them over into trousers for Kate's brother to wear at the Games the next day. She herself did not have the time as she had to go to Lochboisdale to gut herring. When she came home, the trousers were ready, but poor Kate got a roasting for accidentally cutting the green velvet table cover.

Rona's photograph of the participants in the South Uist Games in the early 1950s was published in the *Piping Times* in December 2002. It shows John Garroway, Willie M. MacDonald, Neil Angus MacDonald, James MacGillivray, Donald MacLeod, Micky MacKay, Seumas MacNeill, Angus Campbell, John Scott and Adam Scott, Archie MacDonald, John MacLennan, Neillie MacLennan, Rona MacDonald, Archie MacNab, Dr George MacKinnon and John MacDonald, with the three judges, Campbell of Shirvan, Sheriff Grant of Rothiemurchus and Archibald Campbell of Kilberry. Someone commented that it was like looking at a picture of the gods in Valhalla.

Angus Campbell died in November 2002, at the age of 102. His wife Bell had died a few years earlier, and Angus spent his last years in the care of the Sisters at the Old Folks Home in Daliburgh, where he was a great favourite.

Barry Shears names ARCHIE CAMPBELL, known as 'Giad', who in the 1920s played for dancing in Iochdar (see below). Archie may have been one of the Campbell pipers from Benbecula.

MARY ANN CAMPBELL was a pupil of Calum Beaton in the 1990s, playing excellent light music on the full pipe, after only a year's tuition.

In 2003, a letter from Angus Campbell in Florida arrived for the Piping Times editor, with a donation for the College Building Fund. 'We're ex-South Uist' Angus explained, and said his seven-year-old son EWEN CAMPBELL had won 'his first medal' for piping at the Games in Fort Lauderdale. It's in the blood.

The Smiths of Howmore

JOHN SMITH, married to Christina MacMillan, was a piper in the late 19th century. His three sons were all pipers, SANDY SMITH, JOHN SMITH and NEIL SMITH. All three could read music, and were accomplished players of light music, especially for dancing. All three are said to have attended the classes given by John MacDonald, Inverness, before 1914. They were good teachers of piping, and both Donald Morrison and John A. MacLellan had the benefit of their tuition. John Smith later passed it on to his pupil, Calum Beaton.

Another JOHN SMITH was an army piper from South Uist, serving in the Highland Light Infantry (HLI). In 1910, when the first Army Piping Class was held in the Cameron Barracks in Inverness, taught by John MacDonald, Inverness, the first pupil sent to him was John Smith, who was already an excellent player. He passed the course with flying colours, and was followed by other distinguished army pipers. John Smith, wounded in 1914 soon after the outbreak of war, was transferred to another HLI regiment which was sent to Iraq. He died there from dysentery in 1917.

Donald Smith KSG DSM

In 1995, the Gaelic Society of London, wishing to honour the memory of DONALD SMITH, who had been their President and Chief for many years, inaugurated an annual bursary to enable a young piper to attend a course of piping at Sabhal Mor Ostaig, the Gaelic College in Skye.

Donald Smith belonged to a well-known piping family in South Uist, who lived at Ormiclett (there are various spellings of this name, which often appears as Ormiclate). This was where the Clanranald chiefs used to live, with their MacIntyre pipers close by.

Donald was born and brought up in Ormiclett, and served in the Second World War. On his return, he joined the Metropolitan Police in 1946, and rose to become a Chief Superintendent. Living in London, he took an active part in both the piping and the Gaelic world down there, and saw to it that his own family was immersed. Three of his sons and his daughter were pipers, the eldest being John Angus Smith (see below).

After Donald's death, the Gaelic Society of London had five Honorary Pipers, of whom four were the children of Donald, namely JOHN ANGUS, ALASDAIR, DONALD and JOHANNA.

NEIL SMITH was born in 1939 in Glasgow, but his parents were from South Uist. His father taught him his first piping, before he went to Duncan Johnstone and then to Donald MacLeod. He made his career with the Strathclyde Police, which won all the major band championships, and he used to compete in the island games when on holiday in the west. He sometimes taught in the College of Piping in Glasgow, being acknowledged to be a fine player. Latterly he had a holiday house in Spain, where he died suddenly in 2011.

Appropriately, the first winner of the Donald Smith Memorial Bursary awarded in 1996 was INNES SMITH from Bridge of Allan, who was then 15. Applicants had to submit a tape recording of a 6/8 March, and give their views on the relation between the Gaelic language and the oral tradition of the Highland bagpipe. The Bursary enables the winner to take a five-day residential course in piping, which in 1996 was taught by Norman Gillies and John Burgess (neither of whom was a Gaelic speaker). He also received a copy of Kilberry's *Ceol Mor*.

JOHN ANGUS SMITH of London and Hong Kong, whose parents were from South Uist and Eriskay, is a grandson of Donald Smith. As he is currently a competing piper, he will not be discussed at length here. He composed a lively tune called *Ormacleit*.

His father learned his piping by ear, with no formal instruction, playing mainly marches and Gaelic airs. John Angus says that although many of his family, past and present, are right-handed, they were taught to play with the pipe on the right shoulder as if left-handed. Many other island players, especially those in South Uist played this way. It is thought that the army forced many to change to the left shoulder, in order to conform when playing in military bands. Col. David Murray says another reason to change was that when a left-handed player marched round the table in the Officers' Mess, his tassells tickled the officers' heads as he passed them.

Sources

Calum Beaton
Joshua Dickson, *When Piping Was Strong*
Seton Gordon, *Hebridean Memories*
Rona Lightfoot
Piping Times
John Angus Smith

The Steele Family

As well as John Steele in South Uist, composer of *The Hills of South Uist*, there was DONALD STEELE, living in Nova Scotia at Steele's Crossing, Rear Boisdale, Cape Breton. He was born in 1827, the son of Duncan Steele and Raonaid MacIntyre, of Milton, South Uist. Donald was a carpenter and an accomplished piper. He married Mary MacDonald of Glace Bay, and they had six children.

JOHN STEELE, possibly the father of John Steele (below), was living in Stoneybridge, South Uist in 1891, a crofter aged 35, living in a two-roomed house with his wife Catherine (who spoke no English). They had five children aged 7 or under, including twins. There were Steeles also at Smerclett and Kilphedir at that time. John was a piper.

JOHN STEELE, Lochboisdale (1889–1961), who made *The Hills of South Uist*, was an excellent piper and a fine dancer. A pupil of John MacDonald, Inverness, in his army days, he served in World War I, before returning to Uist in the 1920s. He was a first-classs player of light music, excelling especially at the playing of jigs. He had three sons, all pipers, though said not to be the greatest of players. One of them married a sister of Ludovic Morrison. Josh Dickson (2006) has a fuller account of this family.

More South Uist Pipers

NEIL MACLENNAN, Lochboisdale, was a South Uist piper said to be very good. He served alongside Archie MacDonald and John Mac-Donald (Johnny Roidean) as a piper in the 5th Camerons in the First World War. He later became postmaster at Lochboisdale.

General Frank Richardson gave Neil as an example of a very good player whose nervous temperament prevented him from competing (but the General said the same of Lewis Beaton, who did compete). Calum Beaton spoke highly of Neil's playing, but said he died young. The records of the Games in Uist show that Neil did indeed compete, but seems to have restricted his appearances to island games. Of him, Neil MacMillan said 'His favourite tune was *The Earl of Seaforth* – he liked it because of all those top-hand notes, which gave him a chance to wave flies away from landing on his nose'.

GEORGE JOHNSTONE, born in South Uist, served in the 1st Battalion the Queen's Own Cameron Highlanders in Malaya, Tripoli and the Canal Zone. He was a nephew of Pipe Major JAMES JOHNSTONE DCM MM, Sniper Sergeant of the 2nd Camerons at Salonika, in the First World War. George gained his Pipe Major's certificate in 1951, and on leaving the army, he joined the lighthouse service. He composed *Donella Beaton* 6/8 J 4; Donella married Adam Scott, a piper in the Lovat Scouts.

Other compositions by George Johnstone include:

Alan D. Johnston 2/4 M 4
Donald Johnston of Castlebay 6/8 M 4
Jock Masson 12/8 M 4
Nan's Jig 6/8 J 4
Norman Gillies 6/8 J 4
Pipe Major Thomas Ramsey, Irish Guards 2/4 M 4
Pipe Major Willie Kinnear 6/8 SA 1
Plumber's Pipes R 4
SuperScot 9/8 J 4

Note also: *George Johnston*, by J.A. Barrie 6/8 M 4

Pipe Corporal ARCHIBALD LINDSAY from Daliburgh was a piper in the 4th/5th Battalion Queen's Own Cameron Highlanders (Territorial

Army), and in the 51st Highland Volunteers before he joined the Queen's Own Highlanders as a piper in 1971. He served with the 1st Battalion in Germany, Scotland, Northern Ireland and Hong Kong, and then was at the Scottish Infantry depot. He composed *The Sky-lark's Ascension* in 1980, and *The QOH Polka* when in Hong Kong in 1981. *Lindsay's Lament* is a Slow March, composed when his father died.

Archie Lindsay revived the South Uist Piping Club, with its home in Daliburgh Drill Hall. In 1999 about 20 young pipers were receiving tuition there on a weekly basis. Many of them then moved up to join the Army Cadet Force Pipe Band.

In 1995, Archie competed in the Flora MacDonald Competition, held annually in Daliburgh School, and won several prizes. Two days after the competition he was killed in a road accident near his home. He was 47 years old. Angus Morrison commented that the loss of Archie would be deeply felt in the community where he was always more than willing to entertain others with his fine piping ability.

The MacMillans

Barry Shears lists DONALD MOR MACMILLAN among the early piping settlers in Nova Scotia. He and his brothers JAMES (born around 1822) and NEIL MACMILLAN came to Glenmorrison, NS, in 1841. Another piper, JOHN MACMILLAN (born c.1828) married Annie MacMullin or MacMillan, both pipers from South Uist. John may have been related to Donald Mor, as may Annie. Neil returned to Scotland, but his grandson MURDOCH MACMILLAN (died 1940) was a piper and fiddler in Johnstown, Nova Scotia.

ANNIE MACMULLIN belonged to Mira, Nova Scotia, but seems to have originated in South Uist. Her marriage to John MacMillan pro-duced many children, seven of whom she taught to play the bagpipes. She was herself an accomplished player of both light music and Ceol Mor, and Barry Shears says she could sing several piobaireachd works in their entirety, including *The Finger Lock*.

DONALD MACMILLAN (1896–1976) was reckoned to be a first-class player, taught by John MacDonald, Inverness during John's visits to South Uist. Donald joined the Lovat Scouts in 1913, and became Pipe Major of the 1st Regiment in the Great War, serving in Greece, Gallipoli, Egypt and France.

In 1921 he emigrated to the USA. He was 'the most prominent piobaireachd player in the Detroit area of the USA in the 1930s and

40s', according to Ed Neigh. 'He came out from South Uist to be Pipe Major of the Black Watch in Montreal, except that they did not know that if you came from South Uist you had the wrong religion for the Black Watch of Montreal.' Donald with George Duncan 'taught the piobaireachd which they played avidly, but none of the pupils continued on as professional piobaireachd players and tutors'.

In the early thirties he returned to South Uist, but soon went back across the Atlantic, and continued his career as an eminent teacher and judge of piping. On his retirement, however, he was back in Uist for good, a return regarded as a considerable loss to American and Canadian piping; the *Piping Times* commented: 'It was fitting, however, that he came back to his home and enjoyed playing and listening to his beloved music among the crofts and hills of his boyhood.'

His brother GEORGE MACMILLAN was equally good, and also taught by John MacDonald.

Their nephew and pupil was NEIL MACMILLAN, who was an excellent player for dancing, as well as a fine all-round piper. His piping came to him from both sides, as his mother was one of the piping Walker family. A pupil of John MacDonald, Inverness, he composed and made settings of Strathspeys, Reels and Jigs, and his work is to be found in Logan's Collection of Pipe Music. He is immensely knowledgeable about Uist piping in general, and about the state of piping there before the advent of John MacDonald. He says that in his young days, all dance music in Uist, without exception, was played on the pipes.

This is borne out by a passage from Bill Lawson's *Croft History*, quoted by Barry Shears, about dancing in South Uist in the 1920s:

> There was always a dance on the 15th of August (*Latha Feille Muire*), and a few in the springtime, and there was a dance at Christmastime. The music was provided by '*Giad*' – Archie Campbell on the pipes, and he piped the whole night in the old school at Iochdar. We got a gallon of beer before we went, and gave it to the piper. He was the oddest piper to watch, for he always piped for a dance sitting down, but he was the best of pipers to dance to.

Barry suggests that playing sitting down was often an indication that the music was for step-dancing.

An interesting comment of Neil's was about the old piobaireachd songs, sung with Gaelic words (not canntaireachd) to the tunes of the pipe music. When he was young, he said, everyone in the islands knew these songs, and when a piper was playing a piobaireachd work all those present would burst into song, singing along with the player, and he expected this: he would be upset if they did not respond to his playing, and would regard listening in silence as failure on his part to inspire them with his music. This seems to present a new aspect to piobaireachd songs, which many think were sung only by women or those who were not themselves pipers – or had no instrument handy. Neil added that sometimes different islands had different words to a tune, and yiou could tell from the words which island had originated the songs, as they were re-cast to suit local requirements. This is similar to what Jonathan MacDonald said of Ceol Beag playing in Kilmuir, Skye, in the early 20th century, when every township had its own way of playing a tune, and the place could be identified according to the wee embellishments or changes put into the tune by the player.

These piobaireachd songs in the islands should not be confused with the singing of piobaireachd in the vocables of canntaireachd. The songs were in Gaelic, which carried meaning, and were for entertainment; the canntaireachd was meaningless in the sense that it had no grammatical structure but was intended to imitate the music. Its purpose was to teach and pass on the musical tradition, or to illustrate a musical point when a pipe was not to hand. Many tunes, of course, would have both songs and canntaireachd, but they were entirely separate.

Neil has a first edition of Angus MacKay's *Ancient Piobaireachd,* which was given to him by Neil MacCormick in Mull.

Neil MacMillan has suffered greatly from Djupetron's Contracture, a disease of the tissues of the hand which causes the fingers to curl. Nowadays it can be treated by surgery, but in older times it ruined the careers of many pipers. Neil has had several fingers amputated, and today when taking a dram has to hold the glass between the palms of his two hands.

IAIN MACMILLAN played in the Glasgow City Police Pipe Band.

Sources

Calum Beaton
Neil MacMillan
Angus Morrison
Louis Morrison
Ed Neigh
Queen's Own Highlanders, *The Caber Feidh Collection*
Frank Richardson
Barry Shears, *Dance to the Piper*

The Scott Brothers

JOHN W. SCOTT and ADAM SCOTT were brothers born in South Uist.
John went to live in Glasgow, and Adam, who married Donella Beaton,
remained in Lochboisdale, South Uist, after serving as a piper with the
Lovat Scouts. Both brothers composed pipe tunes.

JOHN SCOTT and DONALD MACPHEE from South Uist created quite
a thriving piping community in the Windsor (Ontario)–Detroit (USA)
area, with good quality pipes, in the 1930s.

John Scott was a good composer, whose works include a tribute to
his second wife, a slow air entitled *Katy MacDonald of Croydon*. He
also made at least a dozen other works, which are still played today (see
the list of South Uist works, above).

The Walker Family

This important piping family in Uist is said to have originated in the
Borders, the name being derived, according to Uist tradition, from
'waulker', i.e. one who waulks or shrinks tweed.

WILLIAM WALKER and his brother CALUM WALKER were pipers in
the Lovat Scouts, as were Ronald Morrison, Adam Scott and Angus
MacDonald, the King of Jigs. Calum was competing successfully in
the 1930s, holding his own against opponents from the mainland. The
Walker brothers' sister was the mother of Neil MacMillan. A grandson
KEVIN WALKER, pupil of Louis Morrison, was at the age of 14, after
two years of tuition, playing very competently on the full pipe.

Sources

Calum Beaton
Neil MacMillan
Louis Morrison

Simon and Finlay MacKenzie

Both SIMON MACKENZIE and his son FINLAY MACKENZIE had leading roles in Uist piping, as important and generous patrons. Simon
had his roots in Gruinard, Wester Ross, but had gone to Barra to run
a hotel in Castlebay before he moved to Lochboisdale, South Uist.
There he had a smallish hotel not far from the present Lochboisdale
Hotel but on the other side of the road, closer to the harbour. After
some years there, he built the present-day, much larger hotel, which

his son Finlay inherited on Simon's death. Although many say it was Finlay who worked with Canon MacDougall to organise the classes taught by John MacDonald, in the decade before the First World War, it was in fact Simon. Matching his father in enthusiasm, Finlay took up the cause of encouraging and financing the classes and the Games, and both father and son were unstinting in the help they offered local pipers. The ground at Askernish where the South Uist Games are held belonged at that time to the hotel, which explains the venue, generously offered by the MacKenzies.

FINLAY MACKENZIE (1883–1964), proprietor of the Lochboisdale Hotel for many years, was an important figure in the piping of South Uist in the late 19th and early 20th century, although he was in Canada for some years after 1900. He returned to South Uist after serving in the First World War.

Not only did he support the Piobaireachd Society's scheme to bring prominent pipers to the island to teach the local players, but he put them up in his hotel at his own expense, and treated them as honoured guests. He also ran competitions, and gave the prizes, as well as starting a Piping Club at Borve. When he died, he left money for a Trust to buy good pipes for promising pupils, usually Hardy's or Grainger and Campbell's. Louis Morrison had one, and so did the young John A. MacLellan. The Trust was administered by the Royal Bank of Scotland in Lochboisdale, but the money seems to have run out when the cost of pipes, unheard of in Finlay's day, outstripped the interest from the fund. It has been said that Finlay left the sum of £2,500 as a bequest to pay for one set of pipes for a promising young piper, and in 1966 the lucky recipient was Willie Morrison, Locheynort. It is not clear if this was an arrangement separate from the above-mentioned Trust.

Local people say it was Finlay's idea to bring John MacDonald over to teach in Uist, and they maintain that it was Finlay, and not the Piobaireachd Society, who financed these visits. It was, however, his father, Simon, who started the classes, acting with Canon MacDougall. Probably the Society contributed, possibly paying John a fee while the hotel provided free board and lodging. Margaret Fay Shaw described John's lessons, at which she was sometimes allowed to sit in, just to listen. Some lessons were held in a back smoking-room, at the Lochboisdale Hotel. In the evenings John would sometimes play his violin, with Margaret accompanying him on the piano. Finlay was himself a piper, but his main talent was for organizing and running schemes to promote island piping.

Although they embedded themselves in the life of Uist, these Mac-Kenzies were not islanders. Simon was from Wester Ross, born at Gruinard, near Gairloch. He married a girl from Portree. Finlay himself was born in Inverness, but when he was very young his father took a hotel in Barra, to which the family moved in the late 1880s. In the 1891 Census, Simon was in Barra, but a George MacKenzie from Gairloch had the Carinish Hotel in North Uist, where he had been for some twenty years.

William Matheson said that Ewen MacDonald of Vallay (see below) brought a father and son called MacKenzie over from Gairloch when he needed carpenters for the building of his house, in the 18th century. The father, Andrew, had a son James – he was living at Malaclete, opposite Vallay, in 1764. James had a son Angus whose son Roderick was an excellent shenachie and lived in Vallay, later retiring to Mala-clete. His son, another Andrew MacKenzie also lived in Malaclete. Though no direct link with the hotel MacKenzies has been found, it is possible there was a relationship and that this is what brought the hotel family from Gairloch to the islands. If not, it has to be coincidence that both sets of island MacKenzies came from Gairloch.

The Lochboisdale Hotel was built in the 1890s, when Finlay was a child. The earlier, smaller hotel, across the road, has long since van-ished. It was his father Simon who came to Lochboisdale as a hotelier to run it, before building the present big one, but Finlay was the one who developed the business. He is remembered with affection in Uist, being a jolly and big-hearted man who enjoyed a good ceilidh and wel-comed everyone to his hotel regardless of social status. He married a girl called Millicent Duff, from Northern Ireland. She died before him, and had asked to be buried with her family, so that when Finlay himself died in Belfast, he too was buried in Northern Ireland. Several other members of his family lie in graves at Hallan, near Daliburgh.

It was Finlay's father, Simon MacKenzie, who, with Fr Alexander MacDougall, founded the South Uist Piping Society in 1908.

Finlay died in 1964, and a fine monument was erected in his memory outside his hotel.

Sources

Census records for Gairloch, Barra and South Uist
Joshua Dickson, *When Piping Was Strong*
Neil MacMillan
Margaret Fay Shaw, *Folksong and Folklore of South Uist*

Uist Pipers in Two Wars

In the First World War, a piper called ANGUS MORRISON, serving with the 16th Seaforth Highlanders of Canada, came from a family in Iochdar, South Uist. He was killed in action, recovering guns lost when the Canadians were gassed by the Germans. He was 32 years old.

Another Uist piper in that war was ALEXANDER MACEACHEN, of the Cameron Highlanders. He died of his wounds after taking part in the great charge around Loos. He was wounded in the head by a German bullet. Unusually, his body was brought back to South Uist for burial. Although the weather was stormy and the ground covered with snow, every man in the district turned out for the funeral.

The *Oban Times* in 1916 drew attention to a family in Garryhellie, South Uist, the five sons of Mr and Mrs Ronald Morrison, all serving in the army. Four of the five were pipers. These were the forebears of Young Fred Morrison.

In the sleeve of his CD *Maidean Dubh' an Donais* ('The Black Sticks of the Devil'), Dr Angus MacDonald has a note on the tune he gave the name *The Pipes of St Valery:*

> My first pipes belonged to my mother's brother, ANGUS MACKAY, quoted as 'one of the best jig players to come out of South Uist', who was killed at St Valery, when the Highland Division was routed at the start of WW2. His army pipes and duties were taken over by ALASDAIR MACDONALD, another Uist man and fellow Cameron Highlander who was subsequently captured and spent the rest of the war as a POW.
> To ensure the pipes would not be confiscated by their captors the Uist boys each took a section of the pipes across France and Germany to the POW camp. The re-assembled pipes survived the war and eventually made their way back to South Uist. They remained in the possession of Alasdair MacDonald who on occasion loaned them to a friend who unfortunately died shortly afterwards. His effects were cleared out of his house for burning. Alasdair came across the fire and on seeing the pipes among the ashes, fell to his knees, weeping.

Alasdair may have been the father (or grandfather?) of Fiona MacDonald, who married a Sudanese diplomat and was the mother of piper Yahya Abdelsamad, now living in Japan (see above).

Assorted South Uist Pipers

Dr Angus MacDonald's CD includes (Track 11) the *Luinneag Mhicleoid* (*MacLeod's Song*, translated by J. Carmichael Watson as *MacLeod's*

Lilt), a song made by Mary MacLeod. It has 14 verses of 8 lines each, with a four-line refrain between each. This is the work which shows that Mary was exiled to the island of Scarba.

CALUM BEATON of Stoneybridge held a weekly chanter class, along with Louis Morrison, in the Drill Hall in Daliburgh. For a fuller picture of Calum, see Joshua Dickson (2006). Calum, a mine of information about Uist piping, was taught by his cousin, ALASDAIR BEATON, and by his McKillop uncles, ANDREW MCKILLOP and WILLIE MCKILLOP, who were both army pipers. Willie was married to a sister of Ludovic Morrison. Andrew was known locally as Andrew Scone. Both of the MacKillops were good players.

RONALD I. MACLEAN from Eochar (Iochdar), South Uist, went into the Queen's Own Cameron Highlanders as a piper in 1959. After the amalgamation of the Camerons and Seaforths, he was with the 1st Battalion QOH in the Far East, and later was appointed personal piper to the Commander in Chief, Allied Forces North Europe, based in Oslo.

On leaving the Regular Army he joined the 51st Highland Volunteers (Territorial Army) as a piper, and was also Pipe Sergeant Instructor of the 1st Cadet Battalion, QOH. He had a few years living in Glasgow, but returned to the north to find work in Inverness, where he teaches young pipers. Himself a good player of both piobaireachd and light music, he judges at piping competitions around the Highlands.

His compositions include:

The 1st Battalion QOH's Farewell to South Armagh 9/8 RM 2
Bert Sutherland 2/4 M 4 (Bert was a stalwart of the Inverness Piping Society)
The Eochar Reel R 4
Inverness Piping Society R 4
Johnnie MacIntyre S 4 (Johnnie was Ronnie's teacher, a piper in the Lovat Scouts)
Mr and Mrs Peter MacLean 6/8 J 4 (Ronnie's parents)
Pipe Major R.H. MacPhee's Reel R 4 (Robert MacPhee, Cononbridge, was fifteen years a piper in the QOH, with Ronnie)
The South Uist Hornpipe HP 4
A South Uist Melody 6/8 SM 2

Ronald's brother JIM MACLEAN was also born in South Uist. His earliest recollection of his piping is sitting at the kitchen table practising, at the age of five or six. He went on to become a pupil of Alfred Morrison (senior, father of Young Fred) at school, before joining the

4th–5th Cameron Highlanders Territorial regiment, where he played in the pipe band under Pipe Major John Burgess.

In 1965 he joined the Strathclyde Police, and in 1975 was in their pipe band. He played throughout their triumphant run of championships, until his retirement in 1995. He then taught, first at the College of Piping in Glasgow, then at the Piping Centre. He published the *Culloden Collection of Bagpipe Music*.

CALUM MACDONALD from Uist was the caretaker at Inverness Castle, and taught piping, and formed the Calumdon Ladies Pipe Band. He was a good piper (Chrissie Morrison).

Bill Innes (*TGSI* LXII) mentions ALASDAIR MACCALLUM from South Uist as a piper at Saturday night ceilidhs held by the Edinburgh University Highland Society, when Norman Johnston was a policeman in the Edinburgh City Police Pipe Band.

ANGUS J. MACLELLAN was born into a South Uist family who lived in South Lochboisdale. Taught his piping initially by his father, he lived later in Rothesay where he had lessons from Alex MacIntyre, before in 1946 he met Donald MacLeod on the machair in South Uist, presumably at the Games. This led to his becoming a pupil and friend of Donald.

Angus won the Gold Medal at Oban in 1973, as 'Angus J. MacLellan, City of Glasgow Police' and at Inverness in 1976, simply as from 'Glasgow'. He was a piper with the Glasgow Police Pipe Band, and on his retirement became an instructor at the College of Piping in Glasgow.

In the late 1990s, Angus, who had been suffering constant pain for some years, had an operation to remove a tumour from his spine. This relieved the pain, but made him immobile so that he is now confined to a wheelchair; he says it was well worth it, to be pain-free at last. In 1999, at the Glenfiddich championship at Blair Castle, Angus was awarded the Balvenie Medal for his 'significant contribution' to piping. The presentation, to great acclaim, was made by John Wilson, formerly his colleague in the Strathclyde Police Pipe Band. Angus is still teaching in spite of his handicap, and says he knows how lucky he is to be able to teach and judge, and still enjoy life.

A piper called HECTOR MACLELLAN was named in the 1851 Census; aged 28, he was married to a daughter of a family living at Airdmore, in South Uist. They were Archibald Currie, 53, a Moss Crofter, who had a wife, three daughters and a son. Hector had a baby son, Donald, and lived with his in-laws.

Another Moss Crofter in 1851 was a widow, Mary McInnis, aged

42, at Laisker, North Lochboisdale. Her son, NIEL MCINNIS, 24 was listed as a Piper. There were three other children, none of them pipers.

RONNIE LAWRIE, Oban, had South Uist links, as his mother came from South Lochboisdale.

DR ALASDAIR MACLEAN, one of the five MacLean brothers from Raasay, was a doctor who became the much loved GP in South Uist. He had graduated in 1941, before going into the army, where he served as a doctor in the RAMC in both India and Burma. After the war he had several medical posts before in 1949 he was appointed to South Uist, where he spent the next 32 years. In 1993 he completed his revision of *A History of Skye*, written in 1930 by his uncle, Alexander Nicolson. Published by his son, Cailean MacLean, this has become a valuable contribution to the history of the islands. Cailean re-issued it, with further additions, in 2012.

When Dr Alasdair died in 1981, Rona Lightfoot was inspired by an old South Uist song, *Ach a Dhomhnuill Mhic Sheumais*, to compose a piobaireachd lament, *Cumha Alasdair*, in his memory. She made it in collaboration with Iain Morrison and plays it on her CD *Eadarainn* (issued in 2004, by Macmeanmna, Portree).

Ceolas Summer School

In 1996 piper HAMISH MOORE set up a summer school in South Uist, offering piping, step-dancing, fiddling, Gaelic song, Ceol Mor and Gaelic as its main subjects. The aim is to encourage the study of links between traditional music, song and dance within the Gaelic-speaking community. The courses included piping, but participants had to take more than one course, so that they could appreciate the dependence of, say, step-dancing on piping, or Gaelic song on harp music. All students have to devote at least 45 minutes each day to learning Gaelic, whatever other courses they may be taking. The school was originally run by the National Gaelic Arts Project, but cuts in funding have put its future in jeopardy.

Busy as the students are during the day, the evenings are not without activity – a series of themed concerts features a wide range of skilled musicians, as well as a ceilidh dance in Eriskay. Some years there are house ceilidhs where students enjoy local hospitality and music, often lasting all night. Clearly you have to be young and super-fit to last a Ceolas course.

South Uist Games

At the Games, the Clan Donald Cup goes to the Best All-Round Piper in South Uist, and the Flora MacDonald Trophy was started in 1956. The names which appear engraved on it include William Walker, Angus MacKinnon, Rona MacDonald, John MacCormick, Calum Campbell, Ludovic Morrison, Angus MacKinnon, Angus Morrison, John Burnett, Archie Lindsay, and Donald MacDonald.

Judging at Askernish

The South Uist Games are held at Askernish every July, on land donated by Simon MacKenzie in 1909.

Generally there were two judges at the Games – one an older man, an experienced and knowledgeable judge, the other younger and still learning. The older man advised his companion to divide his judgement into categories, and allot marks accordingly, and said they would compare notes afterwards.

The story is told of one player, who gave an excruciatingly bad rendering of *The Desperate Battle*. The judges, analysing his performance, went through their categories.

'Pipe?'
'Harsh – 3 out of 10'
'Tuning?'
'Poor – 2'
'Text?'
'Too many mistakes – 1'
'Execution?'
'Good idea'

South Uist Games seem to be a breeding ground for piping legend. One year the committee tried out a system of walkie-talkie radio, so that the piping steward could let the loud-speaker announcer know the name of the player currently tuning on the platform and the title of the tune selected for him by the bench. Unfortunately the announcer was not too familiar with piobaireachd titles, and reception was not very good; it was confidently announced that the piper now on the platform would be playing the *Lament for the Yellow Lantern*. The piper, D.J. Mac-Intyre, who had thought he would be tackling the *Earl of Antrim*, was laughing so much that his tuning was threatened.

Sources

Calum Beaton
Joshua Dickson, *When Piping Was Strong*
John MacKay
Angus J. MacLellan
John A. MacLellan
D.R. MacLennan
Fred Morrison
Ludovic Morrison
Ed Neigh
Piping Times
Queen's Own Highlanders, *The Cabar Feidh Collection*
Barry Shears, *Dance to the Piper*
Scott Williams

Benbecula

Benbecula is an island lying between North and South Uist. It is linked to both by causeways, which in former times were tidal fords. The meaning of the name is disputed. The name is pronounced with the stress on the second syllable, Ben-BEC-ula. In Gaelic it is Beinn na faoghla, which appears to mean 'the high(ish) ground between the fords' – but *beinn* seems an odd choice of words when the island has no hills. It is, however, undeniably higher than the fords to the north and south. To reach Benbecula, take a car ferry, either from Uig in north Skye to Lochmaddy, North Uist, a voyage of an hour and a half; or from Oban to Lochboisdale in South Uist (3–4 hours). There is an airport at Balivanich on Benbecula, with links to Glasgow and Inverness.

Tunes Associated with Benbecula

Abercairney Tom, by R.S. MacDonald 2/4 HP 4
Angus MacAulay's Tune 2/4 M
Bertie Glass, by William MacDonald 6/8 SA 2
Bonnie Benbecula, by William MacDonald 6/8 SA 2
Borve Castle, by Archie MacLean 2/4 M 4
Borve Castle 3/4 RM 2
Craigorry, by William MacDonald 6/8 J 4

Creagorry Blend, by Lachlan MacCormick R

The Dark Island, attributed to Iain MacLachlan 6/8 SM 2. The Dark Island is a name for Benbecula. Iain was an accordionist well known for his excellent playing of pipe tunes in particular. He died suddenly in 1995.

Donald MacDonald of Benbecula, by William MacDonald 2/4 M 4

Electric Chopsticks, by Roderick MacDonald

Good Drying, by Roderick MacDonald

Il Paco Grande, by Roderick MacDonald

Last Tango in Harris, by Roderick MacDonald

Lochiel's Welcome to Benbecula

William MacDonald, Benbecula, by R.S. MacDonald 2/4 M 4

See also the list of Calum Campbell's compositions, below.

Benbecula Piping

William Matheson wrote (*TGSI* XLI) that, according to Uist tradition, Mary MacLeod's mother was a Clanranald MacDonald, probably of the Morar branch, and had kin in Benbecula. Local tradition says Mary and her sister lived for a time at Aird, Benbecula, with their mother's people. The sister died there, and as she was to be buried at Rodel, Harris, her body was taken in a big procession through North Uist, with professional keeners singing a lament.

Willie 'Benbecula' MacDonald said that RONALD MACDONALD of MORAR (traditionally the composer of *The Finger Lock, The Red Speckled Bull* and *The Vaunting*) had an uncle, Alasdair, who lived in Benbecula in the 17th century and may have been related to Mary MacLeod. Ronald himself was given a tack (lease) of land at Liniclate, Benbecula, and another to the south of Loch Boisdale in South Uist.

Clanranald's Tutor

In the Canntaireachd Manuscript of Colin Campbell, written probably in the 1790s, Tune no. 58 in Volume I has the title *Taotar Clan Ronail's March,* a curious mixture of Gaelic and English, where *Taotar* represents the Gaelic word *Taoitear,* 'Tutor'. This means much more than a mere teacher: a Tutor was a legal guardian responsible for the upbringing and education of a ward until he came of age. Often the responsibilities included management of the ward's financial affairs as well. The man known as 'Clanranald's Tutor' was Donald MacDonald, of the Benbecula branch of Clanranald. He was a cousin of his ward, Allan, the young Clanranald chief who at the age of 13 had succeeded his father in 1686.

Of the Tutor, the clan historian wrote 'He spared no pains to secure that his young chief should be properly educated and that the flame of loyalty to the exiled house (of Stewart) should burn in his breast with unabated glow. In proof of this we find the gallant boy of 16 accompanying his tutor to the field of Killiecrankie, at the head of 500 men.'

After Killiecrankie, Allan and his brother Ranald, both of them devout Catholics and Jacobites, felt unable to acknowledge the Protestant William as their King, and they retired to the Court of St Germains in France, joining other exiles. There Allan became an accomplished gentleman, who was commissioned into the French Army under the Duke of Berwick.

Meanwhile his Tutor had submitted to the new Protestant government, in order to protect his ward's lands, and his own, from forfeiture, as Catholic Jacobites. In 1696, Allan too was reconciled with Willliam of Orange, and returned to Scotland. He took up his titles and lands in 1704, and built himself Ormiclett Castle in South Uist. He was married but had no sons. In 1715 Allan came out to fight for James VIII at Sheriffmuir, and was killed in the battle. His heir was his brother, but he died soon after this, so that the chief's line became extinct, and the chieftainship passed to the Benbecula branch.

Ormiclett Castle was burnt down, accidentally, on the very day of Allan's death. It had lasted only eleven years. It is now a picturesque ruin. Local tradition has it that, in the absence of the laird, the servants took advantage and gave themselves a life of unaccustomed luxury, which included warmth from huge fires in every hearth. The accidental burning of he castle is attributed to the carelessness of a Uist family who were the cooks in the castle, and this family is still known as Na Cocairean 'The Cooks', a jibe flung at them when a fight is brewing after, perhaps, a funeral or a wedding.

A bard from Benbecula, John MacDonald (Iain mac Dhughaill 'ic Lachlainn), composed a poem in praise of Allan, shortly before the 1715 Rising. In it he said that Allan was a chief of great culture as well as military prowess and courage. The work was published in the *Uist Collection* in 1894. The poet described the social life in Ormiclett Castle:

'N uair chruinnicheas am bannal ud,	When the company is gathered there
Breid caol an caradh crannaig orr'	Adjusting their narrow kerchiefs
Bi 'dh fallus air am malaidhean, a'danns' air urlar deile'	The sweat will be on their brows Dancing on the wooden floor.
'N uair chiaradh air an fheasgair	When dusk fell in the evening
Gu'm bu bheadarach do fhleasgaichean;	The young men would be flirting;
Bhiodh pioban mor 'g spreigeadh ann,	The great pipes would be stirring,
'Us feadanan 'g an gleusadh.	And the chanters at their tuning.

He goes on to praise the young chief's sailing skills, his hunting prowess, and his Clanranald lineage, using phrases which remind us of the *Dan Comhfhurtachd* made by Iain Dall MacKay in 1734, addressed to the MacDonald chief in Skye: both bards refer to the MacDonald coat of arms and clan banner. In Uist, Iain mac Dhughaill 'ic Lachlainn said:

B'e sud an leoghann aigeannach	There the lion would come to life
'N uair nochdadh tu do bhaidealan,	When you unfurl your banners,
Lamh dearg 'us long 'us bradanan,	Red hand and war-ship and salmon,
'N uair lasadh meamna t-eudainn.	When your spirit lights up your face.

In Skye, Iain Dall addressed Sir Alexander MacDonald with:

Croinn-iubheir le brataichean sroil,	Your masts with their silken banners,
Loingeas air chorsa 's ro-siuil,	Your ships along the coast with full sails,
Long a's leoghan a's lamh-dearg	War-ship and lion and red hand
Cra'n cuit suas an ainm an Righ.	Being raised up in the name of the King.

These references to the clan symbols (those of Clanranald included the salmon) were probably part of the conventional praise of a great chief, expected of his bards and expressed in somewhat formulaic phrases – adding little to the artistic merit of a work, but obligatory among the compliments lavished on him. The inclusion of the red hand as a MacDonald emblem is echoed in the piobaireachd title *The Red Hand in the MacDonalds' Arms*.

After the deaths of Allan and his brother, the Tutor became the 16th chief of Clanranald, and spent the next fifteen years living peacefully at Nunton, in Benbecula, his family home. He was described as 'an honourable and chivalrous upholder of the House of Stewart'. His family at Nunton had MacIntyre pipers, related to the MacIntyre pipers of Rannoch (see also above, South Uist).

One of these was ROBERT MACINTYRE, for whom a poem, or possibly a song, was made by Alexander MacDonald, known as An Dall Mor, 'the Big Blind One', a North Uist man. This poem is of particular interest to pipers, not only because it describes this piper from the well-known MacIntyre line, but because it specifically mentions that he was 'the son of Donald Ban from Rannoch'. This confirms the origin of the Hebridean MacIntyres, their descent from the Macintyre pipers in Rannoch. (Angus MacKay maintained that this Robert was the eldest son of the bard Duncan Ban MacIntyre in Glenorchy, but this must be open to doubt. The poem names the father as Donald.)

The poem, which has no great artistic merit, starts with the refrain:

Oidhche dhomh 's mi ann am chadal,	One night when I was sleeping
Chuala mi sgal pioba moire,	I heard the sound of a great pipe,
Dh'eirich mi ealamh a' m' sheasamh,	I rose quickly from my bed,
Dh' aithnich mi 'm fleasgach a bhual.	I recognised the young man who was playing.

It goes on to describe the player, mentioning the lineage of the Clanranald family. Then the poet pictures Rob MacIntyre:

Rob mac Dhomhnuill Bhain a Ranneach,	Rob son of fair-haired Donald from Rannoch,
Boineid is breacan an cuaich air:	wearing a bonnet and a pleated plaid:
Bha suil leomhain 's i na aodan,	He had the eye of a lion in his face,
Coltas caonnaig 'dol 'san ruaig air.	For fighting and putting the enemy to flight.
Chluich e 'Corr-bheinn' air a'mhaighdinn	He played 'Big-hill' on the maiden [his pipe]
(Ceol a's caoimhneil' chaidh ri m' chluasan).	(Music whose sweetness struck my ears).
Nach iarr biadh, no deoch, no eideadh,	She does not ask for food nor drink nor clothing,
Ach aon leine chur mu cuairt dhi.	Only for a shirt to put round her.

Chluich e air maighdinn Clann Raoghnuill,	He played the maiden of Clan Ranald,
Rob a leannan graidh 'g a' pogadh,	Rob her sweetheart, kissing his loved one,
Meal do mheodhair, meal do mheirean,	Here's to your memory, here's to your fingers,
Meal do chuimhne 's do gloir shiobhalt.	Here's to your remembrance and your great glory.

A few verses about Clanranald follow, then:

'S e Rob maighstir gach piobair',	Rob was the master of every piper,
Bha'n urram greis an siol Leoid ac',	the clan of Leod once had their honour
'N uair bha 'n oinseach aig na daoin' ud,	When the Oinseach was owned by those men,

[reference to the MacCrimmon pipers to MacLeod of Dunvegan – their pipe was called the Oinseach 'The Idiot']

Bha i 'n sin aig Clann Mhic Artuir',	As she (the pipe) was then with Clan MacArthur,
Piobairean sgairteach na caonnaig,	Pipers shrilling in battle,
Tha i 'nis 's a' Chaisteal-Thioram.	She is now at Castle Tioram.

and the poem ends with the poet saying that so long as Rob is alive, the pipe will remain with Clanranald. This was published by the Rev. Archibald MacDonald of Kiltarlity, in 1894, in his *Uist Collection* of Gaelic poetry. We assume that *Corr-bheinn* 'Big hill' was the name of a tune or a dance. It is not clear whether the reference to the piper kissing his instrument is to be taken literally: it occurs elsewhere in Uist poems, possibly based on John MacCodrum's *Dispraise* (see below), and may mean merely the piper having the blow-pipe in his mouth – or it may be an extension of the idea of the pipe being a maiden, his sweetheart. The MacCrimmon pipe was called the Oinseach, usually translated as the Idiot, but really it means a half-witted female who squeals if you squeeze her. The image of the pipe as the player's sweetheart is commonplace in Gaelic poetry, where terms such as *leannan, gaol, maighdean* frequently occur, the language of love.

The references to the MacCrimmons and the MacArthurs seem to be part of the literary convention in writing about pipers: possibly it was a trend started by John MacCodrum with his *Dispraise of Donald Ban's Pipe* (see below, North Uist), but the Torloisg song has a similar tribute, probably earlier.

Sources

William Matheson, *TGSI* XLI
Colin Campbell, Canntaireachd Manuscript (1790)
Rev. A. MacDonald, *The Uist Collection*
Rev. A. and Rev. A. MacDonald, *The Clan Donald*
Barry Shears, *Dance to the Piper*

PATRICK MACMILLAN of Glen Morrison, Cape Breton, Nova Scotia, whose surname is sometimes spelled McMullin, was of a family who came from Benbecula, and was said to be a 'legendary piper' (Barry Shears). He was a nephew of NEIL MACMILLAN who emigrated to Cape Breton in the early 1800s, but Neil returned to Scotland in the 1830s or 40s. He too was an excellent player. DONALD MACMILLAN, known as Donald Mor, born around 1811, was another early immigrant piper listed by Barry Shears. He settled at Glen Morrison, N.S. in 1841, and may have been related to Patrick and Neil, above. He had a piping brother called JAMES MACMILLAN, also born around 1811, and they emigrated together. Some of these Benbecula pipers were listed as being from South Uist, but appear to be from the same stock. (See above, South Uist.)

MacCormick Pipers

William Matheson, in his paper 'Notes on North Uist Families' (1982) *TGSI* LII, mentioned two men called JOHN MACCORMICK in the North Uist Independent Company in 1745; they were said to be related to the MacCormicks in South Uist and Benbecula. The tradition was that the first of these MacCormicks was Neil, who was brought over from Donegal to Castle Tirrim (Tioram), to build and repair war galleys for MacDonald of ClanRanald. This was possibly in the 17th century, or even earlier. In North Uist they were lime-burners, and in 1799 were living at Bagh nan Faochag, Lochmaddy. In the early 19th century, a piper named ALLAN MACCORMACK emigrated to Nova Scotia and settled at West Lake Ainslie, listed by Barry Shears as an early immigrant, possibly from South Uist – but he may have been related to Lachie Ban MacCormick of Benbecula.

Another gifted MacCormick piper was 'LITTLE' KATE MACCORMICK, daughter of Donald, son of Neil. Her father and grandfather had emigrated, possibly from South Uist, but more likely from Benbecula, around 1840. Kate was born in Cape Breton in 1872. She was also a talented dancer. Her brother DUNCAN MACCORMICK was another Cape Breton piper.

Lachlan Ban MacCormick

LACHLAN BAN MACCORMICK was born in Creagorry in about 1853–60 (the date depending on the source of information), and received his by-name Ban because he had very fair, almost white, hair and a fair complexion. His father was a piper, and also a skilled stone-mason; his mother was Catherine MacPherson, a relative of Iain (John) MacPherson in Barra, known as 'The Coddy'. Lachlan lived latterly at Hacklett, near Creagorry.

Frederick Rea met him, probably in the 1890s, and described him as 'a peculiar looking man with almost lint-white hair, smooth hairless face, of squat figure, and spoke no English'. In this last, Rea was mistaken: Lachie could speak English but often chose not to. Rea goes on: 'there was no doubt about his ability as a piper. His speciality was pibroch, and as he played the others seemed to listen to him in awe – I believe he read and wrote music for the bagpipes and was a composer himself. I heard afterwards that he subsequently carried off many valuable prizes for pipe-playing at the various annual Highland gatherings held in many parts of Scotland'.

Again, Rea was probably mistaken about Lachie's achievements, as he does not seem to have travelled much to mainland Highland Gatherings.

Rea was later told by his neighbour that Lachie's prowess was the result of his being a seventh son. The father and six of the sons were fine pipers, 'in great requisition for special weddings, dances and so forth', but the youngest son, Lachie, was the exception. He could not play even the chanter, much less the bagpipes. All efforts to teach him failed, and he took to wandering the hills by himself, with his chanter in his pocket. There follows the familiar story of a meeting with a little old man who took him into a cave leading to a large underground chamber, full of little people, all dressed in brown, dancing to pipe music. His companion seized the pipes and took up the dance tune, embellishing it with 'trills, runs, grace-notes, and wonderful airs'. Then he thrust the pipes into the young man's hands, saying 'Play!' And 'to his surprise and delight he found himself fingering notes with ease and confidence, and tunes and airs came to him spontaneously. As he played on, the joy of it made him feel that he wished he were playing for ever. Suddenly all went dark, and the bagpipe set was snatched from his hands.' He groped his way out of the cave, and made for the dance where his brothers were playing. He took the pipe from his brother's hands and astounded the company with a range of airs and melodies they had never heard before; everyone thought he had been taking lessons secretly and merely pretending he was no good. He became *the* piper of the family, respected and admired by all, including his brothers.

This story is familiar on several counts, and variants of it are told of pipers in Mull, Skye and other islands, to account for exceptional prowess in a piping family – even the MacCrimmons. Clearly it is related to even more numerous tales of a piper with his dog entering an underground passage, the piper never seen again but the dog emerging some distance away, completely hairless. Several things make this particular story unusual, however: it relates to someone the story-teller knew, a piper currently still playing in the community, the fairy folk are in brown rather than green, and there has been no long passage of time when the young man emerges from the cave. Frederick Rea, an Englishman, in recounting the tale, remarked somewhat patronisingly that he and his family 'forebore from laughing' at the story, clearly unaware of its long history as part of island folk-lore. In support of this story we might note a hillock just south of the Hallan Cemetery, not far from Daliburgh, on the west side of South Uist: it is called Sithean a'Phiobaire, 'the Fairy Hill of the Piper'.

Despite his poor eyesight, around 1889 Lachlan joined the 3rd Camerons, a Gaelic-speaking battalion largely made up of islanders (all their instructors had to be fluent Gaelic speakers). Described by D.R. MacLennan, who was very tall, as a 'nice little chap', Lachlan Ban was 'a good player and a composer of note' (David Murray). He made a two-part strathspey *The South Uist Golf Club*, a reel called *Creagorry Blend* and another Reel which was nameless. *The South Uist Golf Club* was recorded by Dr Angus MacDonald, who described it as 'a powerful composition' when he played it on his CD *Maidean Dubh' an Donais* ('Black Sticks of the Devil'). Lachlan was able to write down his compositions in staff notation; this may be why some of them are said to have been attributed to him but were possibly made by his son Allan.

Lachlan won the March, Strathspey and Reel competition at Inverness in 1895. The Notices of Pipers say he was a good instructor, whom they describe as being 'numbered among the best pipers of his day from the Hebrides'.

Willie Benbecula said Lachie Ban made a recording for his 90th birthday, when someone else blew the bag for him and he did the fingering. Willie thought it was done for the Irish Folklore Society, possibly by Calum I. MacLean, and Willie heard it when he was in America. 'He played about 16 tunes on the recording, and I only recognised two of them. The tunes that man used to play were extraordinary'. That, coming from Willie Benbecula, was quite a tribute, as he himself knew an amazing number of unusual tunes.

Willie said: 'Lachlan Ban was a very good piper and I just used to sit in the house as a young boy because there was nothing else you could do unless there was dancing or something on. And he was a very educated man although he had been slightly blind all his life. He played on the right shoulder so I used to get a shot at his pipes, and he was very good for some of the history of tunes. But he played them all different'.

In 2004, Willie heard a recording of piobaireachd played in 'the old style', as preserved among pupils of the Bruce family in Australia, and his immediate reaction was that he recognised the style at once: 'Lachie Ban played just like that', he exclaimed joyfully.

Willie told how he had met Archibald Campbell of Kilberry in London, and Kilberry had asked after Lachlan Ban, saying he had heard him playing the *Battle of Waternish* at the South Uist Games, and couldn't make head or tail of what he was playing. Next time Willie saw Lachlan (when he was 'climbing up to a hundred'), he told him what Kilberry had said. Willie remarked: 'I'm not going to say what Lachlan's comments were, they were too rude', and he asked Lachlan how he had played it. The timing was completely different, and, as Kilberry said, made the tune almost unrecognisable to the modern listener. The same was true of *MacLeod's Salute*, which Lachlan knew as *Lament for Donald MacDonald of Grisirnis*. He said it was based on an old Irish song, and given the name of Donald MacLeod of Grisirnis (Greshornish), who had been a 'bit of a pirate', hence the secondary name, *The Rowing Tune*.

Willie gave several examples of works which Lachlan played quite differently from the settings in the book (dismissed by him as 'rubbish'). He also played a number of the old movements, which ties in with the evidence preserved by Dr Barrie Orme in Australia, based on the playing of the Frasers and the Bruces. Lachlan agreed that many of the pipers in the old days played piobaireachd much faster, and more rhythmically, than it is played today. Willie said that people used to claim that Calum Piobaire played the second variation of *Maol Donn* in reel time.

D.R. MacLennan heard Lachlan play on the practice chanter in 1920, and was impressed. 'He was a very fine player, and a great exponent of what we call the "back" gracenote. In some tunes he played the gracenote on the note after the accented one, which is a very tricky thing to do. You should try it some time.'

This was the same Lachlan MacCormick cited by Joshua Dickson as one of the few pipers who are known to have been playing piobaireachd in the Uists before the advent of John MacDonald, Inverness. There is a story of him at the Games in Uist, where the pipers were tuning in the vicinity of the platform at Askernish. Another bodach was with Lachie Ban, listening to them, and he began to disparage the local players, scornfully calling them *cluasaichean* ('ear-players', that is, pipers who could not read music off the page). 'Aye', said Lachie, 'You're right, *cluasaichean* – just like the MacCrimmons.'

In his old age, his eyesight failed completely. Catriona Garbutt (then Campbell) remembers visiting the blind man when she was a girl ; she played tunes for him on her chanter, and he put his hands on her fingers as they moved over the notes.

Lachlan Ban died in 1951, aged 98 (the Notices of Pipers say he was 92). Two photographs of him appear in a little book by Ray Burnett, entitled *Benbecula*, published in 1986. One is a rather distant view of him wearing plus fours, playing his pipes, the other shows him as one of a group at Creagorry in the 1920s. Both photographs belonged to Donald MacAulay of the Creagorry Hotel.

Lachlan married a girl from the piping Currie family (the name Currie is a form of MacRury). They had two sons, both accomplished pipers. Allan was a good composer of light music, and the younger son, Calum, was a close friend of Calum Iain Campbell, father of Calum Iain junior, Angus, Katy Mary and Catriona (see below).

A great-grand-daughter of Lachie Ban, Ann, is married to Iain Mac-Donald, one of the three piping brothers from Glenuig. They live in Benbecula where Iain is a piping teacher at the college.

The MacRury Pipers and Others

The cover of Ray Burnett's book *Benbecula* has a photograph of a seated piper, dark haired and bearded (his by-name Ruadh indicates he had red hair, which would appear dark in a black-and-white photograph), wearing a yachting cap and playing pipes on the left shoulder. He is sitting on a wooden chair or stool, outside a croft house, and he has a walking stick leaning on his leg. He was ALASDAIR RUADH MACRURY, from Kilerivagh, near Hacklett, and the picture was taken in the 1920s. All three of these old piping photographs, this one and two of Lachie Ban MacCormick, belonged to Donald MacAulay, proprietor of the Creagorry Hotel, who was a great piping enthusiast.

JOHN MACRURY was the first piper that Willie Benbecula MacDonald ever heard playing piobaireachd. He was in the island after retiring from the militia, where he had been taught by Alexander MacLennan of the 74th (Alasdair Liath, or Grey Alexander). Willie only ever heard John play two piobaireachd tunes: *The Desperate Battle* and *The Battle of the Bridge of Perth*. Presumably John was related to Alasdair Ruadh (above).

Of the MacRury family, William Matheson says that Archibald MacRury, who was a blacksmith in Balivanich, Benbecula, moved there from North Uist in July 1803. He was probably a brother of NORMAN MACRURY (Tormod mac Chaluim mhic Thormoid mhic Phadruig mhic Thormoid Ghobha), 'a noted piper early last (19th) century'. He was a tenant in Knockline in 1799 and 1833. Another of this piping family was JOHN (EOIN) MACRURY who in 1799 was tenant in Vallay, but went to live across the Vallay Sound at Airigh Mhic Ruairidh, which was part of the lands of Vallay. Around 1841, some of the family emigrated to Cape Breton. The tradition in the family was that they had originated in Skye (see also below, North Uist). Descendants were living in Aird, on the west side of Benbecula, in 1901; it is not thought that they were related to Alasdair Ruadh from Kilerivagh.

WILLIAM MACLEAN was known to many as 'Willie MacLean, Creagorry', because although he was born in Tobermory and came of a Raasay family, his father ran the Creagorry Hotel for some years, around 1900. This is at the southern end of Benbecula, and was the inn where travellers waited for the tide to fall so that they could cross the ford to South Uist. Some called him 'Willie MacLean, Benbecula', and he and his father were known respectively as 'Blowhard' and 'Blowharder' because of a tendency to exaggerate when telling a story. Alistair Campsie seems to have thought this invalidated any statement from the MacLean family.

The Creagorry Hotel was notable for an occasion in the 1970s, one summer day after the North Uist Games. An English family were having their evening meal, during which they discussed loudly the piping they had heard at the Games. Questioned by her children about the 'long pieces' they had heard, the mother explained that all the players played the same piece; the judges timed them, and the winner was the one who played it the fastest. Could she have got hold of the wrong end of the stick?

The *Piping Times* for March 1994 published a photo of the Lovat Scouts Band at Balmoral in the 1940s. As well as Wee Donald MacLean of Oban, the band included DONALD MACDONALD of Benbecula, described as 'uncle to Black Willie of Inverness', that is, Willie 'Benbecula' (see below).

Sources

Ray Burnett, *Benbecula*
Alistair Campsie, *The MacCrimmon Legend*
Catriona Garbutt
Willie 'Benbecula' MacDonald
William Matheson, 'Some Notes on North Uist Families', *TGSI* LII

Alexander MacDonald

There is doubt about the birthplace of ALEXANDER MACDONALD (1900–1992): some say he was born in South Uist, some give Torlum, Benbecula, but the records have his birthplace as Kettins, Coupar Angus, in north-east Perthshire, where his father DONALD MACDONALD, a native of South Uist, was piper to W.D. Graham Menzies of Hallyburton, Angus. There is another Torlum in that vicinity, which may have caused some confusion. All of Donald's sons were pipers, taught by their father. Alexander went on to become a pupil of Willie Ross, and he went to John MacDonald, Inverness, for piobaireachd.

He joined the Scots Guards as a piper in 1921, after service with the Gordon Highlanders in the First World War. He became Pipe Major of the 1st Battalion, from 1931 to 1946, before succeeding Henry Forsyth as the King's Piper, and he continued in royal service to the Queen until 1965, so that his by-name in the islands is 'Piobaire na Banrighinn'. An excellent player, he was awarded the British Empire Medal and the Royal Victoria Medal (given by the sovereign for personal service). After being the piping instructor at Eton College for many years, he died in 1992.

The *Piping Times* tribute to him says:

> His performances were always of the highest musical quality . . .
> a well remembered example of his fine playing was at the Cairn at
> Boreraig when in a driving wind of rain and sleet he gave a splendid
> interpretation of the *Lament for Donald Ban MacCrimmon*. On that
> day he seemed impervious to the weather, though the MacLeods had
> serious worries about the effect on his health. A quick rush to the car
> and a liberal intake of well deserved whisky and coffee staved off any
> serious effects. This was one of the most outstanding performances of
> piobaireachd ever heard at the Cairn. All who have known Alex will
> remember him with gratitude, for the beauty of his playing, for his
> splendid appearance and for his kindness to those keen to learn.

It is believed that Alex MacDonald played a pipe which had been left in his safe-keeping by King Edward VIII on his abdication in 1936. It is thought to have been of MacDougall making, but there seems to be some doubt as to how many pipes the King had, when he was Prince of Wales.

William MacDonald, Benbecula

WILLIAM MACDONALD was often known as Willie Benbecula, mainly to distinguish him from the other Willie MacDonald also then living in Inverness, William M. MacDonald, who was called 'Willie Tot', or 'Watery Willie'. Some refer to Willie Benbecula as 'Black Will', from the colour of his hair as a younger man – this was an army by-name. He was also known sometimes as 'The Muc' ('The Pig'), but not in his hearing. The origin of this is obscure; it was not his own by-name, but that of his father, DONALD MACDONALD, also a piper, a Pipe Major in the Highland Light Infantry, who had had tuition from Willie Lawrie before joining the army. Willie Benbecula had a list, given to him by his father, of all the pipe majors in the HLI since its inception. His uncle was a piper in the Lovat Scouts, and started Willie on the pipes.

Willie Benbecula was born in Glasgow, in 1927, when his father was a serving soldier, but he was brought up by his grandparents in Benbecula. After himself serving with the HLI, he re-enlisted in the Camerons in 1958. The regimental account says: 'His reputation as a piper of ability and skill had preceded him to the extent that he was appointed to the rank of Corporal on the day he reported for duty. He served with the 1st and 4th/5th Battalions of the Camerons until he was discharged on medical grounds in 1963.'

In a photograph of the march of competing pipers at Oban in 1957, published in the *Piping Times* in December 2008 and February 2009, Willie Benbecula appears, walking, as always, 'on the wrong side of his pipes', i.e. with the drones on his right shoulder – but he was not playing at all, his left arm swinging free. This was because the pipers were playing *The Campbells Are Coming (Bha mi aig bhanais am Bail' Inneraoro:* 'I was at a wedding at Inverary'), as they always do as they approach the games field of the Argyllshire Gathering – and pipers in the Camerons never played that tune. Doubtless his MacDonald blood was a factor, too.

As a young man Willie had a reputation as 'a bit of a heller', given to wild exploits when he had drink taken, but this was regarded as normal for a Hebridean far from home. He married another islander, Margaret Stewart, who came from Muck, one of the few natives of that island. Like her husband, she had an extensive knowledge of pipe music.

Described by Colonel Fairrie as 'a most musical player with a fund of obscure but authentic tunes', Willie competed only occasionally, playing on the right shoulder, as did many island pipers. His rare appearances were highly successful: he won the Gold Medals in 1965 (Inverness) and 1967 (Oban), the Senior Open at Oban in 1969 and 1973, and the Clasp in 1967. The regimental account adds: 'His repertoire of Ceol Beag tunes is inexhaustible, and several of the tunes in this collection (*Cabar Feidh*) were first heard played by him on the line of march.' Col. David Murray particularly praised his playing of strathspeys.

There is a story, probably apocryphal, about a gathering of army Pipe Majors being asked how many tunes they knew. Willie Benbecula emerged as the clear winner, with 'about 150 tunes more than anyone else'. A modest man, he denied all knowledge of this occasion.

He lived latterly in Inverness, and until his health began to fail (2009) was an excellent teacher of piobaireachd, with a fund of knowledge about the music. A judge at the Games and at the Northern Meeting, his decisions were widely respected. He served for some years on the Music Committee of the Piobaireachd Society, and on the General Committee. In any team quiz based on knowledge of piping, the team which included Willie usually won.

After leaving the army he worked as a nurse in psychiatric hospitals; he had a deep understanding of the problems of those afflicted with mental illness, and went out of his way to encourage them. He made regular visits to any acquaintances of his confined in psychiatric wards, and they greatly appreciated his calm and matter-of-fact attitude towards their illness. He has been described as 'a very kindly and interesting man, but eccentric'.

He and the other Willie MacDonald from Inverness (Willie M. MacDonald) made a formidable bench when judging together at Nairn Highland Games every August. One year, Duncan Watson appeared before the two of them, and was asked to name his three tunes. 'Well', he said, 'Not *The MacDonalds are Simple*, that's for sure.'

It was always a pleasure to act as steward to Willie when he was judging piobaireachd at the Games, as he had a wealth of interesting things to tell about the background of each tune. It was also fascinating to see his method of judging, which was meticulous, thorough and effective. He gave full credit for a musical performance and always judged the performance as heard on the day, not affected by reputation or background or any personal interests – and he never asked the piper the name of his teacher. He was kind to the juniors but judged them rigorously. At Tain, a very small boy once appeared before him and announced he was going to play a tune called *Susan MacLeod*, adding anxiously 'Do you know it?' Without a glimmer of a smile, Willie said gravely that, yes, he thought he could remember it.

An American player, Patrick Regan from Texas, was doing the rounds of the Games in the north one year, and had appeared on several occasions to play his piobaireachd before benches which included Willie. Towards the end of the season, Patrick was at Glen Urquhart Games, where the Inverness Legion band was playing. When not marching round the ring, Willie, the Legion's Pipe Major, was wandering about the games field in full rig. He happened to met Patrick, who exclaimed 'Hey, Willie, I never knew you were a piper!', to which Willie replied 'Funny thing, that – I wass thinking the same about yourself.' (Ouch)

He gave two amazing talks to the Piobaireachd Society Conference on the backgrounds to piobaireachd works, opening the eyes of certain gentlemen from England to the realities of life in the Outer Isles when Willie was a lad.

An interesting term he used is *calpa*, meaning the basis or background of a tune, giving rise to its content. (Josh Dickson seems to be mistaken in his assertion that Willie used the term *calpa* as a local Gaelic word meaning Urlar or Ground of a piobaireachd.) As an example Willie gave the *Battle of the Bridge of Perth*, which he said you play 'with the head moving from side to side, and slow', to indicate the men 'all spread along the river in the long grass, watching what's going on on the other side. Then they get the word and they run across the bridge, and when they got into position they would sharpen their swords and they paired off, one facing the other, lifting the swords up. And that was the *calpa* of plenty of battle tunes'. Questioned about this, he was emphatic that *calpa* meant the background or circumstance of the incident which caused the tune to be made, often reflected in the music itself.

There is a story of Willie at a band practice, probably in a Legion hall. He was walking slowly round outside a ring of pipers, listening carefully to their playing, and puffing away at his pipe, which kept going out. He struck match after match, and rather than throw them on the floor, as he blew each one out, he dropped it neatly into a drone of the piper in front of him. How would that affect the sound?

In his talk to the Piobaireachd Society, he spoke of the lack of available teaching in Benbecula in his boyhood. He appears to have had very little tuition from his own family, though his father and uncle were both army pipers. It was his uncle who started him on the pipes, but gave him little in the way of tuition, being away in the army most of the time. Willie was too young to have benefitted from the visits of Willie Lawrie to Benbecula in 1911–12, to teach a piping school, or to have been taught by Willie Ross there, after the First World War. These teachers were sent out by the Piobaireachd Society to promote the playing of pipe music, and especially of piobaireachd, in the islands.

Willie, growing up in Benbecula, had a next-door neighbour, James MacLeod whose father was from Scalpay, Harris, and grandfather from Skye. James had a son who was a very good piper but went to Canada in the 1930s – the son was named MURDO MACLEOD, after his Scalpay grandfather. He was a pupil of DONALD DUAGHAL MACPHERSON (mac Dhomhnall a Chriogair, son of Donald the Knocker), and he used to get home to Benbecula about once every three years. He gave Willie lessons in piobaireachd, teaching him the *Lament for the Union* in a most unusual setting. Willie did not know where Murdo learned this. It seems an extraordinary choice to teach a beginner, but 'Wee Donald' MacLeod sometimes taught it to a first-timer too.

Although Josh Dickson describes Willie as a pupil of Lachie Ban MacCormick in the Benbecula of his youth, Willie himself made it clear that he had no teaching from Lachie Ban. He heard him play often enough, and they often discussed piping matters. Willie greatly admired Lachie's playing, especially for its musical quality, but he said he was never a pupil of Lachie.

Willie played on the right shoulder, with what might be termed an individual way of holding his pipe. In 1950 a critic wrote 'The chief feature of his playing was the way he holds his pipes. Never have I seen such an awkward stranglehold as the pipes have on him. The nearest description heard was that he looks like a man playing the pipes on the top deck of a crowded bus while many people are rushing on and off.'

Whether playing or judging, Willie would be accompanied by his wife, Margaret, who took a keen interest in the music. If it was indoors, however, she was sometimes overcome by the warmth, and would fall asleep on her chair, after asking the person next to her to hold on to her and not let her fall off in the middle of a tune. 'Willie would be so cross' she would murmur as she nodded off, leaving her neighbour hanging on for dear life.

They had a dog, 'a kind of a labrador', as Willie put it, and he asserted that it was an expert judge of piping. In her obituary of Willie in the *Piping Times*, Jeannie Campbell tells how on one occasion the dog was howling during rather a poor competition, and Willie was asked to take it out. He said 'No, the dog's fine', but the steward insisted he must stop it howling. Willie's response was 'If you knew anything about piobaireachd, you'd be howling, too.' The dog never howled at the Games, but would sit at Willie's feet and appeared to be listening intently.

At a Conference of the Piobaireachd Society, one of the members was being teased about not being a proper Scot because he was born on the wrong side of the border, though of Scots parents. 'Ach' said Willie, 'If the cat gives birth in the oven, it's not scones she has.' That settled the matter.

Willie was Pipe Major of the Inverness Legion Pipe Band of which he had long been a stalwart. This being a band of ex-army pipers and drummers, the average age was quite high. Someone once commented on this to Willie, whose response was 'Oh aye, we always carry a coffin in the boot of the bus'.

He played in the band for many years, marching up and down hills as vigorously as ever, even though he had undergone a quadruple heart by-pass operation, followed by an operation to remove a blood clot from his brain, and another for a strangulated hernia. This made him an inspiration to other pipers who have suffered heart-attacks and fear their piping careers are over. Willie was tough, brave and hardy, and, as someone once remarked, looked as if he would last for ever. Alas, his health deteriorated after the death of his wife in 2008, and he died in Inverness in May 2010.

RODERICK MACDONALD is the son of Willie Benbecula, and a piper whose playing of Ceol Beag is greatly respected by his fellow pipers. He does not often compete, as he lives either in the south or abroad, but the few performances heard are memorable. He gave an enjoyable recital to the Inverness Piping Society in the Station Hotel, Inverness, in the 1980s, including in his programme a fine performance of the *Marquis of Argyll's Salute*.

Roddy is, like his father, a good composer of light music. He and Willie published a collection of their tunes entitled *The Clanranald Collection* (1987). In 2003, Roddy issued a CD called *Good Drying*, which Rona MacDonald in her review said proved Roddy to be 'an accomplished and versatile composer' whose work includes *Good Drying, Electric Chopsticks, Il Paco Grande,* and *Last Tango in Harris*. Rona says his work is sometimes confused with that of Gordon Duncan, whose style is similar. Bruce Campbell described the album as 'superbly crafted, with technically dazzling fingerwork on a hot sounding instrument'.

Roddy was taught by John Hunter in Inverness, who was tutor to the Inverness Boys Brigade Pipe Band. Roddy later played with the

Inverness Legion, Invergordon Distillery and British Caledonian Pipe Bands, as well as with the Balmoral Highlanders showband in London. After 26 years in London, he went to live in Australia and Japan, with his Japanese wife.

Sources

Joshua Dickson, *When Piping Was Strong*
Angus A. Fairrie
William M. MacDonald, *The Glencoe Collection*
Archie MacLean
William MacRobbie
Piping Times
Proceedings of the Piobaireachd Society Conference
Queen's Own Highlanders, *The Cabar Feidh Collection*

DR GEORGE MACKINNON was at one time piper to the Gaelic Society of London, but he left the south to practise (as a doctor!) in Benbecula. He was considered a fine piper, and he often sat as a competition judge.

Angus MacAulay

ANGUS MACAULAY (1902–1995) came from Benbecula, of an old Benbecula family. They were not related to the MacAulays who had the Creagorry Hotel, to which Donald MacAulay belonged. Taught his piping first by his father, Angus is believed to have been in John MacDonald's Daliburgh class before World War I, and around that time, as a lad of no more than 11, he also joined a class in Balivanich, Benbecula, held by Willie Lawrie.

It is said that he first met Willie Ross in the Creagorry Hotel in 1922, when Willie was recruiting pipers for the Lovat Scouts Band; Willie's playing made a deep impression on him. Angus joined the Lovat Scouts, serving as their Pipe Major for some years.

Described as 'a very nice player' by D.R. MacLennan, he played at the Empire Exhibition in Glasgow in 1938, and the following year he won the first Jig competition ever held at the Northern Meeting in Inverness.

Angus won the Bratach Gorm in London in 1948 and 1949, and the Open Piobaireachd in London in 1952. He became the official piper to the Gaelic Society of London when he moved there after World War II to become a Highland dress outfitter.

In 1948, he was playing in the show, *Brigadoon,* in London, taking over from Wee Donald MacLean, to play *MacIntosh's Lament* (Ground only) and 'that ghastly Brigadoon tune', as another piper put it.

In 1952, Angus emigrated to New Zealand when he was offered the post of Pipe Major to a New Zealand band. He died there in 1995. Before he left he sold a pipe to Calum Iain Campbell, for his daughter Catherine (now Catriona Garbutt) to play. She still plays it (see below).

There is a photograph of Angus MacAulay in Joshua Dickson's book *When Piping Was Strong*. He is shown playing at the South Uist Games in 1931. The same book has a plate of an 'unidentified piper competing at the South Uist games, 1981': Catriona Garbutt has identified him as her brother, Calum Iain junior.

Young Piper of the Year

In 1990 a contest was started in Benbecula, the Young Piper of the Year competition, with entry restricted to those under 30, organised by the Piobaireachd Society of Uist and Barra. The first winner of the title was American piper ERIC RIGLER, from Los Angeles, who had been living in Scotland for some time. The local event was won by JOHN BURNETT, Benbecula, winner of the Open Senior piobaireachd. The judges were Ronald Morrison and Dr John MacAskill, two noted Hebrideans.

Othe Benbecula Pipers

DUNCAN JOHNSTONE is associated with Benbecula in that his father belonged there; and he had relatives there and in South Uist. But his mother was a MacMillan from Barra, the sister of the famous Father MacMillan, and Duncan is generally regarded as being a Barrach (see above). The *Piping Times* obituary mistakenly stated that his mother was from Benbecula and his father from Barra – it was the other way round.

NORMAN MACLEAN was born in Glasgow but was evacuated during the Second World War, first to relatives at Strathan in Lochaber, and then to Benbecula. Many believe he was born in Benbecula, and certainly he had many relatives there. In 2009 he was living once more in Benbecula.

JOHN A. MACLELLAN, of Liniclate in the south of Benbecula, was a piper, and third cousin ('a sort of uncle') to Deirdre, the wife of Young Fred Morrison, South Uist. She is a fine musician who makes her living with her fiddle. She was brought up in Benbecula, and is a native Gaelic speaker.

John A. MacLellan came originally from South Lochboisdale, where his father lived next door to the father of Angus J. MacLellan; John went away to sea when he joined the Merchant Navy. Later he worked in the pulp mill at Fort William (where he met his wife Mary. Her father was from Eriskay). They came to Liniclate on John's retirement. One of the teachers of Calum Beaton in South Uist, John was a mine of information about pipers and piping in the Uists, also very active in helping to run piping events. He died in 2000.

He is sometimes confused with John A. MacLellan of Dunoon, from an older generation of pipers, and both have occasionally been confused with Captain John MacLellan of the Army School of Piping. Three very fine pipers.

DUNCAN MACLELLAN (1924–2001) of Kyles Flodda, Benbecula, was a piper who was largely unsung outwith the islands, but spent much of his life passing on his piping skills to local lads. In 2000, he was taken to the Glenfiddich competition in Blair Castle, where, to his astonishment, it was announced that he had been awarded the Balvenie Medal for services to piping.

He lived most of his life at Kyles Flodda, apart from six years working for Rolls Royce in their factory at Hillington, Renfrewshire. He said:

> My father wasn't a piper or anything like that. I was taught the pipes by a man Archie MacPhee, who was taught by Willie Ross before the war. I also had a brother in law who played the pipes and tutored me as well. I just went on myself from then. I didn't have a set of pipes until I was in my 50s. I couldn't afford them. When I did get a set they cost me £12.
>
> I started teaching the children when piping lessons began in the schools. Some of the parents asked me to help their children who weren't getting on too well. It just snowballed from there. I had more pupils than I could cope with.
>
> One of my first pupils was DONALD BAN MACDONALD, formerly of the Queen's Own Highlanders and now the Pipe Major of the local band. I am very proud of him, and was particularly so when he passed his Pipe Major's certificate at Edinburgh Castle.' [Donald Ban was a relative of Duncan's. He is now (2012) the schools instructor in Benbecula.]
>
> I see a real future for piping in the islands, but the children need constant teaching from local tutors. A week-long school or *feis* is fine but it is not enough to keep things going through the winter. It is also good if we can a visit from a professional piper. That always encourages them a lot. They believe what they are being taught is right then.
>
> I place a lot of emphasis on correct fingering at the initial stage, more so than the music. They can develop that later. I teach three nights a

week, two on the pipes and one on the box [accordion]. It keeps me going and I can tell you that I have no thoughts of retiring [he was then 76] ... I had a struggle getting tuition when I was younger, and I always said to myself that if I could help anyone with their music in my life, I'd do my best for them. That's what I've tried to do.

In his introductory speech announcing that Duncan had been awarded the Medal, Dr Angus MacDonald said that in his view, music taught in a community situation was music likely to last, and those who knew of Duncan's work in the islands were delighted when he was honoured.

Duncan died in December 2001, and at his funeral service the organ and choir were replaced by pipes and accordions. His obituary, written by Donald Murray, in the *Piping Times* (March 2002) commented:

> He spent some of his time at the Uist and Benbecula Accordion and Fiddle Club, where the sharpness of his wit was almost as much in evidence as the speed of his fingers on his beloved box. Once a fellow judge at a piping competition commented on the fine dress worn by one of the competitors. Duncan was not so easily impressed. Noting that this individual had made a few mistakes, he commented: 'You keep looking at their socks, I'll stay listening to their playing.'

The night before his funeral there was a concert in the school at Lini-clate, at which a large number of Duncan's pupils, newly formed into a pipe band, played their tribute to him in a 'stirring display that would even have met Duncan's exacting standards'.

Donald Murray adds:

> The greatest honour – and the one which Duncan would most have appreciated – was the way so many pipers and musicians travelled to Benbecula to play at his graveside. The sad tenderness of Iain MacDonald's lament echoed over Nunton cemetery to mark a life worth living. One spent in the service of both music and his fellow men.

Sources

Catriona Garbutt
Dr Angus MacDonald, reported in the *Piping Times*
Donald Murray, *Piping Times*

The Campbell Pipers of Benbecula

Barry W. Shears names a piper, fiddler and bard, ANGUS CAMPBELL, who left Benbecula around 1840 to settle at Salmon River, Nova Sco-tia. Some of his songs were published in *Gaelic Songs of Nova Scotia*, edited by Helen Creighton and Calum MacLeod (1979). Barry Shears writes that Angus was described as 'one of the sweetest singers that Gaelic poetry could ever claim', and once he was asked if the gift of song was brought over from Scotland. His reply was that there was no one who appreciated a good poem in America. In Scotland a poet was given a pound or even a guinea for an ordinary song, 'and then he could afford to forget even the ordinary cares of life while he was composing a much better one'. In Nova Scotia, however, there were no such patrons, and he had to earn a living by farming and lumbering. None of his pipe or fiddle music has survived.

A cousin of Angus Campbell, Frobost, South Uist, was CALUM IAIN CAMPBELL, a fine piper, whose four children were also excellent players, taught by himself.

Calum Iain's daughter Catriona has written an account of the family. I am indebted to her for permission to use it here:

> Our childhood home on the outskirts of Balivanich Township, in the island of Benbecula, was, like many homes in other parts of Uist at the time, well known as a centre of piping and the love of piping. My father, Calum Iain Campbell, the youngest of a large family, all pipers, was an enthusiast about everything to do with piping, and was always in demand to play locally at dances, weddings and funerals. He did not take part much in competitions, just occasionally would play a march or jig in the local Highland Games, North and South Uist. His favourite competition march was 'Abercairney Highlanders'. He was, however, noted for his skill in being able to string in succession many of the *puirt bheaga* (little tunes), strathspeys and reels for dances such as Highland Schottische and Eightsome Reel. The names of some of these tunes are lost in the mists of time, but realising later on that they were important, I recorded them as I had learned them from hearing my father play them. I have noticed, too, that when some of these tunes are published, they differ from our versions! On a trip to Cape Breton, Nova Scotia, in 2009, I played some of these tunes on the practice chanter for John MacLean, who played them right back at me, slightly differently, from the Cape Breton tradition (with roots in South Uist!). This meeting was facilitated by Tiber Falzett, a student from Canada studying at Edinburgh University, who took a great interest in the little tunes.
>
> My earliest memories are of evenings when young pipers gathered in our house to play the pipes, turnabout, getting tuition from my father, exchanging tunes, getting reeds trimmed, drone reeds matched and just generally enjoying each other's music. I am trying to remember their names: Willie and Donald Morrison, Fearchar MacLennan, Duncan MacLellan, Donald Allan MacIsaac, Angus John MacPhee,

all neighbours or near neighbours, and of course others who came to listen. Small wonder, then, that at a very young age we children started learning the art, my two brothers, Calum and Angus, sister Katy Mary and myself. My father was quite strict; we had to master the gracenotes, movements, etc. (Logan's Tutor) before being allowed to learn a tune. My first tune was '72nd's Farewell to Aberdeen'. I found out later that it was rare for a girl to play the pipes at that time.

I remember too that my brothers and I used to 'act out' piping competitions up on the moor above our house, using a small broom as pipes and singing the tunes. We played in character(s), up to three each, with weird names, some of these characters being 'good' players (winning!) and others to 'break down' or make playing errors. I remember Calum once saying to me 'Dhiochuimhnich mi dhol cearr' (I forgot to make a mistake).

From these capers we moved to real competition life – chanter, then pipes, mainly at the South Uist games in the summer. Big names started to come to South Uist then (1950s onwards), but local pipers still held their own in the prize list. Pipe Major Angus MacAulay, Ronald and Fred Morrison, William Walker, Adam Scott, Angus Campbell, Angus MacDonald and others. We were in awe of these players. This was the heyday of the 'Under 18' competitions, with as many as 20–30 competitors, all local. The standard was high, and the prize lists don't tell the whole story. Again, I remember some of the names: Neil MacMillan, George and Angus MacKinnon, Finlay MacDonald, Donald Morrison, Donald A. Morrison, Neil and Rona MacDonald, the MacKillop brothers, Archie Lindsay, Calum Beaton, George Johnstone, Calum, Angus and myself. I remember one year, my brother Angus, aged 14 or 15, won 5th prize in the Ceol Mor Open competition, playing 'The Earl of Seaforth's Salute', and so impressed the judge, Campbell of Kilberry, that he presented Angus with a copy of the Kilberry Book. This was around the time that Ceol Mor tuition came in the shape of Pipe Major Robert Nicol, who held evening classes in Kildonan School. My father took Calum and Angus to these classes, and Pipe Major Nicol 'gave' them separate tunes so that they could learn from each other. These classes were very well attended. (I had left home for school in Fort William by this time, and later got Ceol Mor tuition from William M. MacDonald, Inverness.)

While at school in Fort William, I stayed in the Convent of Notre Dame, where life was strict and focussed. I was fortunate to have an uncle, Roddie, my father's brother, living nearby, and I was allowed out for two hours every Friday evening to go to his house to keep up my piping practice, and had a tutor to boot, Sandy Smith, a lovely man, who lived in Inverlochy and came to Roddie's on the Friday night. He was from a notable piping family of Smiths in middle district, South

Uist (see above), and played in the Lochaber Pipe Band. I recently received a photograph of him from Iain MacDonald, and treasure it.

A year into my time in Fort William, aged 12, I was asked to open the local Mod concert in the Town Hall, with Sandy in tow to keep me right. I walked on to the stage, realised that the blow stick valve was not operational, and had to retreat! Sandy took a penknife out of his pocket, gave the valve a few thumps with it and that fixed it. I think I got an extra-large cheer when I went back out to play!

My two brothers left school at 15, and after some local work in the Iochdar Tweed Mill went off to Greenock (Calum first) to learn a trade. Why Greenock? Well, several lads who had gone from the islands to Glasgow at that time suffered from malnourishment and even illness while apprentices, because of unsuitable exploitative accommodation. So my father, ever resourceful, arranged with his married sister, Marion, in Greenock, that they would stay with her during their training years, and both were apprenticed with local firms in the town. Calum became a joiner and Angus a plumber (although he secretly wanted to be a chef). Angus was a bit more fortunate in a way, as he was apprenticed with W.M. Rourke in Kilblain Street. Calum suffered a bit of ribbing in his workplace (though he never said much about it) as 'Torlum School' on an application form did not disclose his religion. They both did well, and featured each year in the prize list at the James Watt College night classes. Piping was not forgotten, my aunt loved music, her own children being accomplished violinists. The boys soon discovered that Fred Morrison (senior), brother of Ronald and Bell, was nearby, so they had many a good piping session with Fred, on their evenings off night school.

By this time I was at Glasgow University and my sister was training to be a nurse in the Southern General Hospital, and so we were all able to meet up regularly. One year we were all at the Pipe Band Championship in Bellahouston Park, the boys playing in the IBM Greenock Band. The parade was being led by, of all people, Bobby MacLeod, from Mull, whose music we all danced to in the Balivanich 'gym' and whom we knew well as our father played the pipes with him. He saw us and came over – and the parade had to pause. 'How's Calum Iain?' says he, and after a short chat the marching continued.

But all four of us were longing to come back home, and we did, and were able to get work in our own island. It was Calum, though, who kept on competing (Angus having turned his attention to the accordion) and after working at his trade for some years, he was appointed piping instructor in the North Uist schools (8 schools at that time). There was already an instructor in the South Uist schools. By this time Calum was married to Marion MacRury and they had 8 children. Our mother's people came from North Uist, and he loved working there. It may be that this was what inspired him to compose, as he began to churn out tunes, some of which I didn't even know of until his untimely death in 2005. The best known of these tunes is probably 'Hercules the Bear', written while sitting in Tigharry School. The teacher, Mrs MacDonald, had barricaded the doors and windows against a possible visit from the bear which had escaped from his owner, wrestler Andy Robbin, during a photo shoot; the animal was known to be in the area. Calum said later 'I just pictured Hercules loping along sadly, looking for Andy.' The story of Hercules was headlines right across the globe.

Calum continued to win piping prizes at the Games and in the Flora MacDonald competition where he consistently won the beautiful 'Flora' trophy. It became a fixture on their sideboard and was never damaged by his many children. His dear wife Marion, who predeceased him in 2001, polished it assiduously before each 'Flora' night. Recently it was won by Ashley MacDonald, a local girl and one of Calum's pupils. She gave it to me to keep for a weekend and we took photos.

Calum also got recognition for his compositions. In 1988, the Trustee Savings Bank sponsored the National Mod (held in Glasgow that year) and sponsored also a competition to compose a pipe tune for the event. From over 200 entries, Calum won with the 6/8 march we still call 'The TSB'. He was also the only Scot to win a prize in the competition set by the National Piping Centre in Glasgow in 1998 in honour of Princess Diana. He renamed that tune 'Schottische on Benbecula'! Another tune, written for a little girl in his chanter class in Iochdar school, 'Eilidh Campbell' (because she was a Campbell), was played a couple of years ago by local piper, Calum Anthony Beaton, at Eilidh's wedding to Harold MacDonald. It is interesting to note in passing that Eilidh is a grand-daughter of the bard Donald John MacDonald, 'Domhnall Iain Dhonnchaidh' of Peninerine, South Uist.

So how did all this come about? Why were we all as small children learning to play the chanter? There were other piping families at the time, those of Angus MacAulay, Lachie Ban MacCormick, the MacDonald family at Hacklet and others. It must have just been the natural thing to do. I have already mentioned that our father's six brothers and possibly his sisters were pipers, and my grandfather Calum played as well. One of my older uncles, Michael, once told me 'I remember as a boy, watching my father, then gravely ill (he died soon after) playing the chanter, and this is the tune he was playing', and he sang it to me. It was the tune we know in Benbecula as 'Angus MacAulay's Tune' – it doesn't seem to have been published anywhere.

What was interesting for me as I grew older and got to know my Campbell family tree was that I discovered a good many of the pipers we encountered on Askernish Machair [at the South Uist Games] were related to us! – all descended from one 'progenitor', Calum

Ruadh Campbell, who married Penny Johnston around 1832. His son, Alexander – Alasdair Mac Chaluim Ruaidh – was my great-grandfather, and from his brothers and sisters came the families of Neil MacMillan (from a sister), William Walker (sister), the MacKinnons of Askernish (sister), Neil and Rona MacDonald (brother) and last but not least, Angus Campbell, Frobost, Aonghas Neill 'ic Catriona (brother, who therefore was my father's 2nd cousin. They even looked like each other. Angus was the oldest of all these cousins that I knew best; we used to visit him and his wife Bell [Morrison] often, especially after the 'Flora' competition, when he would carry out the 'post-mortem' on the prize list ! Around 3 or 4 in the morning he would say '*tha sibh trath gu leoir*', 'you are early enough' i.e. 'are you going already?'

Angus helped Calum and me with the timing details of the Ceol Mor – tunes about which he was very meticulous, the 'song' as he always put it. He frequently stressed the importance of the 'song' in piobaireachd. In that family there was a history of longevity as well as piping – five of the family totalled between them 366 years! – and Angus died at the age of 102.

Because we returned home to live, no one seems to know who we are! No matter – it's the music that counts. I leave the last word to Aonghas Neill: '*Nach ann tha math an ceol*' (Nothing is as good as the music).

Calum Iain senior is remembered as being an exceptionally good piper, and this is borne out by the standard of playing achieved by his children, taught by himself. One of his sons, also called CALUM IAIN CAMPBELL, was a joiner who went to Greenock to serve his time, and worked there for some years, playing in the IBM Pipe Band. On his return to the islands, he became a joiner there, until he gave it up on his appointment as the schools piping instructor in Benbecula and North Uist. It is said that he, above all others, was an important influence on island piping, and kept it going in Benbecula and North Uist.

Calum's brother ANGUS CAMPBELL became a plumber; he too was a fine player, as were their two sisters, CATRIONA and KATY MARY CAMPBELL. Both Calum and Angus as boys had the benefit of tuition at summer schools with Bob Nicol, but the girls did not have this privilege. Their father had encouraged all his children to leave home and go to the mainland for their main education, and they duly received qualifications and practical training – but every one of them eventually found they could not live away from the islands, and returned to settle in Benbecula or South Uist.

Angus had attended the Ceol Mor classes held in South Uist in the late 1940s. He was then a young boy and recalled that he fell off his father's lorry going round a sharp corner, on his way home after one of the classes.

The names of the Campbell youngsters figure frequently in the records of the Uist games (see Joshua Dickson, *When Piping Was Strong).* Catriona was a great rival of Rona MacDonald in South Uist, in junior chanter competitions.

CATRIONA CAMPBELL, now Mrs Garbutt, who was a schoolteacher in Barra, is an excellent piper with very good fingers and great musical feeling – she plays with that special Hebridean 'lift' that is characteristic of players in the islands. While living in Barra, she met Willie M. MacDonald, whose duties with the county water board took him to the islands. He was interested in Catriona's piping, and in the late 1950s sent her a tape of his playing to help with her tuition. As there was at that time no electricity in Barra, she was unable to play the tape immediately, but had to wait until she was home in Benbecula, where she bought a machine (reel to reel), and only then discovered she had something special – a tape of Willie's excellent light music which is probably unique: the rest of the recordings he made are all of piobaireachd works. She points out that the boys, her brothers, played to the same timing, all their tuition being from the same source, John MacDonald, Inverness, who taught both Bob Nicol and Willie M. MacDonald.

Catriona regrets that Willie never heard her play *Donald of Laggan* or *The Wee Spree,* which she was learning at the time, and now she plays 'only for my own enjoyment and satisfaction'.

Her sister KATY MARY CAMPBELL, now a district nurse, also played well, but her work prevented her giving as much time as she would have liked to her music. The family was described as 'a line of Campbell pipers who kept piping going in the islands'.

Catriona now has three pipes which are family heirlooms. Her own pipe is one bought for her by her father from Angus MacAulay, before he emigrated to New Zealand in 1952. She also has the very old pipe which belonged to her cousin, Angus Campbell, Frobost, who died in 2002 at the age of 102, and had been a pupil of John MacDonald, Inverness. This pipe had previously belonged to Roidean, father of Seonaidh and Roddy Roidean (MacDonald), in Daliburgh, South Uist. The pipe is difficult to play, being very strong and needing a strong reed to bring out its full tone. The drones are believed to be old Henderson's. Catriona's third pipe is her nephew's. She has the help of Young Fred Morrison and Iain MacDonald in keeping these instruments in good trim, and she plays them regularly.

In 2006, she played on her own pipe a tune named *Peter Eden*, and one called *Angus MacAulay's Tune* which dates from her father's era. The latter is sometimes given a title 'something to do with Morag', but locally it is known as *Angus MacAulay's Tune*. It is a competition 2/4 March. Then Catriona picked up the older pipe, and gave a first-class performance of the piobaireachd work *MacFarlane's Gathering,* which demonstrated the high standard of the Campbell family's piping.

On hearing a recording sent from Australia of piobaireachd played in the 'old style', i.e. as played in the early 19th century, long before the Piobaireachd Society published its version of the music, Catriona was amazed and delighted. 'I could play like that', she exclaimed, 'it is a revelation to me'.

Calum Campbell composed many good tunes, mainly light music. Some have been lost, and some claimed by other composers, but among those known to have been his work are:

Failte Mhuinntir Cheap Breatainn (gu Ceolas) – composed for the
  Gaelic culture summer school
Nameless (2/4 March)
The 'D'
The Opening of Carinish School Extension
Hercules the Bear (one of Calum's most popular pieces, composed
  when a performing bear, Hercules, escaped and was on the run in
  the islands)
Nameless, 9/8
The Hills of North Uist (to match John Steele's composition, *The Hills
  of South Uist*)
Over to Ruaidheabhal
*IDP Jig (*this is a reference to a firm who do a lot of fencing work in
  the islands)
Welcome to the Isles
Schottische on Benbecula (a prize-winner in the competition held by
  the Piping Centre in Glasgow, for composing a tune in memory of
  Princess Diana)
Three nameless tunes
Marion Margaret MacRury
Calum Iain Campbell, Balivanich (his father)
Eilidh Campbell, Peninerine (a pupil of Calum)
The Changeling
Am Barpa Beag
Bain's Welcome to Creagorry

Nameless, 9/8
MacKay's Favourite
TSB Competition June 1988 (winning tune at the National Mod)
Pipe Major Andy Venters' Farewell to Colinton Dell
Neil MacIsaac of Balivanich
Benbecula Isle
Fr Toal's Farewell to Ardkenneth
*Batal Chairinis (*The Battle of Carinish)
Dunskellar (1992)

There were others, not acknowledged. A work called *Calum Campbell's Caprice* is named, not for Calum of Benbecula, but for an army piper of the same name, who came from Lewis.

His sisters would be grateful to hear of any other of Calum's compositions, named or nameless.

On 11 January 2005, Calum, his daughter Murdina, her husband Archie MacPherson and their two young children tragically lost their lives in a storm of hurricane force. Their cars were swept into the sea as they attempted to cross a causeway in the south of Benbecula, in the early hours of the morning. They were all drowned.

Calum's sister, Catriona Garbutt, is collecting his compositions for publication as a memorial to him.

To add to the family tragedy, Calum's brother Angus died a few months after the drowning. A heart condition was exacerbated by the shock of his loss, 'intensity of grief' one of the causes listed on his death certificate. Their two sisters are still struggling to come to terms with the events of that year.

College on Benbecula

Among the instructors at the College is IAIN MACDONALD, one of the three MacDonald brothers from Glenuig whose aunt married a Morrison from South Uist. Iain is possibly the least well-known of the three because he does not compete as his brothers do, nor does he appear so often on television. His brothers, however, maintain that he is every bit as good a player, and Dr Angus says Iain has the best ear of the three of them. Iain is married to a great-granddaughter of Lachie MacCormick.

The Flora MacDonald Trophy

'The Flora' to which Catriona refers in her account (above) of the Campbell family is a competition for the Flora MacDonald Trophy, inaugurated in 1936; it was named for the Jacobite heroine who, before her marriage, lived at Milton, South Uist. Entry is confined to local pipers, those living in the Uists or Benbecula. There are sections for both adult and junior players, and for both Ceol Mor and light music. It might be seen as a reflection of the state of piping in the islands: when the entry is high, piping is fit and well, but a drop in numbers may be ominous.

Catriona has always regarded 'the Flora' as primarily a Ceol Mor competition, but in 2013 she was dismayed to find there was no adult piobaireachd at all, and the juniors had to play only an Urlar. Plenty of local pipers (including Catriona herself) still play Ceol Mor, but nowadays are less inclined to regard it as a competitive sport.

Roddy MacLeod

RODDY MACLEOD, a leading player and Director of Piping at the National Piping Centre in Glasgow, has roots embedded in the islands, making him as Hebridean as his teacher, Duncan Johnstone. Roddy's mother was a Buchanan from Benbecula, with connections in Eriskay; her family is related to the Campbells in Benbecula and South Uist, and so to most of the piping families there. His father's MacLeod line is from Balallan in Lewis.

Sources

Ray Burnett, *Benbecula*
Jeannie Campbell, *Highland Bagpipe Makers*
Joshua Dickson, *When Piping Was Strong*
Catriona Garbutt
Dr Angus MacDonald
William 'Benbecula' MacDonald
William M. MacDonald, *The Glencoe Collection*
Archie MacLean, Inverness
William Matheson, *TGSI* XLI and LII
Barrie M. Orme, *The Piobaireachd of Simon Fraser*
Frederick Rea, *A School in South Uist*
Barry Shears, *Dance to the Piper*

North Uist, Grimsay and Vallay

To reach North Uist, take the car ferry from Uig in Skye to Loch-maddy, a crossing of about 2 hours. There are flights from Glasgow to Benbecula, which is connected to North Uist by a causeway.

Tunes associated with North Uist include:

Lament for MacDonald's Tutor, by Ewen MacDonald of Vallay P 10 (see below)

Lament for Sir James MacDonald of the Isles, by Charles MacArthur P 4

The MacDonalds of Baleshare, by Angus Lawrie S 4

Sir James MacDonald of the Isles' Lament, possibly by William MacDonald of Vallay P 4 (see below)

Sir James MacDonald of the Isles' Salute, by Ewen MacDonald of Vallay P 11 (see below)

Tha Mi Duilich (I am Sorry) 6/8 SA 2 was a traditional Gaelic tune to which the words were written by the North Uist bard Donald MacDonald (1887–1967). He was known locally as Domhnall Ruadh Choruna (Red Donald of Corunna) because his great-grandfather had fought at Corunna in the Peninsular Campaign of 1809; the family had the by-name of 'Corunna' from that time. Donald himself was wounded at the Somme in 1916, serving with the Cameron Highlanders.

The Trees of North Uist, by William M. MacDonald 6/8 M 4. Willie added a note: 'While being chauffeured from Sollas to Westford Inn by John MacLean, Iain MacFadyen and myself were discussing the tune *The Hills of South Uist* [by John Steele] and other tunes, with our host. I remarked to John "It's a pity there are no trees in North Uist'. He said 'Look to your left round the next bend", and lo and behold, there was a forest of young Scottish fir! I said "Well, John, that deserves a tune", hence this title.'

Vallay Island, by William M. MacDonald SA 2. This appears in Book 2 of Willie's *Glencoe Collection,* and the composer explains that he made it at the request of John Morrison, North Uist, as a lament for John's two brothers who drowned while on a fishing trip off Vallay.

North Uist Poems about Pipers

An 18th century bard, Alexander MacDonald was known as An Dall Mor as he had lost his sight through smallpox as a boy, and was called Mor (Big) to distinguish him from another blind bard, who was smaller. He and his family were sometimes known as Muileach from his father having lived for a time in Mull, but they belonged to North Uist, and returned there. An Dall Mor had a phenomenal memory and could recite the whole of the Shorter Catechism and most of the Bible, which led to his being appointed catechist for the parish of North Uist. He was a big, stalwart man who is believed to have made many more poems than the three which have survived. One was addressed to Ewen of Vallay, grandson of the Ewen who was friend to Sir James MacDonald; another was for Ewen's brother Alexander, and the third was addressed to Robert MacDonald MacIntyre, piper to the Clan Ranald chief. This last was composed at Nunton in Benbecula, where the chief was living (see above, South Uist and Benbecula; also below, Vallay).

Another North Uist bard was Archibald MacDonald, known as Gilleasbuig na Ciotaig (of the Left Hand), so called because he was born with a defective arm and hand. Born at Paible in North Uist around 1750, he proved an expert at handwriting and became the factor of the Clan Ranald estate in South Uist. He composed – and wrote down – a number of poems, mainly Gaelic satires and lampoons, including two about a piper called IAIN RUADH MACCUITHEN. The first was an *Elegy for Iain Ruadh the Piper*, the second his *Resurrection*, both considered to be masterpieces of wit, so much so that even Iain Ruadh enjoyed them, and paid the bard a sum of money in reward (see above, South Uist).

North Uist Pipers

Donald Boyd

The *Lament for the Union* is usually attributed to DONALD BOYD, who was said to be piper to King James VI (James I of England). His name seems to be derived from the Gaelic name Bòd (long o) for the island of Bute, and, possibly for that reason, the unusual structure of the work is considered to be a 'Lowland' innovation. It has 20 very short variations, which are not divided into groups of two or three (Singling,

Doubling, possibly Trebling), each developing the same pattern, as might be expected; instead, it has the Urlar followed by a Dithis with three Singlings and three Doublings, then a Taorluath similarly with three Singlings and three Doublings, and likewise the Crunluath has six parts. It may be that this was an accepted form in the early 17th century, rather than an aberration, but it is by no means certain that it was a Lowland form, nor that Donald Boyd belonged to Bute.

Professor William Matheson said that there was a family of Mac-Donalds in North Uist; Donald MacDonald (Domhnuill mac Iain mhic Sheamais) was famous in Uist as the leader of a force who beat the MacLeods in the Battle of Carinish in 1601. He was an ancestor of the MacDonalds of Kingsburgh, Skye, the family into which Flora Mac-Donald married, in the 18th century. Around 1630 or a little earlier, Donald in North Uist sent his son John to Bute, to be fostered there.

On his return, he was always known as Iain Bòid ('of Bute') or am Bòdach ('the Bute one'), which became the family by-name, Boyd. Descendants were living in Malaclete, North Uist, and gradually spread across the islands: some were in South Uist, others in Barra, where Flora Boyd was a singer of canntaireachd. Some of these Boyds in Barra later took the name of Johnson.

Another source of the name Boyd in North Uist was a corruption of the by-name (Mac Iain) Buidhe ('yellow, yellow-haired'). There were two unrelated lines of Boyd families in South Uist: the ones descended from the Bute fosterling were buried at Kilmuir, those from the Mac Iain Buidhe line were buried at Clachan Sands.

Boyd the King's piper, although he seems to have been at court before the time of the Bute fostering, might have been of Hebridean origin, with links to North Uist. (See also above, South Uist.)

Hugh Macleod

According to the *History of Skye*, the MacDonald chiefs kept a piper in all three of their baronies, Sleat and Trotternish (in South and North Skye), and North Uist. This seems to have been in the 18th century. A Uist piper at that time was HUGH MACLEOD, whom the MacLeod chief brought to Harris as his piper there, in 1707. The records say he was brought from Uist to Harris, but they do not specify to which of the Uists he belonged. It was probably North Uist, since it, like Harris, was a Protestant island.

It is not certain how long Hugh MacLeod was in Harris. After 1711, the Harris records stopped naming the individual estate employees, and began to lump them all together according to their occupations, without naming them or stating their individual salaries. This means that we do not know if one of them was still Hugh MacLeod the Piper, but it is possible that he was there in Harris until 1725, when Malcolm MacCrimmon was brought over from Skye at the express wish of the MacLeod chief, to be his Harris piper.

DUNCAN MACPHAIL, described by Barry Shears as 'a piper, bard, fiddler, harper and composer from North Uist', had fought in the Battle of Sheriffmuir in 1715, before he emigrated to Nova Scotia. Barry adds: 'He was also credited with composing an elegy for James MacDonald to the melody of the piobaireachd 'Sir James MacDonald of the Isles Salute'. Duncan died c.1795, aged 104.

Dispraise of the Pipes

The Gaelic bard, John MacCodrum, was born in Paible, North Uist, around 1700. In 1763 he met his young chief, Sir James MacDonald of Sleat, who appointed him his official bard – but he continued to live in North Uist. He made a clever poem in Gaelic, known as the *Dispraise of Donald Ban's Pipe (Diomoladh Pioba Dhomhnaill Bhain)*, in reply to a song made in Uist by a man called John MacPhail, praising a Paible man, DONALD MACAULAY (known as Donald Ban) for the excellence of his playing. (This Donald Ban has no connection with Donald Ban MacCrimmon, for whom the great lament was composed.)

The praise of Donald's piping was so extravagant that John MacCodrum composed his Dispraise to ridicule it.

He starts by saying John MacPhail was wrong: in overpraising Donald, he had left out MacCrimmon, Condullie and Charles, the three giants of piping in the 18th century: MacCrimmon was probably Patrick Mor, though it could have been Patrick Og, since MacCodrum died in 1769, around the time of the death of Patrick Mor; Condullie was Condullie Rankin, in Mull, famed as a piper and teacher in the first half of the 18th century; Charles was Charles MacArthur, who died around 1780, and was the renowned piper to MacDonald of Sleat.

MacCodrum said:

> Of all pipers, MacCrimmon was king, with beautiful notes of most melodious acclaim – their liveliness would restore a sick man to health. Sweet-sounding march, brisk and impetuous, that chases away faint-heartedness and fear; valour and hardihood are a virtue of the Idiot (MacCrimmon's pipe), the noble foster-mother of the MacLeods, inciting them with vigour. [This is William Matheson's translation.]

Air na piobairean uile
B'e MacCruimein an righ,
Ri pongannan alainn
A b'fhonnmhoire failte –
Thairrngeadh an caileachd
Gu slainte fear tinn.
Caismeachd bhinn,
'S i bras dian,
Ni tais' is fiamh fhogradh;
Gaisg' agus cruadal
Tha bhuaidh air an Oinsich,
Muim' uasal nan Leodach
'G an spreodadh le spid.

Of Charles MacArthur, he said:

The gay sportive one (pipe) that Charles had and used to kiss. The musical pretty one of sweetest voice; the Gaels are so fond of listening to her blandishments, and all the English-speaking folk in Edinburgh dote on her; [obscure phrase] engraved with devices, strong-sounding, impetuous in pursuit of an enemy.

A' bhairisgeach sporsail
Bh'aig Tearlach 'g a pogadh,
An t-ailleagan ceolmhor
As boidhche guth cinn;
Tha na Gaidheil cho deidheil
Air a manran a dh'eisdeachd,
'S na bheil an Dun-Eideann
De luchd Beurl' air a ti;
Breac nan dual
'S neartmhor fuaim,
Bras an ruaig namhaid.

(The term bairisgeach 'gay, merry' might be the name of Charles' pipe, as Oinseach was that of the MacCrimmons, but it may be merely descriptive. The reference to Edinburgh is Charles' service with MacDonald of Sleat, in St Andrews and Edinburgh.)

The poem then turns to Condullie Rankin:

If it were heard in Mull how thou didst pass over Condullie, they would deem it but fitting that thy blood should be on the top of thy head; she (his pipe) was the most zealous on the right hand of the battle front, beating out the wild airs most vengeful in the charge. 'Tis no small loss that you are without a head under George's oppressive bondage; the wry-mouthed ones (the Campbells) tormenting and banishing you, they did by violence deprive you of your rights.

Nan cluinnt' ann am Muile
Mar dh'fhag thu Con-duiligh'
Cha b'fhuilear leo t'fhuil
 Bhith air mullach do chinn;
'S i bu ghreadanta dealchainn
Air deas laimh na h-armachd,
A'breabadh nan garbhphort
Bu shearbh a'dol sios.
Creach nach gann
Sibh gun cheann
Fo bhruid theann Sheorais;
Luchd nam beul fiara
'G ur pianadh 's'g ur fogradh,
Rinn iad le foirneart
Bhur coir a bhuin dibh.

(This refers to the Campbells taking Duart Castle, in 1692, from the MacLeans, who had had the Rankins as their pipers there. The decline in the Rankin piping school at Kilbrennan seems to have started then as a result of their expulsion.)

The next verse tells us that the Laird of Vallay was a great admirer of Charles MacArthur, and the poet blames John MacPhail for praising a worthless player, and 'sealing up a treasure without flaw', Charles' piping, 'the tree of musical excellence that would inspire the rocks with melody by the dancing of his fingers, and would not suffer *odrochan* to raise its head':

Craobh nam buadh ceolmhor'
Chuireadh fonn fo na creagan
Le breabadaich mheoirean'
'S nach fhuilingeadh oodrochain
A thogail a cinn.

(O-drochan is a phrase of vocables used in canntaireachd, a system for singing piobaireachd without an instrument. Here the poet uses it as a term of contempt.)

We then have a glimpse of the unfortunate Donald Ban, who was not good enough to play in a hall but had to sit on the furnace in a sooty kiln, playing 'a plaguy scrap of a tune, noise of a bad drone, smell of a decaying body: music as loathsome as the screeching of rooks or young birds pained by lack of food'.

Plaigh bhloigh puirt,
Gair droch dhuid,
Aile cuirp bhreoite:
Ceol tha cho sgreataidh
Ri sgreadail nan rocas,
No iseanan oga
Bhiodh leointe chion bhidh.

Is it not a fine laughing-stock to splutter away at a theme without playing of variation or lovely gracenotes, ramming *odraochan* in the tail of *odrochan*, ramming *odrochan* in the rear of *odrovi;* a narrow crooked bag, half-full of slavers, a wind like the chill of frost through the squint holes that the fingers cannot cover, only *ohon* and *ohi* can be understood aright.

Nach gasda chuis-bhuirt
A bhith cneatraich air urlar'
Gun phrannadh air lutha,
Gun siubhalaichean grinn,
A'sparradh o-draochain
An earball o-drochain'
A'sparradh o-drochain
An toin o-dro-bhi;
Mal caol cam
Le thaosg rann,
Gaoth mar ghreann reota
Throimh na tuill fhiara
Nach dionaich na meoirean,
Nach tuigear air doigh
Ach o-theoin is o-thi.

(The canntaireachd used here is not that used today, and probably represents a system used in the islands.)

The next three verses give the sad history of Donald's pipe, largely fanciful, it being under water when the Ark was closed, so that it decayed, and the rotten drones made *odrochan* pithless with the groaning. Then the Irish had the pipe, which deteriorated further until it came into the hands of local lads: Iain Og used enough straw reeds to feed cattle, Hector's son mistreated the mouth-piece. The wood was dirty and the instrument needed too much wind to blow.

The pipe needed re-hemping, and the bag evidently leaked so badly that the player's side was chilled. The drones screeched, the bag had to have hoops to hold it together, and the poet was scathing about the noises emitted. Donald's playing was so bad that reels danced to his music fell into disarray, and his music lacked any sort of martial quality.

The last verse of the Dispraise goes:

> The wind of the rotting bag puts a thrill in the drones, she (the pipe) is ever in haste to prop up *odra;* the slender hanging chanter is under attack from eight fingers, a stream of spittle choking it, reducing bad music to silence; a noise like a gong for frightening horses, a chant that would put out a heath fire: I shall say no more in dispraise of pipes, but to let it be heard that I've routed MacPhail.

> *Bidh gaoth a'mhail ghrodaidh*
> *Cur gaoir anns na dosaibh'*
> *I daonnan 'n a trotan*
> *Ri propadh o-dra;*
> *Bidh sionnsair caol crochta*
> *Fo chaonnaig aig ochdnar'*
> *Sruth staonaig 'g a stopadh'*
> *Cur droch cheoil 'n a thamh;*
> *Fuaim mar ghlag*
> *Dh'fhuadach each,*
> *Duan chur as frithe:*
> *Chan abair mi tuilleadh*
> *Ri diomoladh piob',*
> *Ach a leigeadh a chluinntinn*
> *Gun thill mi MacPhail.*

His *Dispraise* was not of pipes in general, merely an attack on poor Donald Ban, his playing and his instrument, in order to humiliate the poet John MacPhail, MacCodrum's neighbour.

Pipes and pipers seem to have been a topic of some interest to the bards of the islands, especially those of North Uist: the *Uist Collection,* published in 1894, has a number of such works, by John MacCodrum, Archibald MacDonald (Gille na Ciotaig), Alexander MacDonald (An Dall Mor) and Neil MacVicar.

NIALL RUADH MACVICAR (1779–1861), of Catalone, Cape Breton, Nova Scotia, was a veteran of the Napoleonic Wars. He had been a shepherd in North Uist before he emigrated in 1828. Scott Williams says he was a noted fiddler, piper and bard (see also below, Vallay).

JOHN MACINNIS from North Uist settled in Nova Scotia, according to Barry Shears, who quotes an account of John from a book about Cape Breton piping:

> Piper John MacInnis of Kennington Cove near Louisburg [Cape Breton] was the official wedding reel piper in that district. Every time

he would play the reel 'More Rum for the Piper' he was given a water glass full of rum. When he thought he had enough he let the rest of the 90-over-proof down the blowpipe. My late father used to tell me when the instrument got warm you'd swear there were doves flying out of the drone. In the wee hours of the morning when the pipes would stall he would walk home with two gallons of rum in an oversize bag – sheepskin with no cover on it.

A Wedding at Lochmaddy in 1829

In Volume I of his *Reminiscences of My Life in the Highlands*, Joseph Mitchell, a road engineer, recalled a visit he made to North Uist in June 1829, 'crossing the Minch on professional duty'. Sailing from Dunvegan in Skye, he found himself with a party bound for Lochmaddy to attend the marriage of the eldest Miss MacDonald (daughter of Lord Godfrey MacDonald) to the Earl of Hopetoun. The MacDonalds were the proprietors of most of North Uist at that time, and North Uist was one of the three estates where they maintained a piper – but it is not clear just why the wedding was held in Lochmaddy.

On arrival, Mitchell was welcomed into the wedding party.

Numerous boats laden with guests were entering the harbour. The morning was calm and beautiful. The several vessels lying in the bay were gaily decked with flags. Parties in their holiday attire from various quarters of the island were arriving in gigs, in carts, and on horseback, and all as they came were liberally and plentifully supplied with refreshments. At four o'clock a large party in the house sat down to a most sumptuous entertainment – salmon and other fish, with beef and mutton, besides no end of other viands. Then came the whisky toddy, with speeches of affection for the Chief and the happiness of the young bride.

Outside there was a large gathering of the common people, who were profusely entertained. Bagpipes discoursed inspiriting music to all. About eight in the evening the numerous party from the house assembled in a large barn, where, under the inspiriting bagpipes, the dance was prolonged to an early hour. The feast was continued over the second day. Never was a merrier party of simple but earnest folk . . . It has remained to me a puzzle for more than half a century to understand where all the people slept.

(This is probably the most complimentary account of pipe music penned by Joseph Mitchell, who was not a piping enthusiast. His references are usually scornfully disparaging. He was of the school that thinks a gentleman is someone who can play the pipes but doesn't.)

Pipe Music for Funerals

In the Statistical Account of 1837, the North Uist minister the Rev. Finlay MacRae wrote:

> At funeral processions . . . the pipes, in strains of pathos and melody, followed the bier, playing slow plaintive dirges, composed for and used only on such occasions. On arriving near the church yard, the music ceased, and the procession formed a line on each side, between which the corpse was carried to its narrow abode.

MacDonalds of Baleshare

A piper named ANGUS MACRURY was, according to Barry Shears, a half-brother to Donald MacDonald of Baleshare, who sent him over to Ireland to learn the Irish method of curing bacon. Angus took his pipes with him, and while over in Kilkenny he met Irish pipers; they found they had tunes in common, but the tunes had different names (see also above, MacRury pipers in Benbecula).

Another North Uist piper was ANGUS MACDONALD (1922–2000), Baleshare. At the age of seventeen, he joined the (Territorial Regiment of the) Cameron Highlanders, and was called up in the Second World War. He benefited from instruction by Pipe Major Willie Young at the regimental barracks in Inverness early in the war, when he was barred from joining in the British Expeditionary Force landings, because he was too young, not yet eighteen.

General Tam Wimberley was looking for a piper who could both speak and write Gaelic, to act as his personal piper and bodyguard, and Angus filled the bill. He played for Wimberley at ceremonies and social functions, and was then sent to North Africa to join the 51st Highland Division. He led troops into battle at El Alamein, an experience he later recalled with horror.

Re-joining the Camerons in 1943, he was with them for the D-Day landings the following year, and, when still only 22, he was Pipe Major of the 5th Camerons for the final push into Germany.

After the war he went to the Glasgow City Police, after a brief spell in the prison service. With the police he played in the Pipe Band, of which he became Pipe Major in 1958. He set about recruiting top class players who laid the foundation for the later outstanding success of the band. Under Angus himself, the band won every honour except the World Championship. He competed a little as a solo player, mainly at the Games.

After retiring from the band, handing over to Ronnie Lawrie, Angus rose to the rank of Chief Inspector, and when he left the police he ran a kilt-making business in Glasgow, and took an active part in running piping functions in the city. His son IAIN MACDONALD is also a piper.

DONALD EWEN MACDONALD, from Balranald, North Uist, was a second cousin of the mother of Iain Archie MacAskill of Bernera. He fought in the First World War in the Cameron Highlanders, and was one of several who were promised their own crofts on their return. But the landlord, Ranald MacDonald of Balranald, broke his word and refused to give them their crofts. They made a march to the place in military style, with Donald Ewen piping in the lead, all carrying stakes to knock into the ground to mark their plots of land. All were arrested, and appeared in court, receiving prison sentences of between three and six months. But the Sheriff who heard the case said that the evidence was in writing that Balranald had made that promise, and when the men had served their sentences, he must keep his word.

Norman Johnston said that Donald Ewen had a set of pipes which are very old. They are known as the Corunna pipes because they were played at the Battle of Corunna in the Peninsular wars (1809), 'and they were very old even then'. Were these the pipes which Tommy Pearston heard about in Glasgow, believed to have belonged once to Patrick Og MacCrimmon (died 1730)? Seton Gordon took this a generation further back, saying he and his wife had been to North Uist to see the pipes that had belonged to Patrick Mor (died c.1670).

There is a story that a man called MacAulay was the son of one of the imprisoned crofters. He was a man of strong views, concerned about the safety of these ancient pipes, and decided to do something about them. So he went and asked to see them, and simply took them away with him, and presented them to the Museum in Lochmaddy.

Donald Ewen went to the police to report that they had been stolen from him, and MacAulay was obliged to return them. (Some say this was not in the time of Donald Ewen, but of his father Angus MacDonald.) The matter is not fully settled yet, nor is the truth of the story established – but the pipes are still in North Uist.

John Angus Smith says he got his first pipe from Donald Ewen, who, like John Angus' father Donald, was a self-taught player, learning by ear and not from the book.

Ferguson Pipers

There were two North Uist men fighting at Corunna in 1809: one was Angus Morrison from Sollas, the other a piper named DONALD FERGUSON. He appears in a list of men recruited by Captain Ewen MacDonald of Griminish for the short-lived Regiment of the Isles in 1799. Domhnall mac Mhurchaidh mhic Iain mhic Mhurchaidh, he was the son of Murdo Ferguson at Illeray. On discharge from the army, Donald Ferguson went to live at Corunna, North Uist, a township named after the battle. He had a brother, JOHN FERGUSON, also a piper, who served in the Peninsular War. In 1829 John was living at Malaclete as an army pensioner. Donald's son, another JOHN FERGUSON, was a piper, too: he died at an advanced age in 1915.

Barry Shears listed ROBERT FERGUSON as a piper from North Uist who settled at Catalone, Cape Breton, Nova Scotia, around 1829, describing him as having served in the Black Watch, and a veteran of the Battle of Waterloo. One source calls him 'Master Piper of the Black Watch', which may mean Pipe Major. Robert's grandson, 'BIG JOHN' HOLLAND, was also a piper.

Piper Donald W. MacKinnon

DONALD W. MACKINNON in 1995 sent an interesting letter to the Editor of the *Piping Times*, in response to a request for information about piping in Prisoner of War camps. He said that, although he was not an army piper, he had played at home in North Uist before the war. While a prisoner he had tuition from 'Big Donald' MacLean from Lewis and Bob Hill; two sets of pipes were sent by the Red Cross in 1943, followed by a consignment of five sets, one of which went to Donald MacKinnon, who made a reed from a clarinet reed. Soon a pipe band was formed, sometimes with as many as 16 pipers, including two good Canadian players.

Pipe Major John Maclean

Pipe Major JOHN MACLEAN was a piper in the Scots Guards and later in the HLI. He came from North Uist. He enlisted first as a piper in the Gordon Highlanders in 1918, and served for a few years in the Middle East. Later he joined the 1st Battalion Scots Guards. In the 1950s and 1960s he judged many Pipe Band competitions.

His son ARCHIE MACLEAN was born in Glasgow, but both his

parents were from North Uist. He studied sculpture at the Glasgow School of Art, and became an art teacher, latterly at Dingwall Academy, exhibiting his work in many venues. Many of his paintings have piping themes. He plays an active part in the piping life of the Highlands, judging at many competitions and organising piping events. Now living in Inverness, he was for some years a leading light in the Inverness Piping Society.

Archie Maclean has kindly sent an account of his father's life, which is reproduced here. It has also appeared in the *Piping Times*, December 2010–January 2011:

> John Maclean was born in the solitary house on the small tidal island of Kirkibost, on the west side of North Uist, where his father, Angus Maclean, was the herdsman. John's birth certificate shows his birth date as 23rd April 1900 – there was no doctor present at the birth, and 'farm servant' is entered as his father's occupation. John was the oldest surviving of ten children of his mother, Mary Flora MacDonald, three dying in infancy.
>
> His letters from the Normandy campaign during WW2 show that he had a very good education in various schools in Uist as his father moved from one township to another, depending on where there was work – Clachan Sands, Claddach Illeray, and Locheport.
>
> Who initially taught him piping is unknown. John joined the 1st Btn. Gordon Highlanders in 1918 (his army record states that, like his father, he was a 'farm servant') and was posted to Turkey. In his photo album from the time, he has written *Piper John Maclean 1st Batt. Gordon Highlanders, Haidar Pasha, Turkey 7/10/21*. He left the Gordons in 1921.
>
> After 5 years in and around Glasgow, where he took a variety of unskilled jobs during the Depression, he joined the Scots Guards in 1926. By 1928 he was Pipe Corporal in the 1st Btn, under Pipe Major John D. MacDonald from Melness in Sutherland, a fellow Gaelic speaker. In the famous photograph of 1928 (see Scots Guards Book 1), showing the pipers wearing new feather bonnets, John is the Pipe Corporal seated front left. The other Pipe Corporal standing at the back is J.B. 'Robbie' Robertson (Dundee). Also in the photo is Peter Bain from Skye and Malcolm 'Baggy' MacMillan (Glenlyon, Perthshire) – quite a collection of top players!
>
> John followed the pipers' course at Edinburgh Castle and was taught by the great Willie Ross, himself a former Guardsman. John Burgess and Peter Bain told a story of John Maclean and Willie travelling somewhere together by train. Willie was uncharacteristically quiet and apparently not in good humour. Noticing this, John reached into his pipe case and produced a half bottle of whisky and offered Willie a taste. 'Maclean, I'll make a piper of you yet!' exclaimed Willie.

Obviously someone who showed initiative such as this would go far! John Burgess recalled that Willie thought highly of John Maclean – quite a feat as Willie was not prone to praise many!

By 1929 John was Pipe Sergeant of the 1st Scots Guards. In 1930 he was Strathspey & Reel champion at Oban and second in the Young Pipers piobaireachd competition playing 'The Big Spree'. At the Northern Meeting that year, he was second in the Gold Medal to R.B. Nicol (Balmoral), piper to King George V – both had played 'Cille Chriosd'.

Nicol was first in both the March and the Strathspey & Reel competitions, with John second on both occasions.

In 1931, John spent a few days at Angus MacPherson's Inveran Hotel in Sutherland, preparing for the Nothern Meeting. As a memento, there is a postcard showing Inveran Hotel (see *Piping Traditions of the North of Scotland*, p. 276). Angus has written on the back –

> 'Inveran Hotel, Invershin, Sutherland
> *Sept: 12th–16th 1931*
> where J. McLean played well for the medal.'

John did play well for the medal, coming in fourth. It was another MacLean, 'Wee Donald' from Glasgow, who was first.

John was second in the Marches, playing 'Highland Wedding', beaten by John Wilson, and he was third in the Strathspey&Reel competition, to Robert Reid and David Ross.

In 1931, John's Pipe Major, John D. MacDonald ('John the Bap') was invalided out of the army due to TB. John was Pipe Sergeant to his replacement, Alec MacDonald, who later became Piper to Queen Elizabeth II.

In 1932, the 2 Pipe Sergeants of the Scots Guards came first and second in the Gold Medal at Oban, J.B. Robertson beating John into second place. John played 'MacLeod of Raasay's Salute'.

At Inverness that year, John, playing 'Bonnie Ann', was second to Charlie Smith in the Marches, but was the Strathspey&Reel champion, ahead of David Ross and Charlie Smith.

In 1933, John was promoted to Pipe Major of the 2nd Btn. Highland Light Infantry (74th Highlanders). He was presented with an engraved practice chanter by the Highland Society of London. The plaque reads –

The Highland Society of London
Presented to
Pipe Sergt. John Maclean
1st Btn. Scots Guards
on his promotion to
Pipe Major
2nd Btn. HLI
1933

This promotion effectively finished his competing career. It appears that even more top prizes would have come John's way, but it was not to be. The late Alan Ferguson (Inverness) who served as a piper under John in the 2nd HLI, said, 'The Gold Medal was waiting for John – but he joined the HLI and was abroad for years'.

John then saw the next 5 years' active service in India and the North-West Frontier, and a year in Palestine and Egypt between the wars.

When he was home on leave, John was able to visit his old pipe major, John D. MacDonald (Melness), who had been invalided out of the army in 1931, due to TB. John would visit him at Invergordon hospital. P.M. MacDonald later died in Lairg, 1941.

John's impressive array of campaign medals show he was involved in Sudan and Eritrea against the Italians after war broke out. In Lt Col. Oatts's classic history of the HLI, *Proud Heritage*, he notes that with yet another defeat of the Italians in 1941, '*On 1st April, the 74th arrived before Asmara, the capital of Eritrea, and marched in with all pipes playing, led by Pipe-Major McLean*' (the 'HLI spelling' of his surname which is still on his leather pipe case). Alan Ferguson (Inverness) was with John later in the Western Desert fighting Rommel's Afrika Korps. He recalled, 'John was a veteran compared to us youngsters. When the barrages came in, we pipers would be cowering in terror, but John knew how to keep us distracted. He would take a practice chanter from his bag pack, and kindly order someone, including me, to play a tune. That soon diverted our thoughts from the incoming fire! We concentrated so hard on getting the tune right, that we soon forgot the shelling! He was a wonderful man.'

In 1943, John returned home with the HLI as Home Defence forces and to prepare for the Normandy landings. Stationed in various parts of northern Scotland, his letters show that, when home on leave, he was kept busy playing for ceilidhs in North Uist. He also began courting Jessie Ann MacAulay from Illeray. It is from that period that his wonderful letters to her give insight into those times.

Before he landed in Normandy on 23rd June 1944, he wrote to Jessie, 'All ready now, and not long to go. I have sent my pipes and some peacetime clothing home. They will be upset by it, but it is all part of a soldier's life.'

By then he was no longer Pipe Major of the 2nd Battalion, but Company Sergeant Major of HQ Company, 1st Battalion HLI (71st Highlanders), part of Montgomery's 21st Army Group. His pipes were looked after by a piping friend in Uist and played by him 'to keep them warm' until John returned. (John's pipes were originally Robertson's. However, later on the two tenor drones were damaged during active service and replaced by Henderson tenors. In the 1950s, Peter

Henderson's shop in Glasgow – managed by Bob Hardie – turned a new lower bass section, so now they are regarded as 'Henderson's'.)

The fighting towards 'The Killing Ground' of Falaise was ferocious. John writes, in various letters –

> 'we had a church service today before starting out. A lot of faces missing, Jessie, but we are left to carry on the good work. The Americans are going well on their front, but we are having a hard time of it.'

> 'Better sign off now. It's dangerous to write out here. You don't know if it's your turn to get it. I just pray that it's not my turn. If I get out of this alive, I'll never complain again' – and he didn't.

> 'A lot of flies everywhere in the heat. As bad as the Western Desert' – with the hot summer in France, corpses and dead animals produced plagues of flies.

Other letters show a lighter side in contrast to the dreadful carnage.

> 'The sergeants and I have found a place for the night. We have two bottles of Johnnie Walker, for tomorrow we are back into action.'

> 'The Pipe Major is in the trench beside me, reading my Oban Times.'

The Pipe Major (1st HLI) was Donald James 'Muc' MacDonald, from Benbecula, father of Willie Benbecula.

> 'Received the socks. Gave a pair to the Colour Sergeant. He was delighted, socks all the way from the hielans.'

> 'Spoke Gaelic to a man from Islay. It was just like being back home.'

> 'Am witnessing a beautiful sight here, Jessie. German prisoners marching down the road with their hands above their heads.'

The remaining Germans in the Falaise pocket surrendered. However, the fighting in Belgium was relentless. John's HLI were sent down to the Ardennes as part of Monty's British 2nd Army, to bolster the American positions after the fierce German breakout which became known as the Battle of the Bulge.

The HLI fought on through Holland and across the Rhine into Germany, via the Reichswald Forest, and on to Hamburg in 1945. After the German surrender, John was promoted to Regimental Sergeant Major of the 5th HLI BAOR [British Army of the Rhine]. A letter to him, and to others who had performed 'outstanding service, and shown great devotion to duty, during the campaign in North West Europe', was signed by *B.L. Montgomery, Field Marshal, Commander-in-Chief, 21st Army Group.*

John returned home in 1946, as Regimental Sergeant Major of the 71st Primary Training Centre and Depot at Maryhill Barracks, Glasgow. There he kept his pipes going, and was known as 'Pipey'. A humorous story from that time tells of John and his friend, PM 'Big Donald' Maclean from Lewis. Donald asked RSM Maclean 'Well, John, and how is the pipe going?' John replied, 'She's going so well she's *speaking* to me'. A Gaelic conversation, of course!

The late Norman Gillies recalled that a few of the HLI pipers were heading out for a night on the town when John asked them 'Well, lads, where are you going?' 'We're heading out for a pint, sir' was the reply. 'I don't think so, said John, 'get your pipes and let me hear how you're all playing'. Norman recalled that the comments later by the pipers, whose evening had been 'interrupted', weren't printable!

In 1947, John married Jessie in a Gaelic service at St Columba's Church ('The Gaelic Cathedral') in Glasgow. The best man was PM 'Big Donald' Maclean (Lewis), and the piper was PM Donald James 'Muc' MacDonald (Benbecula).

On Assaye Day (23rd September) of that year, John handed the Assaye colour to General Urquhart, Colonel of the Regiment in preparation for trooping the colour – the special occasion being that Princess Margaret had become Colonel in Chief of the Regiment, and also that the HLI had been restored the right to wear the kilt.

John left the army in 1948 with 25 years' outstanding service behind him, and became an employee of the Bank of Scotland. He was much in demand for the rest of his life as a judge for both solo and RSPBA (pipe band) competitions.

Always smart and neat, whether in kilt or civvies, John was a stickler for appearance. One unfortunate Scots Guard piper appeared at a competition which John was adjudicating, properly dressed in Scots Guards attire from the waist up – but improperly dressed in borrowed civvy kilt, sporran and kilt hose – a big mistake, especially in front of a former Scots Guardsman!

John taught individually as well as being tutor to the Glasgow Academy cadets' pipe band for many years. Over the years he was very much part of the Glasgow piping scene which included Robert Reid, Hector Maclean, Big Donald Maclean, Nicol MacCallum, Bob Hardie, Angus Morrison, PM John MacDonald (South Uist – Seonaidh Roitean), the MacFadyen brothers – John, Iain and Duncan – Ronald Lawrie, Seamus MacNeill, Young Peter MacLeod, Hector MacFadyen (Pennygael), Donald MacLeod, Andrew Wright, Dr John MacAskill and Kenny MacDonald.

In 1956 John was one of three North Uist who were presented to Queen Elizabeth II after playing her ashore at Lochmaddy, and later playing for her at Locheport, during her first visit to the Outer Isles.

John and Jessie had three children, Angus, Archie and Donald. Archie was a successful competitor during the 1970s and 80s, playing his father's pipes, and is now a piping adjudicator.

John kept closely in touch with his Uist background, speaking Gaelic whenever possible throughout his life. He would return home to the croft in Uist annually, sometimes judging at both the South and North Uist games.

He suffered a stroke in the mid-1960s, but this did not prevent him judging. In 1970 he was diagnosed with cancer, and bore the last months of his life with his usual quiet, uncomplaining dignity. He died peacefully at home in 1971, the day before his 71st birthday, surrounded by his family. At the Scottish Pipers' Association in Glasgow, where John was a regular attender, the audience stood in silence as Iain MacFadyen played a Gaelic slow air in memory of John. There were huge attendances at both of his funeral services, in St Columba's Glasgow, where he had been an elder, and at Carinish Church, North Uist. John's coffin was draped in his Scots Guards Royal Stuart plaid with which he had been presented when he left the Guards. His friend, PM John MacDonald, who had retired home to South Uist, played the laments at both Carinish Church and the graveside at Kilmuir, North Uist.

The Pipe Major John Maclean Memorial Trophy is the overall prize at the North Uist games, the first winner being Roddy MacLeod. Other names on the trophy are Alasdair Gillies, Gordon Duncan, Fred Morrison and the MacDonald brothers from Glenuig, Allan and Dr Angus.

John was a kind, unassuming, modest man of great courage, with a wonderful sense of humour. His son Archie says he would have been horrified at being publicly called courageous. Many who knew him described him as 'a real Highland gentleman'.

John Maclean, North Uist

In 2011, Elaine MacLean from Paisley wrote to the *Piping Times* about her father, another North Uist piper called JOHN MACLEAN. A German piper, DR CHRISTIAN GROSSER, had written to ask if anyone knew the former owner of a set of MacDougall pipes he had bought in 2006, and Miss MacLean answered: they had belonged to her father. She outlined his career: he was born in 1922, at Hougharry, North Uist, and became a piper in the 5th Battalion of the 51st Highland Division, the Queen's Own Cameron Highlanders, and served from 1938 until 1946. He saw active service in North Africa, Sicily, France and Germany.

His daughter says he piped at El Alamein (where Duncan MacIntyre was killed with his pipes in his arms), and he played in the Victory

Parade at Bremerhaven – and a picture of him on that occasion was published with the article.

After the war he worked for a time on the mainland and taught many youngsters to play, before he returned to North Uist. He became President of the island Piping Society, continuing to promote piping as well as supporting the piping at the island Games. He composed a Lament for his uncle, Angus MacLellan of Vallay, and called it *Inverness to Dunskellar*. The *Piping Times* published it alongside Miss MacLean's letter.

See also below, Vallay.

Sources

John D. Burgess
Alan Ferguson
Norman Gillies
The Inverness Courier
Bill Lawson, *Croft History in North Uist*
Iain MacFadyen
Archie MacLean
Elaine MacLean, Paisley
William Matheson, *TGSI* XLI
The Oban Times

North Uist Pipers

Bill Lawson, well known Harris historian and genealogist, in his book *Croft History in North Uist*, wrote of two pipers there who while playing the pipes passed a preacher, Finlay Monro. He looked at them and said 'No burial earth will cover either of you.' One of them went to Australia and drowned falling between the boat and the jetty; the other went down with his boat, fishing from North Uist.

NORMAN JOHNSTON lives in a lovely 18th century house in Lochmaddy, the Old Courthouse (now a guest-house). When a schoolboy at Heriott Watt School in Edinburgh, he was taught his piping by James Sutherland. He later joined the army, to become a piper in the Black Watch; then he went into the City of Edinburgh Police, where he played in the pipe band.

Bill Innes (*TGSI* LXII 2002) wrote: 'A young policeman, Norman Johnston, off duty from the City of Edinburgh Police Band, enlivened proceedings' at ceilidhs held on Saturday nights by the Edinburgh University Highland Society.

A young piper with North Uist connections is ALEXANDER LEVACK, now living in Maryburgh, Easter Ross. He is of Polish descent on his father's side, but his grandfather, also called ALEXANDER LEVACK, lived for a time in North Uist and married a girl who belonged there. She was related to the family of Norman Johnston. Alexander senior was a piper, too, a very musical man, who became an English teacher at Dingwall Academy. He went later to live in Helmsdale, on the east coast of Sutherland. The young Alexander was a pupil of John D. Burgess until John's untimely death in 2005; after that he went to Iain MacFadyen in Kyle, as a pupil at the School of Excellence, Plockton.

Grimsay

Grimsay is a Norse name meaning 'the island of (a man called) Grim' – quite a common personal name in Norway and Iceland, not necessarily implying a dour nature.

LACHLAN MACDONALD, a piper in Grimsay, to the east of North Uist, was described in the 1891 Census as a 'weaver of wool', living with his wife and son. None of them spoke English. (Note that there is another Grimsay in the south of Benbecula).

Vallay

Vallay is a Norse name, meaning possibly 'fields island' because it was so fertile, or because it had ground cleared for cultivation. It is pronounced VAL-ay.

Sir Donald MacDonald, 11th of Sleat, was prominent among the Stuart adherents at the time of the Battle of Killiecrankie (1689), though he himself was taken ill before the battle and had to go home, leaving command of his men to his eldest son. His third son was WILLIAM, TUTOR OF MACDONALD (for whom the piobaireachd *Lament for Mac-Donald's Tutor* was composed. Tutor means 'guardian' rather than 'teacher'). William married Catherine, daughter of Cameron of Lochiel, and they had a large family who became the MacDonalds of Vallay.

The family supported the Stuart cause in 1715, and William and his brother James fought at Sheriffmuir. For this, they forfeited their lands, but William negotiated with the Crown Agents to have the estates restored to himself. On receiving them, he handed them over to the rightful heir, his eldest brother. In return he was given the farm of Aird, near Duntulm in Skye, and a perpetual feu of the Island of Vallay for one shilling per year.

It is said that William was a fine piper and composer, and that it was he who made the *Lament for Sir James MacDonald of the Isles*, referring to the 10th Chief of the MacDonalds of Sleat who had died in 1678. This is what Angus MacKay said, but this chief was not 'of the Isles', and some maintain that the title refers to Sir James MacDonald, son of Angus, 7th of Dunyveg, the last claimant to the Islay/Kintyre remnant of the Lordship of the Isles. This Sir James died in 1621, and if that is right, the composer would not have been William the Tutor. It seems likely that two traditions have become fused.

The Sir James who died in 1678 had a brother Archibald, known as An Ciaran Mabach ('The Tawny Stammerer'). He was a bard who lived in North Uist; he had been a soldier and deer-stalker. In his elegy for his brother Sir James, he mentions a piper called DOMHNALL ODHAR ('Dun Donald') who was a good player but known to be a coward in battle. On one occasion when playing his clansmen into battle, he was seized with such fear that he stopped playing and began to sing 'some dolorous song to a lachrymose air', which his fellow soldiers picked up. They used it to mock him, and the tune came to be a symbol of cowardice, sung to anyone who showed signs of fear. It is not certain where Dun Donald lived, but it was probably in North Uist. Was his lachrymose air perhaps a piobaireachd work, sung in canntaireachd? If so, what tune would he have sung in the heat of battle? *Too Long in this Condition*, perhaps?

William's third son EWEN MACDONALD became 1st Laird of Vallay in 1727, and was a later Sir James' factor for North Uist between 1733 and 1740. He was a famous piper and composer of pipe music: he composed *Sir James MacDonald of the Isles' Salute*. This was for Sir James MacDonald of Oronsay, the 14th Chief. Ewen was Sir James' tacksman (tenant), and it is likely that it was he who made *Lament for MacDonald's Tutor* when William died in 1730.

The North Uist bard, Alexander MacDonald, An Dall Mor, who composed a poem to Clanranald's piper, Rob MacIntyre (see above), also made two songs in praise of two of the Lairds of Vallay. One is addressed to Ewen Og, the subject of the other is not named but was Ewen's younger brother, Alexander. Naturally their characteristics are similar, being the expected conventional praise for lairds: their prowess as hunters, hill-walkers and sailors, or in Ewen's case, a swimmer, not to mention his wisdom and generosity. Neither poem refers to the pipes, but Ewen Og, we are told, was an expert dancer and fiddle-player.

Norman Johnston was taught a Gaelic song by Willie Matheson in Edinburgh, a dance tune with words about Ewen of Vallay and the gille-phiobair who carried his pipes. Ewen, it says, wore his hair drawn back in a queue or pigtail behind his head, a common style in the 18th century, especially among military men.

Ewen was one of the finest swordsmen in the Isles. He once fought a duel with MacLeod of Bernera (not Sir Norman, but probably his grandson) and beat him. This was the last duel fought in North Uist.

Ewen was married to a daughter of a minister in Coll, but 'she is not favourably spoken of by tradition', according to William Matheson. Their house in Vallay was built by Ewen, and was one of the first slate-roofed houses in the parish. To celebrate his marriage, his initials and those of his wife were engraved on the lintel of the door, with the date 1742. The house is now derelict.

When Ewen died, possibly in 1769, his funeral was in North Uist and seems to have been a great affair, with two pipers, one of whom was a MacArthur (from Skye? Charles? His son Donald?). Seven gallons of whisky were provided, and consumed, but history has not recorded how many people drank it.

The story told about *Sir James MacDonald of the Isles' Salute* is that a shooting party was out hunting in North Uist when young Sir James was accidentally shot in the leg, a severe injury which endangered his life. This happened in 1764, and the shot was fired by Colonel MacLeod of Talisker's gun, which went off accidentally when the trigger caught in a sprig of heather. Sir James' men – one version says the crofters of North Uist – were incensed and threatened to kill the Colonel if their Laird died of the wound, but fortunately he recovered, and the Salute was made 'to evince his joy in seeing Sir James' restoration of health' (Angus MacKay). As Ewen of Vallay was host to both Sir James and the Colonel that day, his relief must have been heart-felt. Ewen was Sir James' first cousin.

Some say this was William, not Ewen, but he had died some years previously. Alexander Nicolson said that the wounded Sir James, whose health was never robust, was carried to Ewen's house in Vallay, and while he was recovering, Ewen beguiled the time for him by playing many a piobaireachd, and even composed a song, *Cumha na Coise* (Lament for the Leg) – presumably when he was well out of danger. Nicolson quotes a verse from it:

Mo ghaol, mo ghaol do chas threubhach	My love, my love (is) your firm leg,
Dh'an tig an t-osan 's am feile;	Comely with hose and kilt;
Bu leat toiseach nan ceudan,	You would be first among hundreds,
'N am feidh bhith gan ruith.	When following the deer.

William Matheson (*The Songs of John MacCodrum*) said this Cumha was a piobaireachd as well as a song. We may speculate whether this was the work to which the Campbell Canntaireachd gave the name *Porst na Lurkin* (*Port na Lurgainn*) 'Tune of the Shank' – which appears in Angus MacKay's manuscript as *King James the 6th's Salute* (wrong James).

There is also a *Lament for Sir James MacDonald of the Isles*, composed by Charles MacArthur, and included in the MacArthur manuscript. This Sir James was the 16th chief, who died young, in Rome, in 1766 (he was the same Sir James for whom the Salute was made, after he had been shot. He was not in fact 'of the Isles', as that designation referred to the MacDonalds further south, based on Islay and Antrim. Sir James was 'of Sleat').

To add to the confusion about these works, Fred MacAulay said that there was a strong tradition in North Uist of a lost piobaireachd lament for MacDonald of Vallay (which one?). The words were still known and sung, but the piobaireachd itself has vanished, although it is only two generations since it was played. Was this the *Cumha na Coise*, Lament for the Leg? But that was not a lament for a MacDonald of Vallay. Maybe there was a lament for Ewen himself, perhaps going with the song that Norman learned from Willie Matheson.

Barry Shears has written of a bard, fiddler and piper, NEIL MACVICAR, known as Niall Ruadh Mor 'Big Red-Haired Neil' (1779–1861). He left Vallay in 1828/9 for Nova Scotia, where he lived at Catalone, Cape Breton. He had previously been a shepherd in North Uist, after fighting in the Napoleonic Wars. He seems to have been remembered more for his Gaelic poems than for his piping. Some years after suffering a terrible injury while cutting timber in the woods, he died in 1861.

One of his poems, composed before he left Vallay, was the curious *Oran nan Cat*, 'Song of the Cats', which tells of a piper who played 'hundreds of marches' at a fiddler's wedding, before laying down his pipe at the end of the evening. A group of cats had gathered and that night they fell on the pipe, devouring the leather bag and fighting so fiercely over it that they suffered various injuries. The rest of the poem is the cats' reflections on their actions, concluding that they would have been better to leave the pipe for Donald the piper to produce his music from under his arm.

ANGUS MACLELLAN was a fine piper in Valley in the 1920s and 1930s. At that time there were three pipers in that district, Angus in Valley, KENNETH MORRISON in Griminish, North Uist, about a mile away to the south-west, across Valley Sound, and a third player, possibly a MACRURY, at Malaclete, a mile and a half to the south-east, across Valley Strand. (Malaclete is about three miles from Griminish). On fine calm summer evenings, according to Norman Johnston, these three formed a piping triangle, exchanging tunes across the water, each outside his own home. Pipe music travels amazing distances over calm water.

Angus was the uncle by marriage of JOHN MACLEAN, an ex-army piper in North Uist who had returned to the island and was a leading figure in piping there (see above, North Uist). When Angus died, John composed a short lament for him, as a tribute to a fine player. He called it *Inverness to Dunskellar*, published in the *Piping Times* in December 1985 and July 2011. John had escorted the car which took Angus' remains to the cemetery at Dunskellar, not far from Malaclete, on the north side of North Uist.

Sources

Frans Buisman and Andrew Wright, *The MacArthur–MacGregor Manuscript*
Colin Campbell, Canntaireachd MS
Alec Haddow, *The History and Structure of Ceol Mor*
Bill Innes, *TGSI* LXII
Norman Johnston
Fred MacAulay
Rev. A. MacDonald, *The Uist Collection*
William M. MacDonald, *The Glencoe Collection*
Angus MacKay, Manuscripts
Archie MacLean
Elaine MacLean, Paisley
William Matheson, *TGSI* LII and *The Songs of John MacCodrum*
Joseph Mitchell, *Reminiscences of my Life in the Highlands*
Alexander Nicolson, *History of Skye*
Piping Times
Barry Shears, *Dance To The Piper*
Scott Williams, *Pipers of Nova Scotia*
Statistical Account 1837

Duncan Johnstone, 1925–1999.
Courtesy of the College of Piping

Neil Angus MacDonald teaching piobaireachd to young pupils.

Above. The ruins of Ormiclett Castle in South Uist, formerly the strongholdof the chiefs of Clanranald. Built in 1704, it burned down accidentally in 1715.

Right. Ludovic (Louis) Morrison, who does so much to keep piping alive in SouthUist. He belongs to the branch of the Morrison pipers who come from Loch Eynort district, and is an important source of South Uist piping tradition.

Left. Seonaidh Roidean, or Johnny Roidean, John MacDonald of the City of Glasgow Police Pipe Band. He belonged to South Uist, and was a pupil of John MacDonald, Inverness, but his playing retained its island tang. He died in South Uist in 1988. *Courtesy of the College of Piping*

Below. The house near Daliburgh, South Uist, where Seonaidh Roidean lived. It burned down in 1987.

(Left to right:) Robert Reid, Roddy 'Roidean' MacDonald, 'Wee Donald' MacLean, Peter MacLeod junior. *Courtesy of the College of Piping*

Bob Nicol's class in South Uist in the 1950s: (left to right) Calum Campbell, Andrew MacKillop, Willie Morrison, Rona MacDonald (now Lightfoot), Bob Nicol, Calum Beaton. *Courtesy of the College of Piping*

Above. Rona Lightfoot, née MacDonald, daughter of Archie MacDonald, niece of Angus Campbell, South Uist, and cousin of John MacDonald of the Glasgow City police. As well as being an excellent piper, Rona is well-known as a fine Gaelic singer. *Courtesy of the College of Piping*

Left. Angus Campbell, South Uist, a pupil of John MacDonald. He lived to be 102, and had great influence on piping in the Outer Isles. *Photograph kindly lent by Catriona Garbutt*

Above. Angus Campbell, known as Angus Frobost from the name of his home, in piping conversation with his relative Catriona Garbutt (née Campbell). *Photograph kindly lent by Catriona Garbutt*

Right. Calum Iain Campbell senior was from a well-known family of pipers and taught many pupils, including his four children. *Photograph kindly lent by Catriona Garbutt*

Four piping Campbells, children of Calum Iain Campbell, all good players. (Left to right:) Calum Iain junior, Katie Mary, Angus, Catriona. *Photograph kindly lent by Catriona Garbutt*

Left. Catriona Garbutt, née Campbell, playing Ceol Mor at her home in Uachdar, Benbecula, in 2006. *Right.* Catriona Campbell as a girl of fifteen. *Photograph kindly lent by Catriona Garbutt*

Pipers at the South Uist Games at Askernish in the 1950s. It was remarked at the time that it was like seeing a picture of all the gods in Valhalla. See the text, Angus Campbell, South Uist, for identification. *Courtesy of the College of Piping and Rona Lightfoot*

Calum Beaton, who with Louis Morrison is keeping the piping tradition going in South Uist. Calum is a tradition-bearer with a vast knowledge of piping history in Uist.

Willie MacDonald, known to many as Willie Benbecula, from his childhood home. He was sometimes called 'The Muc', a by-name inherited from his father. Here he is seen playing in the Inverness Legion Pipe Band, of which he was Pipe Major.

Pipe Major John Maclean when he was with the 2nd Battalion Highland Light Infantry, in the late 1930s. This photograph was probably taken in Egypt. *By kind permission of Archie MacLean*

Norman Johnston from Lochmaddy, North Uist, here seen at the dedication of a cairn to Willie Ross in Glen Strathfarrar, in 2007. He is talking to Alex Mackenzie.

Valley Sound from Malaclete, on the south-east side, looking west. Around 1930, Angus MacLellan was the piper on Valley, one of a trio of pipers exchanging tunes across the water.

The old Gunnery at Risgary, Bernera, the contents of which were described by Mary MacLeod in her poem *Luinneag Mhic Cleoid* (mid-17th century).

The stones in the foreground are all that remains of the house at Risgary, Bernera, said to have been granted to Mary Macleod by her chief, Sir Norman Macleod. Some say that Mary was born at Risgary, others believe she was born and buried at Rodel, Harris.

Left. Duncan MacLean from Scarp, when he was living in Ardrishaig.

Below. 'Wee Donald' MacLeod and 'Big Donald' MacLean (front row, third and fourth from left) in the 2nd Seaforth Highlanders, in 1939. *Courtesy of the College of Piping*

John Morrison in 1904, before he moved to Assynt House, Stornoway. Here he is pictured (right) with Pipe Major Charles MacIver, when the Lewis Pipe Band was started. *Courtesy of John MacQueen, Stornoway*

Ardvar, Stoer, Sutherland, where Thomas MacKay's father Hugh may have been estate shepherd in the early 19th century. Hugh was the great-grandfather of John Morrison of Assynt House.

The small township of Nedd, in the north of Stoer, Sutherland, under the shadow of the mountain Quinag. Thomas MacKay, grandfather of John Morrison, lived here after his marriage in 1842 to Flora MacRae, who belonged to Nedd. They later moved to Stornoway.

This painting of a Masonic Meeting in Stornoway depicts an occasion in 1847, a celebration of the laying of the foundation stone of Stornoway Castle. The painting may have been made later, possibly based on a photograph, or the key may have been added later, as it names Sir James and Lady Matheson (nos.32 and 33), and the baronetcy was not conferred until 1851. This is the only known image of Thomas MacKay (no.13), Sir James' piper, who was the grandfather of John Morrison of Assynt House. *By kind permission of Neil Campbell McGougan*

List of names for the key to the picture of the Masonic meeting opposite

1 Roderick Morrison, Banker, RWM
2 James Robertson McIver of Gress, SM
3 Daniel Lewis McKenzie, Shipowner, SW
4 John Furse, Supervisor of Inland Revenue, JW
5 Norman McIver, Banker, DM
6 Colin Morrison, Merchant
7 Roderick McKenzie, Town Clerk, Secretary
8 Donald Beaton, Tailor
9 John McAulay, Merchant
10 Malcolm McAulay, Merchant
11 John McKenzie, Contractor, Bible Bearer
12 John White, Inland Revenue, JD
13 Thomas McKay, Piper
14 Rev. John Macrae, EU Minister
15 Hugh Suter, Mason
16 Alexander Gair, Mason
17 John McKenzie, Shipmaster
18 James Christie, Mason
19 David Rae, Painter
20 Dr A. McIver
21 John McLeod of Hudson's Bay
22 —— McDonald
23 John Reid McKenzie, Shipowner
24 Chas Wilson, Architect
25 Hugh Brown, Jailer
26 Thomas Clark, Baker
27 Captain Neil Morrison, RN
28 Donald Munro, Procurator Fiscal
29 Daniel Murray, Tidewaiter
30 Captain R. T. Hudson, Hutchison's Stmrs
31 Roderick Nicholson, Shipowner
32 Sir James Matheson, Prop. of the Lews
33 Lady Matheson
34 Mrs Watt
35 Captain Benjamin Oliver
36 Sheriff Substitute Andrew McDonald
37 Captain Richard Barnaby, RS&M
38 Robert Grant Massou, the Artist
39 Charles Howitt, Architect
40 James Perrie, Solicitor
42 John Scobie, Chamberlain
43 Kenneth Morrison, Flesher

44 Rev. George Shipton
45 Master David McDonald
46 Master Duncan McKenzie
47 John Urquhart, Painter
48 William McKay
49 John McAlpine, PM
50 Donald McKenzie, Shipmaster
51 Robert Pritchard, Teacher
52 Corporal James Kielle, RS&M
53 Donald Morrison, Seaman
54 A. T. Chatfield, Compt of Customs
55 John Rae, Shipwright
56 Archibald McLellan, 'Mary Jane'
57 David Corner, Fishery Officer
58 Alexander McKenzie, Joiner
59 Alexander McLean, Ship Carpenter
60 Murdo Lead, Baker
61 Roderick Millar, Surgeon
62 Mrs McLeod, Belleville
63 Donald Matheson, RS&M
64 Roderick McKay, Gamekeeper
65 Henry Stafford, RS&M
66 William Auckburn, RS&M
67 Duncan Grant, Bookseller
68 John Munro, Excise Officer
69 Revd Mr Watson, Uig
70 Peter McNab, Carting Contractor
71 Roderick Nicholson Jnr, now of Tighnabruaich
72 McEachan, Steward of Steamer
73 Colin John Nicholson, Clerk
74 Alex Robertson, Shipowner
75 Angus Mckay, Supt Herring Fishery
76 Robert Wilson, Gas Manager
77 Murdo McKenzie, Shipowner
78 Alexander Morrison
79 W. T. Jeffries, Collector of Customs
80 Alexander McKenzie, Architect
81 Hugh McPherson, Galson
82 Hugh McLachlan, merchant
83 Murdo McIver
84 James Robertson, CE

Snowy MacLeod, Stornoway, was Pipe Major in the 2nd Seaforth at the battle of El Alamein. He later became Drum Major in the Lewis Pipe Band. *Courtesy of John MacQueen, Stornoway*

Willie MacLean. Although born in Tobermory, Mull, of a Raasay family, he was known as Willie MacLean, Creagorry, because his father had the Creagorry Hotel in Benbecula. *Courtesy of the College of Piping.*

Harris, Scalpay, Bernera, St Kilda and Outlying Isles

With **Harris** are included the islands of **Bernera** (not to be confused with Bernera, Lewis), **Scalpay, Scarp, Pabay, Taransay, Ensay** and **St Kilda.**

Bernera (Harris) is now linked by a causeway to North Uist, so is regarded by some as belonging to North Uist, but historically it was part of the parish of Harris, and is so treated here.

Although Harris and Lewis are regarded as separate islands and used to belong to different counties, they are in fact one geographical entity, known (sometimes) as the Long Island. Harris is a name thought to be derived from Norse herath, 'district' (Na h-Earradh in Gaelic), but possibly both go back to pre-Gaelic forms, whose meaning has been lost. For many years in the 20th century, Harris was included as a part of Inverness-shire, whereas Lewis was in Ross and Cromarty. Both now come under the Comunn an Eileanan (Western Isles Council).

Harris

To reach Harris, travel to Skye and take the car ferry from Uig, in northern Skye, to Tarbert, Harris. The crossing takes about 2 hours. Alternatively, take the car ferry from Ullapool, Wester Ross, to Stornoway, Lewis (3 hours), and travel by road south through Lewis to Harris. By air, fly from Glasgow or Inverness to Stornoway.

Tunes Associated with Harris

Angus MacLeod of Scalpay's Jig, by J. Smith 6/8 J 4
A Harris Dance (trad., arr. Bruce Gandy) R 2
The Harris Hornpipe, by Donald Varella HP 4
The Kyles of Scalpay, by A. MacIver S 4
Leaving St Kilda, by William Ross 4/4 S 2
The Lewis and Harris Gathering, by Peter R. MacLeod 2/4 M 4
Loch Seaforth R 4
Loch Voshmid, by George MacLeod 2/4 HP 4

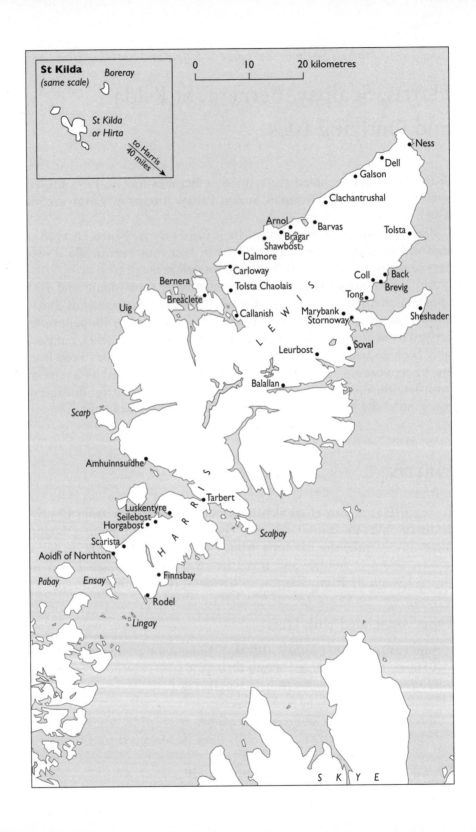

St Kilda
(same scale)

Boreray

St Kilda
or Hirta

to Harris
40 miles

0   10   20 kilometres

Ness
Dell
Galson
Clachantrushal
Arnol
Barvas
Bragar
Shawbost
Tolsta
Dalmore
Carloway
Coll
Back
Bernera
Tolsta Chaolais
Brevig
Breaclete
Tong
Uig
Callanish
Marybank
Stornoway
Sheshader
L E W I S
Leurbost
Soval
Balallan
Scarp
Amhuinnsuidhe
Tarbert
Luskentyre
Seilebost
Horgabost
Scalpay
Scarista
H A R R I S
Aoidh of Northton
Pabay
Ensay
Finnsbay
Rodel
Lingay

S K Y E

The Long Island, by Donald MacLeod 6/8 M 2
Murray of Harris's March 2/4 M 2
St Kilda Wedding R 2

See also the works composed by, and for, Dr John MacAskill (below).

There seem to be no piobaireachd works associated with Harris, although Robert Meldrum in his *Reminiscences* has a somewhat confused note about *Barisdale's Salute*, often attributed to Alexander MacLennan, but associated by Meldrum with Angus MacRae from Ensay, Harris (see below).

The piping traditions of Harris have been obscured by religious opposition to music, ever since the mid-19th century. Even though the piping family of MacCrimmons has traditionally been associated with Scarista, in the south of Harris, the best of them were in Skye as pipers to the MacLeods of Dunvegan, so that their piobaireachd compositions are regarded as Skye works rather than originating in Harris.

The MacCrimmons at Scarista and Rodel

It is not certain where this important piping family came from, though recent opinion seems in favour of Ireland; according to the MacLeod Bannatyne manuscript, however, written in the 18th century, the family was already in Harris before the Norse invasion in the 10–11th centuries, and was one of three old families there – but doubt has been cast on this claim, and it is not borne out by the Harris estate records, such as they are. Alternatives are that the MacCrimmons were of Norse origin, around the 12th century, or that they came over from Ireland in the 13th century, when many artistically gifted families had to leave Ireland for political reasons.

The evidence is thin, and it is not until 1725 that we have irrefutable documentary evidence of MacCrimmon presence in Harris. Oral tradition is strong, but seems to be based largely on 19th century stories, corrupted by romantic notions about the '45 Rising. There was undoubtedly a piping family called MacCrimmon who supplied the Dunvegan MacLeods in Skye with their famous pipers, and had apparently done so for several centuries – but what is the evidence that they belonged to Harris?

In his paper 'Early Harris Estate Papers', given to the Gaelic Society of Inverness (*TGSI* LI), Alick Morrison gave rental and other estate lists, from the MacLeod Muniments, which include three generations of a family in Harris called Mc Cumra. This may be an early spelling of the name we now call MacCrimmon, which throughout its traceable history until the late 18th century always had the vowel *u* in the stressed syllable. The *i* spelling began to come in as an alternative, but very gradually, and no earlier than the mid-18th century – and even then it was rare.

It is not clear why this change in spelling, and presumably also pronunciation, took place; it may have been part of the 18th century's 'enlightenment', an urge to become (or appear) more 'civilised', when Scottish pronunciations began to be percieved as vulgar and unrefined, so that the back vowel *u* was shifted to front vowel *i* (see below).

While the Harris estate clerks were spelling the name Mc Cumra, in Skye the contemporary spelling was MacCrumme, used of Patrick Og in the Skye records in 1688. In that year, Rory Campbell, the Harris agent for the Dunvegan chief, Iain Breac MacLeod, sold Iain a bonnet for 14/- (shillings), which he gave to 'Patrick MacCrumme the piper' – this was presumably Patrick Og, then in Skye. Note that there is no final -*n*. Not long after this, the Skye records began to use the spelling McCrummen. It is, of course, possible that MacCrumme was a scribal error.

Rory Campbell, as Chamberlain of Harris, was in charge of the depository, a kind of warehouse for imported goods at Rodel, in South Harris, where rent items paid to the MacLeod estate in kind, such as oatmeal and cheese, were also stored. Martin Martin, visiting in 1703, said the place was overrun with rats, who bullied the cats brought in to keep them down: the cats, outnumbered by 20 to 1, needed to be pampered with offerings of warm milk to keep up their strength and courage for the fray. Rory ran an import/export business from Rodel. He used to buy cattle, horses, cloth and shoes in North Uist, he and his sons Angus and Alexander sailing round the Hebrides as merchants.

Rory Campbell, descended from the Campbells of Auchinbreck and Barbreck, in Argyll, was a well educated man, who imported from Flanders or France such exotic items as spices, honey, raisins, prunes, salad oil, brandy, wine, and vinegar; he brought in tar (for boats) from the Baltic, flour and meal from Ireland, tobacco from Glasgow and sugar from Greenock. He also imported salt, tallow, soap, herring and biscuits (probably ship's biscuit for long sea voyages) from other parts of Scotland. He sold the everyday utensils of the time: tankards, quart measures, skillets, porringers, trenchers, door locks, clocks, chamber pots, boat cordage, sail needles, mails (big hammers), gimlets, pick axes, iron and steel bars, pipes, chalk and floor nails. His exports were mainly cattle and sheep, and woven cloth.

His accounts give us a glimpse of life in Harris in the late 17th century. The surviving Harris rentals begin in 1678, and continue, though sometimes sporadic, until the estate was sold in 1779. We have rental lists, and in some cases lists of the receipts of a tax on crops known as Cess Money, also another levy called Silver Dutie. All these give us names of the tenants. Later accounts include the factor's outgoing expenditure. Rarely, however, do we have both the incomings and outgoings of the same year, so it is difficult to know how well off each tenant was.

Rory Campbell was a Harris tacksman or tenant until in 1686 he succeeded his father, Finlay mac Finlay, as Chamberlain, taking over also the tenancy of North Scarista. As his power increased he replaced the minister, Mr John Campbell, in the tenancy of part of the island of Ensay, and the district of the Aoidh of Northton, as well as being the tenant of Scarista. In 1703, however, Rory left Harris for Uist, apparently after a quarrel with his MacLeod chief at Dunvegan. Efforts were made to lure him back, but his heyday in Harris was over.

It is clear that from 1686 to 1703, Scarista was in the hands of this powerful Campbell family, and for some years after this, too; the earliest written record of a MacCrimmon at Scarista is dated 1725.*

---

* The terms 'clittick' and 'kinock' are Gaelic words of land measurement, based on an old Norse system. The following conversions may be helpful:
  1 unga (ounceland) = 20 pennylands
  1 pennyland = 4 feoirlins (fardings or farthings)
  1 farthing = 4 cleiteags (clitigs or clitticks)
  1 cleiteag = 4 cianogs (kinocks)
  Cleiteag and cianog were terms used especially in Rodel and Ensay.
  As the extent of a pennyland varied according to the richness of the ground, it is impossible to be precise, but both cleiteag and cionag were pretty small holdings. A tacksman, who held his land on a long lease from the proprietor of the estate, might have several pennylands and let parts to his sub-tenants, who then sub-divided into smaller units.
  In South Harris, North Scarista was four pennylands. Rodel was one pennyland, split into 5 lots, and further subdivided into small holdings of one or a half cleitig each, and some of these were in turn split into lots of a cianog or kinnock. In 1678, the rent for half a cleitig was 10 merks, while the tenant of four pennylands paid 130 merks in cash plus substantial rent in kind – mainly oatmeal and sheep. By 1685 the rent for a cionag was five merks. A merk was the equivalent of a pound Scots, worth one-twelfth of a pound sterling.

It was at this time, when Finlay mac Finlay and his son, Rory Campbell, were successive Chamberlains of Harris, that several rental lists were compiled, which give us some information (but not enough – never enough) about the MacCrimmons. In 1678, Scarista was not the MacCrimmon home, being divided into two parts, South Scarista 'for the Laird his use', and North Scarista and Finnsbay let to 'Finlay mc Finlay ... for wch he payes ane hundreth & thretie merks, ten bolls & ane half meall, threteine stones (of cheese or butter), nine wedders & ane halfe'. In other words, the good and extensive lands of North and South Scarista were held directly by the clan Chief and his Chamberlain.

It is at Roadille (Rodel) that we find Angus Mc Cumra, in 1678, with a holding of 'half a clittick' for which he paid annually ten merks. There is no indication that Angus Mc Cumra was a piper, but his name, in the list of the Rodel tenants, is not in the form of a patronymic: this is another way of saying that Mc Cumra seems to have been his surname, and does not tell us who his father and grandfather were. It was employees of the MacLeod estate whose names were given in this form, because many of them were incomers. Bill Lawson, the Harris genealogist, does not agree that the name McCumra is a form of Mac-Crimmon, but identifies these McCumras with the Gaelic form of the name Montgomery (found in Lewis). He says the McCumras in Rodel came to Harris from Skye. This might be thought to support the theory that they were indeed MacCrimmons – and there is no tradition of any Montgomeries in Harris.

Many tenants in the Harris rentals are given with two, three or even four generations of first names, with no family names, and the use of a family name (surname) often indicates that the tenant was an incomer, brought in by the MacLeod estate for a specific purpose, to act as the estate ferryman, forester, ground officer, carpenter, smith – or musician. It is possible that Angus Mc Cumra was so called because he was there as piper, and that he (or his family) originated somewhere else – but we do not know if this was so. Angus Mc Cumra had two sons, Murdo and John, both later listed as 'son of Angus son of Cumra', in patronymic style, but we do not know who Angus' forebears may have been, or who Cumra was.

Many of the tenants of tiny holdings at Rodel were there by virtue of their office as estate employees. Some received a wage of exactly the same sum as their rent, i.e. they lived rent-free; some were paid half of their rent if their services were not full-time. Some of the Rodel tenants appear to have been just that, tenants, and not employees or

estate servants, and they appear in the rentals listed by their patronymic line, their fathers' and grandfathers' names (sometimes up to
two generations further back than that). This identifies them with
remarkable accuracy, but usually with no indication of the family
surname.

At this time some were beginning to feel the need of a surname and
we find occasionally a patronymic list with an additional 'alias Mac-
Donald' (or other surname), which tells us this man's family. 'Alias'
does not imply anything sinister – it means simply 'otherwise known
as', or, by extension, 'beginning to use the surname of''.

In Iceland, where the patronymic system is still used, it was felt (in
the twentieth century) that too many Icelanders, influenced by Den-
mark and Norway, were beginning to introduce surnames, so a law
was passed, forbidding the use of surnames except in business. Under
this, Sigurthur Eysteinsson Olafssonar might trade under the name of
Nordal, but would vote in elections as Sigurthur Eysteinsson.

This did not happen in Scotland, where one of the consequences
of the Jacobite Risings was the deliberate suppression of Gaelic customs and the introduction of English ways. The patronymic system as
exemplified by the Harris Estate papers is a marvel of accuracy and
(when we get the hang of it) clarity, every man being defined in such
a way that we can tell who his relatives were, and defined in a unique
way, not duplicated by anyone else. We do not have to grapple with
dozens of John MacDonalds, Iain MacKenzies or Alasdair MacKays,
impossible to sort out.

Because of this mixing of surnames and patronymic lists we cannot
be sure if Angus Mc Cumra at Rodel in 1678–84 was the same Angus
who figures in the patronymic line of 'The Widow' Rachel, who is
described as 'daughter of John, son of Angus'. She had three brothers,
John Og, Finlay and Angus, all with the same line, and we know that
their father was known as John (or Iain) Dubh, 'dark-haired John'.
The siblings were all of the tacksman / tenant class with big holdings
of land and enough wealth to pay large rents. It is not certain whose
widow Rachel was, but she had probably been married to Finlay mac
Finlay (Campbell), the Chamberlain of Harris, as she appears as the
tenant of North Scarista and Finnsbay in the year of Finlay's death
(1685) – and was in 1689 joint tenant of 'the two Scarastas' with Finlay's son Rory Campbell; presumably she was Rory's mother, though
this is not certain (she may have been Finlay's second wife). She may
herself have been a Campbell, though this too is uncertain, and her
line could be Campbell or Mc Cumra – or other.

It is possible that Rachel was a Mc Cumra, grandchild of Angus in Rodel, and if so, she and her three brothers had risen in the world, since Angus and his sons John and Murdo were, in comparison, mere peasants, with tiny holdings at Rodel. Was the marriage of Rachel to Finlay Campbell the stepping-stone to this prosperity? Was it through Rachel that the MacCrimmons acquired a claim on tenancy of the lands of Scarista? Or are Rachel and her brothers red herrings, irrelevant to MacCrimmon history?

The name Mc Cumra appears to be a form of MacCruimein, the Gaelic spelling of what we now call MacCrimmon. The piping family in Skye at this time, Patrick Og and his sons, are spelled MacCrumme(n) in the Skye records, but spelling was at the whim of the clerk writing out the names, and we cannot base much argument on the anglicised variants. Mc Cumra was later spelled Mc Cumerad or Mc Cumrait, which looks like the Gaelic form of Montgomery, but there were no Montgomeries in Harris at that time, and this spelling is probably misleading. Alistair MacLeod, formerly the genealogist with Highland Council, with a vast knowledge of island families, is of the opinion that Mc Cumra is a variant of MacCrumme or MacCruimein, and that it was used as a surname in the Harris accounts because the family had come in from somewhere else, so that to give their family line as a patronymic list would have been pointless. Does this suggest that they had come to Harris comparatively recently, and that Angus Mc Cumra was the first of his family to live there? Not necessarily – but it does suggest he was an estate employee.

The reversal of the consonants *m* and *r* presents no difficulty in a Gaelic name: it is a phenomenon known as metathesis, found frequently when *r* or *l* occurs next to another consonant.

As Angus appears in the rental lists up to 1684 as a tenant at Rodel, but not in that of 1685, which gives his son, Murdo Mc Cumra, as the tenant, we assume that Angus died in late 1684 or early 1685. Another son, John, also had a holding at Rodel, but his name does not appear consistently, and we cannot be sure how long he was there. It is possible, but unproven, that this John, son of Angus Mc Cumra, was Rachel's father. Murdo held his cianog of land (1/4 of a clittig), paying 5 merks in rent, until the early years of the 1700s.

Rodel was made up of 4 separate lets, and one of these was divided into 17 parts, each comprising one clittick, and some of these were further divided into four cianogs – so Murdo's holding was very small. Bill Lawson, the Harris genealogist, makes it clear that it was only at Rodel that such tiny holdings were viable – because 'it is different from the rest of Harris in that it has soil', i.e. it was comparatively fertile land. Much of Harris is either bare rock or rock covered by a thin layer of poor soil, so that holdings elsewhere needed to be much bigger.

Harris Estate Pipers

In 1707, MacLeod of Dunvegan, the proprietor of the Harris estate, sent for a piper called Hugh MacLeod, bringing him over from Uist to be the official Harris piper. The inducement was a handsome salary of £40 a year, which contrasted with the £10 or £20 wage given to the official pipers in other MacLeod estates, in Skye. These salaries were often the same as the piper's rent, so that they amounted to his holding his land rent-free, but sometimes the salary was only half the rent. The fact of Hugh's pay being £40 probably indicates that he held the Kirk-penny, part of Scarista, which was the only holding with a £40 rent at that time. This seems to be the first recorded reference to a piper at Scarista – and he was not a MacCrimmon.

Later on, from 1730, Donald Ban MacCrimmon, living in Scarista, received a salary of a mere £28 13s 4d, which was increased in 1738 to £33 6s 8d – so Hugh MacLeod was, we must assume, an excellent piper. Donald Ban was paid as a part-time piper, his salary amounting to only half of his rent – and one year he received a cow instead of half of his pay.

Hugh MacLeod was in Harris for at least four years, probably longer, being named in the accounts until 1711; after that the accounts lump all the estate servants together, unnamed, as forester, ferryman, ground officer, carpenter, harper, violer, piper, porter, gardener and so on, so that we do not know who they were, or what their individual wages were – we have only the sum total of their annual pay as an anonymous group of estate workers.

This continued until 1725, when the young Malcolm MacCrum-men became the Harris piper. In 1728 we find an entry which states that Malcolm MacCrummen, as the tenant of North Scarista, on the express orders of the chief, was to have the large rent of £53 6s 8d paid to him, in addition to his salary as piper, less than half of this. Ruairidh Halford-MacLeod suggests that this gift, which was repeated in 1729, was a form of tocher (dowry) from the chief on Malcolm's marriage in 1728. Malcolm's holding in Harris was probably the Kirkpenny, at Scarista, one of the best tenancies in Harris, carrying with it social prestige as well as a good income. The previous rent of £40 had been raised by then.

From these entries we may surmise that at the time when Murdo Mc Cumra died in the early 1700s, there was no piper left in Harris who was good enough to be the chief's official piper there. This suggests, but does not prove, that Angus and Murdo Mc Cumra had been his pipers but had no sons well trained to replace them (Murdo was succeeded in the Rodel tenancy by his daughter, listed in the 1703 rental as *nien vic Cumerad*, Mc Cumra's daughter), that Hugh MacLeod was brought in to fill the vacancy, and that when he died, or perhaps when he left Harris, probably in 1725, Malcolm MacCrimmon was sent over from Skye, with the inducement of a big holding of good land. Five years later, Malcolm's father, Patrick Og, died in Skye, Malcolm replaced him as the Dunvegan piper, and his younger brother, Donald Ban, took his place in Harris. Donald is well attested as the Harris piper, from 1730 to 1745. Donald, like Malcolm, was brought from Skye to be the Harris piper – there is no sign of him in Harris before 1730.

Donald Ban, born around 1710 as a son of Patrick Og's second marriage, was not the principal piper of MacLeod, never rising above the status of the Harris piper. He was probably not born in Harris, but took over from his brother Malcolm at the age of twenty. His wife Rachel may have been a Harris woman, since she remained there for many years after his death, receiving an annual pension from the chief until the Harris estate was sold in 1779.

Alick Morrison, in his book *The Chiefs of the Clan MacLeod* (1986), said that when Patrick Mor was principal piper at Dunvegan – between c.1640 and c.1670 – his son Patrick Og was living in Harris, and he also said that Isabella, the widow of Sir Rory Mor MacLeod, moved to Harris when her son took over as chief. Living quietly in Scarista, tended by none other than Mary MacLeod, who had come from Bernera to look after her, Isabella was played the *Lament for Donald of Laggan* by Patrick Og every evening (she was Donald's daughter). There appears to be no evidence to set this pleasant fantasy in Harris, and it takes no account of the exile of Mary MacLeod, sent from Dunvegan for whatever reason. What little evidence we have points to all of them being in Skye rather than Harris – but this could be wrong. If Isabella was living in Harris in her widowhood, it would have been at South Scarista, the holding reserved for the Chief himself, or his family.

If Mary MacLeod was indeed sent for, to come to Harris to look after Isabella, is it possible that this was her exile from Skye, and the stories of her being sent to Mull and Scarba are mere stories? The evidence is scant, but we do have Mary's own words in her song *Luinneag Mhic*

Leoid, in which she laments her isolation in Scarba from which she could see Islay and Jura, neither of them visible from Scarista.

Simon Fraser in Australia passed on another tradition which probably came to him from the writings of Niel MacLeod of Gesto, who received much MacCrimmon lore from Iain Dubh MacCrimmon in the early 19th century, or late 18th. This said that Patrick Og was succeeded as the Dunvegan piper by Donald Ban, who was considered to be the best player of all Patrick Og's sons; but we can show that Donald Ban was not Patrick Og's successor, and was never the Dunvegan piper, so the tradition has become distorted, for whatever reason.

Simon Fraser's tradition also said that the composer of the *Lament for Donald Ban MacCrimmon* was Donald Ruadh, brother of Iain Dubh. It is generally accepted that the lament was the work of Donald Ban's brother Malcolm, mainly because Malcolm was the Dunvegan piper at the time of Donald Ban's death, as well as being his elder brother. Donald Ruadh was six years old when his uncle Donald Ban was killed, so presumably he was claimed to have made the composition long after his uncle's death in 1746 – and surely Iain Dubh would have known, if indeed it was made by his own brother, rather than by his father.

But there is something strange going on here: Gesto (or somebody else?) seems to have been set on belittling Malcolm in the MacCrimmon story, and we have to wonder why. Much of what Gesto passed on to the Frasers seems to be rooted in the beliefs of Freemasonry, and there may have been some reason, such as Malcolm rejecting or opposing Freemasonry, which led Gesto to try to denigrate him. It is hard to believe that this came from Iain Dubh, who was a son of Malcolm MacCrimmon, but, of course, sons do fall out with fathers. Would Iain Dubh have publicly dishonoured his father in this way? It seems unlikely, even if they had had a serious disagreement, since Highland tradition of a duty to respect one's father is very strong, and Iain would have been dishonouring himself. Perhaps Gesto 'adjusted' the tradition after the deaths of Iain Dubh and Donald Ruadh, to suit his own purposes.

The late 17th century seems to have been the time when the MacCrimmons in Harris were rising socially, and it is possible that, by marrying into the tacksman class, they established themselves at Scarista, having previously been small tenants in Rodel. We cannot prove this, however.

Possible MacCrimmon Line in Harris

If we were to assume (tentatively) that Angus Mc Cumra and his son Murdo were MacCrimmon pipers in Harris, how would they link up, if indeed they did, with the MacCrimmon pipers in Skye? The tradition of Patrick Mor losing all of his sons except Patrick Og within the space of one year may be borne out by there being no tenants in Harris who were 'son of Patrick son of Donald', and we have to assume that Patrick Mor had no sons in Harris. The patronymic lines of the rentals appear to be meticulously accurate, recorded by factors (chamberlains) who were not only careful record-keepers but had been born and raised in Harris, and knew everybody there.

So we have to look a generation further back, to find possible brothers of Patrick Mor, whose line would be son of Donald son of John (Iain Odhar). Donald Mor died around 1640, less than 40 years before the earliest of the surviving Harris rentals, and well within the memory of living tenants.

There are surprisingly few who were son of Donald son of John, even though these are both names which recur frequently. There was a large family in the small Harris islands of Pabay, Lingay and Ensay where nine tenants were the sons of Neil son of Donald son of John, and there was also Angus son of Donald son of John, and this Angus had a son called Rory – they too were in Pabay. Angus and Neil were brothers who were Pabay tenants in the mid-17th century – Neil died in 1687 – and their sons took up tenancies in the 1680s. Were Neil and Angus sons of Donald Mor MacCrimmon? The dates are right, the *sloinneadh* is right, but we cannot be sure. It would be neat if this Angus was Angus Mc Cumra who died at Rodel in about 1684, and again the dates would fit. And if the Widow Rachel at Scarista was Angus' grandchild, the link is laid out, with Donald Mor as the common ancestor. This is, of course, entirely hypothetical, and no claims are made for its accuracy. Possible, maybe, but proven, by no means.

At Rodel in the 1680s we find a tenant John son of Donald son of John, who had a brother Donald, also with a holding of land at Rodel. Donald's wife was called Mairi (Marie), and took over his tenancy when he died in 1701. Were these two brothers sons of Donald Mor MacCrimmon and brothers of Neil and Angus in Pabay? The problem here is that their names are listed alongside that of Angus Mc Cumra and later Murdo Mc Cumra, and there is no indication that they might be related. Possibly, however, the surname Mc Cumra was used of Angus and Murdo because they were estate pipers, to distinguish them from other tenants, and John and Donald could be of that same family. This, of course, is also speculation.*

According to Alick Morrison, seven of Patrick Og's reputed twenty sons from his two marriages were Malcolm, Angus, Donald Donn, Farquhar, Donald Ban, John and Peter; he had at least one daughter, Rachel (not the Widow Rachel at Scarista). Angus was said to be a piper, but died around 1730. Donald Donn made his home in Skye, as did Farquhar, and John lived in Kintail. None of Patrick Og's sons was in Harris, other than Malcolm in 1728, and Donald Ban, from 1730 to 1745.

Literacy Among the Maccrimmons

How did the MacCrimmon pipers reach such high status as to be the tenants of a whole pennyland at Scarista when they were so young? Malcolm seems to have been only 17 or 18 in 1725, and Donald Ban

---

* Some complications in the Harris Estate papers are:

(1) that the spelling of the names John and Ewen (G. Iain and Eoin) overlap and it is not always possible to tell which is which. John is spelled Ean when it is the first name in a patronymic list, but may be Eane, Ewine, Ewne or Ene further down the line, and may be Eane in one rental but Ewine in the next. This is further complicated by the fact that in the Gaelic Bible, the name John is always spelled Eoin, not Iain.

(2) that in Harris and other islands, the family naming system sometimes led to the same name being used more than once, as children were called after their parents' relatives: a boy Angus could have one or more brothers called Angus, one named for (say) his mother's father, one for his father's brother and one for his mother's cousin. A Harris family, living in Wester Ross in the 20th century, had five sons all named Neil, after their father. They were known as Neil, Neilie, Neilie John, Neilie Angus and Neilie Og. All of these would be in official records as Neil, with the same patronymic line and the same surname, and would appear as if they were one man.

(3) that some of the names are spelled as phonetic renderings of Gaelic pronunciation, such as Mc Coill or MacColl representing MacDonald or son of Donald, Mc Conchie for son of Duncan, Mc Innish for son of Angus, reiwech or reeiveich for ruaidh ('red-haired'), itrawe meaning 'coming from Strath, in Skye'. Many of these are standard in 17th and 18th century rentals and accounts, and we soon become accustomed to them, but they make interpretation of the information more difficult.

a mere 20 when he moved in. Probably the shortage of good pipers in Harris and the chief's wish to have a skilled piper there, combined with their connection to Patrick Og, obviously a favourite with the chief, worked on their behalf. Donald evidently became a respected resident, and in both 1733 and 1735, he was at Dunvegan to sign as witness the Skye factor's accounts for the Harris estate. He used the anglicised forms of his name, signing himself Donald MacCrummen rather than Domhnall Mac Cruimein, with a surname, not a patronymic. This might suggest that he was copying a model supplied by the factor, or that he was literate only in English, if at all. Literacy would have been in English or Latin in those days, Gaelic being largely an oral language among the people.

We assume he was called upon as a witness because he had detailed knowledge of affairs in Harris, or perhaps it was merely that he happened to be in Skye visiting his family when witnesses were required – but the other witness was the Harris schoolmaster, so maybe it had been arranged beforehand. The implication seems to be that Donald Ban was regarded as a professional man rather than a servant.

Does this witnessing by Donald Ban tell us that he was fully literate? Not necessarily, since he may have been merely witnessing a signature, but he seems to have been able to sign a form of his own name with a reasonably firm hand. Literacy at that time was often hit-or-miss in a family: if an educated man died leaving a young family, and the widow had a struggle to bring them up, the children might not become literate, since feeding them would be their mother's priority. Once the family tradition of education had broken down, that branch might not resume it for several generations. In many families, poor or otherwise, it was the mother who was responsible for the children's education, and if she herself was illiterate, they would probably grow up that way.

Simon Fraser, probably drawing on the writings of Gesto, assured the world that Patrick Mor MacCrimmon, who died around 1670, was not only English-speaking and literate but was 'a scholar and a poet', who wrote an account of his family's religious beliefs ('The Failure of Christianity') in a lengthy manuscript, presumably in English. Again, this tradition seems to be bound up with the tenets of the Masons, and, as happens so often with the statements of Simon Fraser, the evidence is lost, this time because Patrick Mor, not wishing his family secrets to be revealed, seemingly gave orders that his manuscript should be buried with him (so why did he write it – if he did?).

We know for certain that his son, Patrick Og, could not write: a report of his evidence to an enquiry into the MacLeod estate rents in

1724 ends with the words ' He depones he cannot wryte' and he had to make his mark instead of signing his name. It does seem odd that if Patrick Mor was so literary, his only surviving son should be totally illiterate. This may, however, have been because Patrick Mor had married the wrong wife. It is possible, of course, that Patrick Og saying he could not write in 1724, when he was an old man, means merely that he was unable to hold a pen at that time because of a physical condition such as arthritis or Djupetron's Contracture. He may have been literate and able to write as a younger man. On the other hand, if he could not hold a pen, presumably he would no longer be able to finger a chanter, either, and would have had to give up his position as the Chief's principle piper. So perhaps we may take it that he was in fact illiterate.

It is difficult to take Simon Fraser's stories about Patrick Mor seriously, or to guess who started them: Iain Dubh? Gesto? Hugh Archibald Fraser, father of Simon? In the tradition received by George Poulter in the 1930s, presumably in Skye, it was Iain Dubh who wrote 'The Failure of Christianity' which was buried with him – three generations after Patrick Mor. A curious discrepancy – especially as the Australian Frasers had their information via Iain Dubh himself (or claimed to).

It seems likely that both Simon Fraser and his correspondent in Montana, A.K. Cameron, developed and elaborated the theories which Simon said he found in the (lost) book and (lost) manuscript of Gesto, but they did not sow the seed. Simon quotes several religious verses (in English) which he says were written (sic) by Patrick Mor, but perhaps he meant they were composed first in Gaelic. He does, however, imply that Patrick was not only literate but bi-lingual, and there is little evidence for either. The theory of canntaireachd (called seanntaireachd or seantaireachd by Simon Fraser) being based on vocables found in the book of Genesis, in the Old Testament, is rooted in the Authorised Version of the Bible, in English, and depends on Patrick Mor being able to read English as well as speak it, in the 17th century. This seems unlikely.

It is difficult to discover if the MacCrimmons as a family were literate, and if so, when (and who). It should be noted, however, that the earliest recorded MacCrimmon was Sir Jhone McChrummen, who in 1533 was in Inverness, witnessing the signature of the MacLeod chief, Alasdair Crotach. 'Sir' was a designation given to a university graduate, and tells us that Sir Jhone was fully literate, probably in both Latin and Scots English, as well as being (presumably) a Gaelic speaker. It is thought that he was a parson, or possibly a lawyer. We do not know if he had come to Inverness with his chief from Skye, or whether he was living in Inverness in 1533. It is possible that he was 'Evanus piper' in Skye, in 1541.

Certainly Donald Ban seems to have been able to read and write in the 1730s, when he witnessed the MacLeod accounts for Harris. At the very least, he could sign his own name, using that anglicised spelling, possibly copying a written model. But in 1791, one of the two MacCrimmon brothers, presumably Donald Ruadh, had to make his mark rather than sign his name on receiving his salary of £4 as piper to MacLeod – and there is evidence that he learned to write some time after this, in adulthood, around 1800. Up until then, his handwriting was quite wobbly and unformed, but it improved steadily as he wrote more letters. He was possibly in his late forties when he learned to write. It is not always easy to judge if the writing in his letters is his own, as some have survived in clan muniments (e.g. the Seafield papers) only as copies made by clerks.

Less convincing evidence is Seton Gordon's story of MacCrimmon (unspecified and undated) writing a tune in the wet sand of the beach as the tide began to ebb, and telling his pupils he expected them to be able to play it before the incoming tide washed it away (*A Highland Year*, 1947). Written in staff or canntaireachd? Both seem unlikely.

Like his brother, Iain Dubh clearly knew, and used, canntaireachd, but probably could neither read nor write it. Canntaireachd was traditionally a medium for singing, not intended for writing down, but Iain must have been present when Gesto and Hugh Archibald Fraser began to transcribe it into written vocables. Simon Fraser said it was his father, Hugh Archibald, who did the actual transcribing, and wrote down the vocables from Iain Dubh's singing. Eye-witness evidence of the manuscripts, however, makes it clear that the tunes were written in more than one hand. We have to wonder if perhaps Gesto (who was certainly literate) did some of the work himself, but we cannot be sure. Possibly his breathing problems made sustained efforts of writing difficult – or his social position as laird meant that he was accustomed to having professional scribes act for him.

The 1790s saw the start of attempts to record piobaireachd works in written canntaireachd, Colin Campbell in Nether Lorne apparently being a leader in this field. William MacMurchie in Kintyre may have attempted it as early as the 1760s, but his writings of music have been lost, and it is not certain whether he wrote it in canntaireachd vocables or staff notation, nor indeed if he was writing out pipe music or that of the harp. Joseph MacDonald wrote his *Treatise* in 1762, but he used staff notation and did not attempt to write down canntaireachd vocables – his work was first published in the early years of the 19th century, and may have been a spur to Gesto and Hugh Archibald Fraser. Joseph's brother Patrick also wrote out some piobaireachd in staff, published in 1784.

Supply of Pipers from Harris to Skye

A son of Patrick Og was John, who soon after 1715 was living at Leacachan, on Loch Duich, and was probably the composer of *The Glen Is Mine*. He is said (by Alick Morrison) to have been born at Scarista; do we assume then that Patrick Og did not live in Skye until his father, Patrick Mor died (around 1670)? We have only the word of Alick Morrison for John's Harris birthplace and for Patrick Og's home being in Harris. There seems to be no other evidence. Certainly there is no trace of Patrick Og, or of the birth of John, in Harris in 1710; indeed, the records do not tell us that any of his sons were born in Harris, traditionally at Scarista. Patrick Og married twice, but the Harris records, which start in 1678, do not name him. The strong Scarista / MacCrimmon connection probably arose in tradition no earlier than the time of Malcolm and Donald Ban, between 1725 and 1746. And there is no suggestion that Macrimmon pipers were in Harris after that. Donald Ban's children were probably there, but do not seem to have been pipers.

It looks as if the MacLeod tradition of a family of MacCrimmons at Scarista made up of accomplished pipers, a pool of talent on which the chief could draw at any time, may be mistaken – unless there were MacCrimmons in Scarista much earlier, in the time of Iain Odhar and Donald Mor, a time when records are thin, during the 16th century. The possible descent of some Harris tenants from Donald Mor (see above) may be evidence, but we cannot depend upon it.

When Donald Mor was away in Sutherland, said to be fleeing from the retribution of MacKenzie of Kintail, he was absent from Dunvegan for some twenty years, approximately from 1603 to the early 1620s, yet tradition has not given us the name of a substitute piper there, MacCrimmon or other. There is documentary proof that Donald was a piper with the MacKays of Strathnaver in 1612–14, but who was his stand-in, in Skye? Was it another MacCrimmon, brought over from Harris? Tradition is, uncharacteristically, silent.

A link with Rodel, Harris, was Mary MacLeod who lived for a time in Bernera, but possibly was born at Rodel, around 1610–15. The facts of her life are vague and unconfirmed but oral tradition says Rodel was both her birthplace and her burial place, although she said herself that she was brought up by a foster-mother in Skye (see also Alick Morrison's theory that she was servant to the Dowager Isabella in Harris). Her grave, unmarked, is said to be under the floor of the side chapel on the south side of Rodel Church. She died around 1705.

Alick Morrison said her unmarked grave was outside the church, but gave no reason for this opinion. As her beloved chief, Sir Norman MacLeod of Bernera, is buried outside the church, perhaps it is unlikely that Mary herself would merit a burial inside, along with the Dunvegan chiefs. The graves of Sir Norman and his son, John of Contullich, are in an elaborate mausoleum beside the church, on its upper (southern) side, and close by, to the west, there is a single upright stone of rough uninscribed rock. It is tempting to suppose that this is Mary's resting place, close to that of her chief.

Hugh Macleod

(see also above, North Uist)

The Contullich accounts for the MacLeod estates in Skye and Harris mention that in 1707, a piper called HUGH MACLEOD was given 'pr. MacLeod's verbal order as an Encoragement for his coming from the Isle of Wist to Harries of yearly Sallary £40'. This was the year after Patrick Og received a tocher of £228 from the chief on his second marriage; Patrick was piper at Dunvegan, and this payment to Hugh MacLeod to persuade him to come as piper in Harris suggests that in 1707, none of Patrick Og's sons was old enough (or skilled enough? willing enough?) to become the official Harris piper, and that there were at that time no accomplished pipers in Harris.

£40 yearly salary was considerably more than Donald Ban received, but it may have been related to his rent. The precision of that £40 salary suggests Hugh was installed in a holding with a £40 rent, which was probably the Kirkpenny at Scarista. (There were only two Harris tenancies with a £40 rent, the Kirkpenny and Drumphoint, but by 1702, the latter had risen to £50.) He appears in the accounts in the Contullich papers, still receiving £40 per annum, until 1711, when his name is coupled with that of NORMAN(D) MACLEAN, another piper, in Skye, who received only £20.

We then lose sight of Hugh and Norman as individuals, when the accounts begin to list them along with other estate workers such as foresters, ferrymen, ground officers, porter, gardener and violer, none of them named. Their salaries are given jointly as a sum of hundreds of pounds, which tells us little. We do not know exactly when Malcolm became the Harris piper, living at Scarista, but he was there in 1725. His name is not in earlier rentals. We assume that Hugh either died or retired, leaving Harris around 1725.

If Hugh MacLeod was in the Kirkpenny, holding it rent-free, and presumably taking much benefit from this rich tenancy, he may have set a precedent for this particular land at Scarista becoming the perquisite of the Harris pipers. Not long before Hugh was brought in, the Kirk-penny had been held for some years by the Campbell chamberlains, but Rory Campbell had fallen out with the MacLeod chief and had gone to Uist. This may explain why the Laird broke the tradition of the Kirk-penny being a Campbell holding, and gave it to the newcomer.

As far as we know, the next occupant was Malcolm MacCrimmon in his capacity as the Harris piper, followed in 1730 by his brother, Donald Ban. Malcolm, however, was not paid £40, and the rent had gone up by then: Malcolm appears to have been paid £26 13s 4d, half the sum of his rent. Does this mean he was an inferior piper compared with Hugh MacLeod? He was, of course, very young, a mere teenager. Perhaps his duties were part-time? Or was the MacLeod estate just economising?

A Piper in Harris, 1786

In his report to the British Society for Extending the Fisheries, in 1786, John Knox described how he was in Harris, staying with a Highland gentleman called Captain MacLeod, who lived at Rodel. After a week there, Knox wanted to move on to Stornoway, and Captain MacLeod offered to escort him. Their boat was escorted by a pinnace 'well manned' and one of the crew 'was equally qualified for managing the sails or the bagpipe, which he carried with him'.

Captain MacLeod was similar to his predecessor at Rodel, Rory Campbell in the late 17th century, in that he maintained a large store-house for such items as salt, meal, casks, etc, and he had a 'manufacturing house for spinning wool and linen thread, and twine for herring nets'. He also owned a large number of boats of different sizes, built roads and a schoolhouse and a public house at Rodel, as well as restoring St Clement's Church 'out of the ruins of an old mon-astery'. We might wonder if the sailor with the bagpipe was Captain MacLeod's personal piper, but Knox goes on to describe a wedding they all attended at Tarbert, Harris, where there was dancing: it seems likely that the pipe on board the pinnace was taken for that purpose, to play for the wedding dance.

In his report, John Knox described the suffering of the local men ('native Hebrideans') in their Highland boats, returning from their fisheries:

> The wind being contrary, these poor people were forced to labour at the oars from ten to twenty, or twenty-five miles, before they could reach their respective huts. They take the oars alternatively, and refresh themselves now and then with water, though generally in a full sweat. They sing in chorus, observing a kind of time, with the movement of the oars. Though they kept close upon the shore, and at a considerable distance from our vessel, we heard the sound from almost every boat. Those who have the bagpipe, use that instrument, which has a pleasing effect upon the water, and makes these poor people forget their toils.

Angus Morrison

Barry Shears lists among the early piping settlers in Nova Scotia a Harris man ANGUS MORRISON (1792–1878). He arrived at St Ann's, Cape Breton, in 1826. Born at Stroud, Harris, he had as a young man been an accomplished piper, but Barry tells us that at the age of 26 he 'adopted the stricter tenets of Protestantism, to the detriment of his musical talents'. He gave up piping, as he found it 'tended to lead him into temptation. In later life he refused a handsome sum of money for his pipe, nor would he give it away, saying that it was an injury to himself and he could not pass on an injury to anyone else. So he tied a stone to the instrument and threw it in the sea'. We are reminded of an uncle of John MacDonald, Inverness: after serving as piper to the Prince of Wales, William MacDonald retired to Glen Urquhart and, in a fit of religious zeal, he burned his pipes.

Kenneth MacDonald, 1880s

Lord Dunmore had an estate in South Harris, and from 1881 to 1886 his piper, living at Rodel, was KENNETH MACDONALD. Kenneth won the Gold Medal at Oban in 1888, and later went to live in Glasgow. (This is not the Kenneth MacDonald from Tiree, who much later won both Gold Medals in 1959 and 1962.)

Alex John MacLeod and John MacKinnon

In 1998, an interesting letter appeared in the *Piper Press*, written by DUGALD C. MACLEOD in Portree, about MacRae tuning slides. He said he played MacRae pipes himself, bequeathed to him by his father, ALEX JOHN MACLEOD, who had been the Gaelic teacher at the school in Tarbert, Harris. Dugald's mother was Dolina MacPhail from Bragar in Lewis, and she told him the history of those pipes.

A Harris man, JOHN MACKINNON, had emigrated to North America before the First World War, but returned with the Canadian army in 1914. He remained over here and married a cousin of Dugald's mother, a girl called Effie MacPhail. John used to play the pipes at ceilidhs and dances in Glasgow, along with his friend DONALD RUADH MACLEOD from Arnol. Donald, however, developed miliary tuberculosis, which killed him. Unfortunately the two friends had shared the same set of pipes. On Donald's death, John's wife decreed that he must never share pipes again, so she commissioned MacRae to make him a pipe of his own. It was a silver and ivory set, but the silver was found to be flawed and had to be done again. Dugald attributed the weightiness of them to this mistake. John's wife paid £26 for them – and that included a silver mounted practice chanter.

Not long after he had started playing the Glasgow circuit on his own, John MacKinnon said he had had a vision of himself walking into Hell with his pipes on his shoulder, and he underwent a religious conversion, with the result that he gave up piping, and offered his pipes for sale (could have saved his wife £26). When Alex John MacLeod came back from service in the Second War, he bought the pipes for £50, which, as Dugald said, was quite a price for someone connected with the family.

Dugald played these MacRae pipes, and in the late 1950s had them re-conditioned by Wee Donald (presumably MacLeod, rather than MacLean of Oban). He played them with a Naill chanter and a modern blowpipe with integral valve, and suggested that tuning slides 'do not adjust easily to modern day central heating and this may be the reason for their present rarity'.

Emily MacLeod MacDonald

EMILY MACDONALD, wife of Dr Angus MacDonald, the piping GP in Portree, Skye, is a MacLeod whose family emigrated in the 19th century from Horgabost, beside the Luskentyre sands, in the west of Harris. Many Harris families had moved to Victoria County, Nova

Scotia, and Emily was born in South Haven, Victoria County in 1952, her parents being Robert MacLeod and Eveline Dunbar.

Emily studied piping at St Ann's Gaelic College, and played for some years in the College pipe band, in the late 1960s and early 70s. She is also an accomplished Highland dancer. She went on to travel in Canada and the USA, competing and playing, in both solo and band competitions.

Having taken her BA degree and followed it up with a BEd teaching qualification, she went to Scotland to work, and renewed her acquaintance with Dr Angus MacDonald, whom she had met previously in Nova Scotia. They were married in 1985 and went to live in Nova Scotia when Angus took up an appointment as a doctor there. Their two children, Mairead and Allan, were born there, but in 1993 Emily and Angus decided to go to live in Skye in order to bring up their family in a Gaelic environment. Dr Angus is a partner in the medical practice in Portree. They lived in Camustianavaig, near Portree, for a time, before they built a new house nearby, at Comhnardan, where they have a 200-acre croft, on which they are growing trees. The house looks across the Sound to Raasay.

Today Emily teaches piping to youngsters in Portree. She is the Hon. Secretary of the John MacFadyen Memorial Trust, and runs such functions as the annual lecture and recital before the Piobaireachd Society's annual conference, and the Silver Chanter evening at Dunvegan. Her husband is a leading competitor in solo piping, but Emily is one of the powers behind the scenes without whom piping would be much the poorer. Though efficient and well organised, she has a pleasantly laid-back manner, and manages to instil confidence without becoming bossy. Tribute was paid to her in the *Piping Times* in 2004, for her excellent friendly stewarding of the Skye competitions.

Harris Postman

It is said that there was a postman in Harris who did his rounds on a bicycle. He was a piobaireachd player and enjoyed singing piobaireachd as he sped from house to house. One day a car drew up beside him, and some tourists asked him the way to Tarbert.

'Och, you just keep on along this road, you canna miss it', he said.

'And how far is it?'

'Well, now, wi' the wind behind you, it would be twice through *Mary MacLeod* and well into the second variation of *Donald Ban*.'

Scalpay

Scalpay is reached by a bridge from Harris, not far from Tarbert.

ANGUS MACLEOD of Scalpay was a famous Gaelic singer, who was also a good piper. Seumas MacNeill recalled (*Piping Times,* November 1995) a visit he made for the Arts Council to Jura. He and John Mac-Fadyen, with two well-known Gaelic singers, IAIN DARROCH of Jura and Angus MacLeod of Scalpay, were there. Iain was keen for the two pipers to play on top of a particular hill, and after they had climbed the hill and the pipers had performed, he asked John if he could borrow his pipe to play a tune himself. On this, Angus asked to use Seumas' pipe, and he too joined in – to everyone's surprise.

Bernera, Harris

There are three islands called Bernera on the west side of the Outer Isles: one is near Barra, to the south of Mingulay; one is in Lewis, connected to the mainland of Lewis by a bridge, whose opening was commemorated by Donald MacLeod with his jig in four parts, *The Bernera Bridge.* This Lewis Bernera, sometimes known as Great Bernera, should not be confused with the Bernera which is part of the parish of Harris, even though it is now linked by causeway to North Uist. Bernera, Harris, is the island where the Prince of Wales, as a young man, went to spend several weeks learning about the crofting way of life.

Sometimes the name is spelled Berneray; it is a Norse name Bjørnar-ey, meaning the island of Bjørn (personal name, frequently found). It is pronounced with the stress on the first syllable, BERN-er-a.

Bernera, Harris, has several piping connections: Mary MacLeod and her chief, Sir Norman MacLeod of Bernera, lived at Risgary, in the east of the island; John MacLeod of Contullich had family links there; the writer(s) of the MacLeod Bannatyne manuscript were also related to the MacLeods of Bernera, being descended from Sir Norman; and the MacAskill family of pipers lived in Bernera, of whom Dr John MacAskill was the best known in recent times.

Mary Macleod and Sir Norman of Bernera

Sir Norman MacLeod of Bernera was the third son of Sir Rory Mor MacLeod of Dunvegan, which made him brother of the 16th Chief, Iain Mor, and uncle of the next two, Rory Mir and Iain Breac. He was also a brother of Sir Roderick MacLeod of Talisker. He was always known as Sir Norman, although there is no record of his ever having been knighted. The title 'Sir' usually denotes a university graduate, and the title was often used of a clergyman or a lawyer. Sir Norman was neither of these, but he was undoubtedly a graduate.

His exact birthdate is unknown, but he graduated from Glasgow University in 1633, probably then aged about 16, or a little younger. He returned to his birthplace, Risgary, Bernera, to live in Old Bernera House, of which only the turret remains. He then built himself a new residence, Bernera House, a two-storey house with a thatched roof. The walls were still standing until about 1870, but now only the foundations can be seen. He was known for his 'unfailing hospitality', and seems to have been a jovial, larger-than-life character.

A poetic elegy was made by the bard Mary Campbell, in memory of John Campbell of Scalpay, whose family were the hereditary keepers of the deer-forests of Harris (known as foresters, but not tending trees). In her poem, she speaks of Sir Norman's household as being full of music:

Nuair rachadh tu do Bhearnaraidh	When you would travel to Bernera
'S an cluinnteadh gair nan teud,	And would hear the sound of the harp,
Piobaireachd is clarsaireachd	Pipe music and clarsach music
Is fiodhail ard gu seinn.	And the playing of the high-pitched fiddle.

One of the most devoted admirers of Sir Norman was his kinswoman, Mary MacLeod (Mairi nighean Alasdair Ruaidh, Mary, daughter of Red Alasdair), who became renowned as a Gaelic poet, living at Dunvegan before being sent into exile. She was probably not born in Bernera, and either Rodel or Skye has been claimed as her birthplace; but Sir Norman gave her a small house not far from his own, now a grass-covered ruin known as Tobhta Mhairi (Mary's Ruin). Some say he had this cottage built for her. Other houses have survived, or have been restored, at Risgary, giving us an idea of Mary's; they are low, thatched 'black' houses, looking out over the Sound of Harris towards

Rodel. Across the sea from Risgary, the tower of Rodel Church, Mary's burial-place, may be seen on the horizon.

Close by is the Great Well of the MacLeods (Tobar Mor MacLeoid), and to the south, low down in the sand, are the remains of the jetty where Sir Norman's ships used to come in.

At Risgary, the building called the Gunnery was Sir Norman's arsenal, where he kept his armaments. It was fortified against attack, with gun-slits in the walls, and lower walls built around the building as defences. This building has survived, and Mary MacLeod mentions it in one of several poems she made in praise of Sir Norman and his family. In the *Luinneag Mhic Leoid* (*Lament for Mary MacLeod*) she says:

Gheibhte sud ann ad fhardaich,	In your dwelling would be found,
An caradh air ealachainn,	Ranged upon the weapon-rack,
Miosair is adharc is rogha gach armachd,	Powder horn and shot-horn and the choice of every armoury,
Agus lanntainean tana	And slender sword blades,
'O 'n ceanaibh gu 'm barra dheis;	Tapering from the hilt to the tip;
Gheibhte sud air gach slios dhiubh	On each side of them would be found
Isneach is cairbinn	Rifle and carbine
Agus iubhar chruaidh fhallain	And bows tough and sound
Le'n taifeidean cainbe;	With their bowstrings of hemp;
Agus iubhar chruaidh fhallain	And bows tough and sound
Le'n taifeidean cainbe;	With their bowstrings of hemp;
Agus cuilbhearan caola	And narrow culverins
Air an daoiread gu'n ceannaicht' iad;	Expensive to buy;
Glac nan ceann liobhte	A handful of polished arrows
Air chur sios ann am balgaidh	Thrust down into quivers
'O iteach an fhir-eoin	With flights of eagle feathers
'S o shioda na Gaillebhein.	And the silk of Galway.

Sir Norman fought at the Battle of Worcester in 1651, and was taken prisoner. He was tried for his life, but acquitted through a technical error in the indictment – his name, MacLeod, had been confused with that of a notorious Welsh rebel, ap Lloyd. After 18 months of harsh treatment in prison, he escaped to France, before he returned home, a staunch Royalist for the rest of his life. He became a somewhat romantic figure in the Jacobite world. Alexander Nicolson wrote 'He was blessed with great personal beauty, princely generosity, a gallant bearing, and he was endowed with a lofty purpose and a staunch integrity of conduct'.

He was married twice, first to Margaret MacKenzie of Kintail, by whom he had a son, John of Contullich (subject of the piobaireachd work, *Lament for the Laird of Contullich*), and then to Catherine MacDonald of Sleat, daughter of Sir James MacDonald, who lived at Duntulm in north Skye.

Sir Norman died in March 1705, and Mary MacLeod made a noble poetic lament for him. He is buried beside Rodel Church, in south Harris, in an imposing mausoleum. Mary's own (unmarked) grave may be close by (see above).

John MacLeod of Contullich

Although known as Contullich, and subject of the piobaireachd work composed by Iain Dall MacKay, *Lament for the Laird of Contullich*, John MacLeod was one of the Bernera family, being a son of Sir Norman's first marriage. He acquired the designation of Contullich from possession of a farm in Easter Ross, which came to him from the Munros of Foulis through a series of marriage settlements and debt repayments.

Contullich was a lawyer, trained in Edinburgh, and became lawyer and factor to the MacLeods of Dunvegan. On the death of the 21st Chief, the heir was a mere infant, and Contullich was appointed his Tutor (guardian), taking over the management of the estates, which were deep in debt. Within ten years he had them solvent and in good order, but when his ward, Norman MacLeod, came of age, he was influenced against Contullich by his mother, and took the old man to court, for mismanagement and appropriation of funds. Contullich died, humiliated and disgraced, in 1726. Many in Skye thought he had been treated shabbily, especially as the alleged discrepancies in the accounts were often for tiny amounts, merely pence.

His daughter was married to MacLeod of Talisker, who was the host of the Talisker Circle, a group of the poets and musicians of Skye which included Iain Dall – and probably Contullich himself, who was an accomplished Gaelic poet. Iain Dall made his piobaireachd *Lament for the Laird of Contullich* around 1726, presumably in an attempt to restore the old man's good name. Mary MacLeod, too, made a poem in his honour (*Luinneag do Iain mac Shir Tormoid*) after he had given her a snuff-mull. She used the poem to express extravagant praise of the Bernera family.

She refers to Contullich in conventional poetic terms as:

Fior Leodach ur gasda
Foinnidh beachdail glic fialaidh thu,
De shliochd nam fear flathail
Bu mhath an ceann chliaranach.

A true MacLeod, fresh and spendid art thou,
comely, prudent, wise and generous,
of the race of princely heroes,
and a good host to groups of poets.

This last phrase probably refers to his family's involvement with the 'Talisker Circle', which included Iain Dall MacKay, the Blind Piper of Gairloch.

She also depicts him as a skilled huntsman and horseman, but the gist of the poem is praise for his father and family.

The MacLeod Bannatyne Manuscript

Roderick MacLeod WS (Writer to the Signet, a Scottish lawyer in Edinburgh) was born in Bernera, and was descended from Sir Norman. His son, William Bannatyne MacLeod became Lord Bannatyne of Kames, a Gaelic historian and antiquary who is said to have written the MacLeod Bannatyne manuscript, on which much of the *Book of Dunvegan* is based. This manuscript claims that the MacCrimmons in South Harris were one of three families living there before the arrival of the Norsemen.

William had a sister, Isabella MacLeod of Bernera, who married a minister, and another sister, Margaret, whose first husband was John MacLeod of Colbecks, father of the Colbecks for whom the Lament was made. Her second husband was the Chief Justice of Jamaica.

Sources

I. Grant, *The MacLeods: The History of a Clan*
Alexander MacKenzie, *History of the Munros*
R.C. MacLeod, *The Book of Dunvegan*
Alick Morrison, 'Harris Estate Papers' *TGSI* XLIV
Alick Morrison, 'Early Harris Estate Papers' *TGSI* LI
Alick Morrison, 'The Feu of Berneray' *TGSI* LI.
J. Carmichael Watson, *The Gaelic Songs of Mary MacLeod*

The MacAskill Family

This account is based partly on an article in the *Piping Times*, vol. 61, no.12, which gives further detail about Iain Archie MacAskill.

IAIN ARCHIE MACASKILL from Bernera, who was an uncle of Dr John MacAskill, was a piper who played in the City of Glasgow Police Pipe Band. He was also a well-known Gaelic bard, and published a Gaelic book, *An Ribheid Chiuil* (*The Reed of Music*).

Born in Bernera in 1898, Iain Archie went to Glasgow to become a piper in the City of Glasgow Police band, and also served with the Cameron Highlanders in the trenches, in the First World War, lying about his age when he enlisted at 16. After the war, he emigrated to Australia, where he died in 1933, aged only 35. He bitterly regretted emigrating when he was unable to make his farm near Fremantle pay, during the Depression years. He had huge debts, and died a pauper, longing to be back in Bernera. He was buried in Karrakatta Cemetery, Western Australia. Although he had lost touch with his family in Scotland, his nephew, Dr John MacAskill, went out to try to find his grave; he managed to track it down and erected a headstone over the pauper's grave. Iain Archie's family was trying to raise money to have his body returned to Bernera, to fulfil his dying wish. By 2010 they had achieved this, and his remains have been buried where he had longed to be.

See also Donald Ewen MacDonald, North Uist.

Dr John MacAskill, MB, ChB, DROG, DIH (1943–2003)

This account is largely based on an article written by Seumas Mac-Neill, John's first piping teacher, after John had won the Gold Medal at Inverness in 1972. It was published in the *Piping Times* after John's death in 2003.

John was born and brought up in Bernera, though his brother Iain was born in North Uist. When he was ten his father took him to hear piping competitions in Glasgow, but he was not greatly impressed and expressed no wish to learn himself. Some three years later, however, he changed his mind, and in January 1957 presented himself at the College of Piping in Glasgow, where he was then living, and asked to be taught. He knew absolutely nothing about piping when he arrived, but twelve days later he won third prize in a chanter competition, playing *Scots Wha Hae* (what else?). The judge was Hector MacFadyen.

'John's progress was phenomenal' wrote Seumas.

With two lessons per week he got through Tutor I in three months, completely and perfectly. By the time he went to the College summer school at Dunvegan in July, he was playing competition tunes. He rapidly overhauled everybody of his age-group, although some of them had been playing four or five years before he started . . . He, in fact, caused the College to take a fresh policy on what is the best age for beginners.

He had piping in his genes, which does help. His father was a piper, as were his two uncles, and he was a native Gaelic speaker, brought up in Bernera, soaked in Gaelic tradition. He then moved to Glasgow, with its opportunities for learning to play.

As a boy he played in the SPA amateur contests, and won the Chisholm Cup, the Farquhar MacRae trophy, the Cameron Cup, and then all the College of Piping trophies in the one evening. Next, he came first at the North Uist Games, and by 1962 he was a serious contender, winning prizes in both piobaireachd and light music. He had a distinctive way of playing, with his head thrown well back.

He was not a tall man, but well built, with a stocky square appearance, and an infectious smile. He was known for his wit and humour, and his friendly, sociable manner. A great man for a ceilidh.

In 1964 he won the March at Inverness, playing *Pipe Major John Stewart*. By this time he was a medical student at Glasgow University, which restricted his playing a little, although he found time to instruct juniors at a summer school in Skye. In 1965, he went to New York to help at a summer school, and then with a friend and a tent set out in a small car to see America, coast to coast. 'This is a saga which needs a long night and a peat fire for the proper telling', wrote Seumas.

In 1966 he had no spare time for competing, but the following year he won the March at Oban, and in 1970, the Strathspey and Reel at Inverness. Then, in 1972, without any further competing meanwhile, he won the Gold Medal at Inverness, playing *Lady Anapool's Lament*. His comment was 'I just compete every two years – and then I'm lethal'.

He was not only a good player, but also a good teacher and a good composer. His reel *Lexie MacAskill*, made for his mother, has proved very popular 'and has joined the ranks of the classics'. D.R. MacLennan said he had the best fingers in Scotland, and Seumas added that it would be a great pity if they were not heard in action regularly – and of course they were not. He became a fully fledged doctor, a full-time GP, first in Lairg, Sutherland, and later in Fort William, and became also the team doctor to the Scotland football (soccer) team. He was never again able to give his full attention to competing, but had his awards to remind him and his triumphs to look back on.

He wrote piping articles, letters and reviews, and amassed a great collection of old pipe music, books and tapes. While a doctor in Lairg he made visits to old Angus MacPherson, then living nearby at Achany, and recorded interviews with him, both discussions of piping topics and Angus' playing on the practice chanter, at the age of 84. These are a valuable record of the MacPherson style, which they discussed for the tape.

When Seumas MacNeill died, it was Dr John MacAskill who played at the church before and after his funeral service in Milngavie.

He was teaching more and more, at summer schools in America and Canada, and private pupils at home, notably Johndon MacKenzie from Dornie, Wester Ross, and Leslie Hutt, from Inverness. Both played at his funeral in 2003. He was buried in Bernera. His death from cancer brought letters to the *Piping Times* from his pupils, whose devotion to him was obvious.

One from John Fisher in Nevada, USA, remembered John's passion for 'tightly rolled, stylish, six-inch cigars', and how, at an American summer school, the fire alarms went off and the building had to be evacuated, before John appeared, cigar in hand, wreathed in smoke, asking 'What's going on? What's all this noise?'

John, it seems, set a fashion for wearing sandals with kilt, sporran and hose, at the summer schools. John Fisher ended his tribute with: 'I can hear him playing *Black Donald's March* to a hypnotised crowd. I can see him bow and tip his hand to his brow and sweep it across to the audience, well knowing the playing was perfect and knowing the joy it brought to the listener'.

Dugald Murdoch, writing from Stockholm, Sweden, said 'Dr John was talented in so many ways that you would be lucky to find all his talents in a crowd, let alone in one person. He was outstanding, not only as a piper, but also as a composer, a teacher and a doctor. But John had another quality that not everyone has, moral fibre, and he had it in large measure . . . Whatever he did, he did with total commitment, scorning all distraction and his own comfort . . . When he played, his concentration on what he was doing, and his enjoyment of the music he was producing, was so intense as to be almost tangible . . . As for his company, if you were with him when he was relaxing, then your luck was in, for you would be chuckling at his stories of his experiences for days afterwards – some of them have me chuckling more than forty years after I heard them.'

Leslie Hutt wrote of Dr John: 'His approach as a judge was to know and to be able to play the set tunes himself, criteria which he felt was essential to judge at the highest level . . . He was a thorough and meticulous tutor, keen to pass on his knowledge of the styles and prepared to look at tunes afresh . . . He was a larger than life character, great fun to be with and a great friend – and he had a crunluath which would surpass many competing today.' Quite an epitaph.

Dr John MacAskill's compositions include:

Alena McAskill 6/8 J 4
Alexander MacAskill of Berneray, Harris 6/8 J 4
Andrew Stewart Hills 6/8 M 4
Glenda Douglas R 2
Joy Wallace's Bike 6/8 J 4
Lexie MacAskill R 4
Mrs Angus MacDonald of Tiree 6/8 J 4
Peter MacKinnon of Skeabost R 4
The Sands of Berneray 6/8 SA 2
The Terrible Twins 6/8 J 4. Some say this refers to John MacAskill
    and his friend Kenneth MacDonald from Tiree.
A Touch of the Irish 6/8 J 2
Twelve Torlum 9/8 R 4
Twisted Fingers 6/8 J 4

Note also:

Dr John MacAskill, by John N. MacIver R 4
Dr John MacAskill, by Donald MacLeod 2/4 M 4
Dr John MacAskill's Welcome to Fort William, by Angus MacDonald
    6/8 M 4

Scarp

Scarp is a Norse name, probably *skarfa-ey*, 'island of cormorants'.

Duncan MacLean

DUNCAN MACLEAN, who lived for many years in Ardrishaig, on Loch Fyne, Argyll, was born in Scarp, a small island off the west coast of Harris. His family had a small croft there, and supplemented their income by lobster-fishing.

Duncan, born in 1918, was brought up in Scarp with his two brothers. In the late 1930s he was working at Amhuinnsuidhe Castle in Harris when a fellow estate worker gave him a set of pipes. Duncan then went to work for the post office in Harris, teaching himself pipe tunes and piobaireachd from recordings. On the outbreak of war in 1939, he and his brothers left for the army, and Duncan was taken prisoner at St Valery in 1940.

After years as a prisoner of war in Germany, he returned to Britain and trained as a teacher. He married Peggy MacLennan, of a well-known piping family in Harris, and was a teacher in Orkney and Lochaline before he became headmaster at Achnamara, in Argyll. Forced by ill health to retire at 60, he made his home in Ardrishaig. Both he and his son ALLAN were pipers, and Duncan composed a large number of tunes. He had a great love of piobaireachd, although he never competed. He had lessons from John MacFadyen and was a friend of Donald MacLeod.

A born linguist, he spoke Gaelic, English, French and German, and one of his hobbies was translating English poetry into Gaelic, and vice versa. He also wrote poetry of his own, played the fiddle, painted pictures and was a keen fisherman. He taught himself Italian, for his own amusement. In 2008, he suffered further ill-health and had to retire to a care-home in Benderloch, where he died a few years later.

He remembered many pipers in Harris, including his late wife's brothers and nephews, CALUM, RODDY and NORMAN MACLENNAN. Duncan passed on his pipes to Norman when he was no longer able to play the full pipe. He also recalled 'SWEENEY' MACSWEEN, who held piping classes in Harris during the winter months, a native of Scalpay, born in the mid-20th century; he worked in the shop at Ardhasaig.

Duncan also named Harris pipers such as the cousins RODDY and JOHN MACLEOD and ANGUS CAMPBELL, and GEORGE MACLEOD, 'up in Harris'.

See also *The Piping Traditions of Argyll*.

Ensay

The name is Norse and may be *ennis-ey* 'island of the jutting headland'. It lies in the Sound of Harris, between Harris and Bernera.

Stewart of Ensay

WILLIAM STEWART OF ENSAY was a captain in the Argyll and Sutherland Highlanders, and later a major in the Lovat Scouts. His family had been factors to the MacLeods of Dunvegan and Harris, and had bought one of the MacLeod estates when their lairds fell on hard times. These Stewarts had a bad name for being harsh landlords. They took their designation from the island of Ensay, but did not live there. They did, however, have a house there which they sometimes visited in summer.

David Craig described Stewart of Ensay as the 'arch-evictor', finding the descendants of his tenants still bitter about their families' treatment – and one of them said 'the husband wasn't so bad, but the women were terrible. The husband asked the wife, "Are you pleased now I've burnt the houses?" and she replied "I'll never be pleased while I still see a wisp of smoke between here and Rodel".'

Ensay was the proprietor of the islands of Ensay, Pabay, Bernera and Killigray, as well as much of North Harris. He and another landowner, Lord Dunmore, who had bought Harris in 1834, set about removing the tenants and destroying their houses. One way of forcing them out was to prevent them from making a living by banning them from fishing or owning a boat, and refusing them access to sea-weed or shellfish on the shore. One of David Craig's informants sang a song which he quotes:

> My thousand curses on the old Stewart,
> Before he comes back, that his grave will be ready for him . . .
> The children were better than the parents,
> I want nothing will happen to the children,
> But I hope that the one who is telling them
> To be bad will not be long in this world . . .

A few of the descendants of the victims, however, conceded that Ensay had been a good farmer, with progressive ideas, introducing modern machinery even in the small islands. And three of his beasts, raised on Pabay, won prizes at Smithfield in London for the heaviest highland cattle.

William was a founder-member of the Piobaireachd Society, but fell out with the Campbell brothers of Kilberry (brothers of Archibald) when they objected to the piobaireachd settings published by the Society in its earliest volumes. Ensay, who had compiled the first volumes, played a leading part in the Committee's refusal to climb down and admit faults. Finally, in 1905, the Campbell brothers, their father and other influential members resigned, after Ensay had taken it upon himself to over-rule the judges at Oban and change the prize-list.

Col. Jock MacDonald used to tell how an elephant's foot, carved in ivory and brought from Burma, disappeared from Viewfield one day. Months later, William Ensay appeared with an ivory pipe chanter which he had had made from it. He presented this to Col. Jock, who thanked him politely, though he said later that he had no use for an ivory chanter, and in any case had been quite fond of the elephant's foot.

Ensay, who had become President of the Society in 1904, comes across as a supremely arrogant figure, who with Lord Dunmore represented the 'Establishment' of the time at its inflexible worst. He died in 1908, not a moment too soon, by the sound of things.

There is an account of the controversy surrounding the Piobaireachd Society's early publications in William Donaldson's book *The Highland Pipe and Scottish Society 1750–1950*.

Angus MacRae (1850–1935)

ANGUS MACRAE was born on the island of Ensay, Sound of Harris, and became a piper at an early age, playing on the right shoulder. He learned his piobaireachd from Alexander MacLennan of the Inverness Militia, a pupil of Donald Cameron, and later went to Calum Piobaire MacPherson, at Catlodge, near Laggan. In his march playing he was greatly influenced by William MacLennan (the 'father' of modern march playing). Alexander was a cousin of William's father.

Angus was said in the Notices of Pipers to have been 'unrivalled' in his strathspeys and reels, and is described as 'a good-looking Highlander and a most charming personality'. He had two piping brothers, DONALD MACRAE, who became piper to Lady Scott, and FINLAY MACRAE, who 'did not follow the profession but stuck to the land', according to Robert Meldrum's *Reminiscences*. Both Donald and Finlay were also pupils of Alexander MacLennan, who belonged to the family of the piping MacLennans from Gairloch. These piping MacRae brothers were the sons of Christopher MacRae, a boat-builder who had come to Harris from Kintail; they were the forebears (great-grand-uncles) of FINLAY MACRAE, the Skye piper who settled in Dingwall and has become well-known as a player, teacher and judge.

A great-uncle of the present-day Finlay was also of that name. He became piper/valet to Cameron of Lochiel and his wife Hermione. These Camerons had a house in Ardross Street, Inverness, opposite the Cathedral and handily placed for the Northern Meeting Park.

The Notices of Pipers say that Angus MacRae won the Gold Medal at Inverness in 1881, and the Clasp seven years later; he had won the Gold at Oban in 1883. The Northern Meeting records give different dates: he won the Gold at Inverness in 1879, and the Clasp in 1881. Finlay MacRae confirms the latter account as correct.

Angus had been piper to Duncan MacRae of Kames, Isle of Bute, until 1879, when he went to Raasay as piper to the laird, E.H. Wood, who seems to have been a comparatively benevolent landowner and spent a lot of money on improving conditions for the islanders. Angus competed from Raasay until Mr Wood's death in 1886, when he moved to Callander.

This was just the start of a highly successful piping career. The *Oban Times*, quoted in the Notices of Pipers, said: 'As a piper he won every honour possible. He excelled in every branch of pipe music, and his name will be handed down as one of the greatest pipers of his generation', to which the writer of the Notice added: 'He was a most forcible player', which seems a curious phrase. He was also an excellent dancer, and won many prizes for this, too.

He was involved in the players' protest in 1885 against the meagre prizes offered at the big competitions, and Robert Meldrum tells how Willie MacLennan and John MacColl led the 'strike' in which they refused to play at Inverness. Angus MacRae and John MacDougall Gillies had both added their names to the protest, but in the end both played (and were booed by MacLennan and MacColl). Gillies won the piobaireachd, with Robert Meldrum in second place.

After travelling abroad with Admiral Lord Charles Beresford for some years, Angus replaced Aeneas Rose as Pipe Major of the Athol Highlanders, and was also Pipe Major of the Scottish Horse, but had given up competing, 'to the disappointment of his admirers'.

Finally he was piper to the Earl of Dudley, and lived in London, where he died in 1935. He is buried at Streatham, London.

Pabay

This Norse name means 'island with a hermit-monk' of the early Celtic church. Pabay lies to the north of Bernera and west of Ensay.

Mary MacLeod had a brother who lived in Pabay, and when she was exiled from Skye, she may have been sent there to be under his care for a time. Tradition associates Pabay and the nearby island of Scarp with Mary, but this may be from confusion with another island, Scarba, in the Firth of Lorne, which Mary mentioned in one of her poems (see above).

St Kilda

Transport to St Kilda has to be arranged privately. The name covers a group of islands about 40 miles west of Harris.

The name is thought to be derived not from the name of a saint (there was no saint called Kilda), but from a Norse name *Skildar*, meaning 'outlying islands'. The S became detached and mistaken for S., short for 'saint'. It was a map name, used by English-speaking seafarers. So both *St Kilda* and the *Hebrides* are names which are really copying errors (as is *Grampian*). In Gaelic the islands are called *Hirt* or *Hirta*, which is the name of the only habitable island in the group.

In 1697, Martin Martin, a Skyeman who was factor to the MacLeod estates, visited St Kilda, and published his description in 1703, commenting on the great passion of the islanders for music. He said they used to dance to the Jew's harp, and always had bagpipes at their weddings. One day in June 1697, wrote Martin Martin, the minister married fifteen couples, who immediately after their marriage, joined in a country dance, 'having only a bagpipe for their music, which pleased them exceedingly'.

Some fifty years later, in 1758, the Rev. Kenneth MacAulay wrote that the St Kildans were 'enthusiastically fond of music', any music, good or bad, and they sang all day long while working: rowing songs, grinding tunes, reaping songs, waulking songs. If they were dancing and there was no instrument available, they took it in turns to sing – doubtless this was Port-a-beul.

Before the advent of the Free Church ministers, St Kilda was celebrated for its unusual music, but by the time of John MacCulloch, that scornful and disparaging tourist in the early 19th century, there was 'not a violin or bagpipe left', and he commented that the islanders' music was 'in no respect different from the innumerable ancient compositions of this class which abound in the Highlands'. (This was the man who described pibroch as being of 'very irregular character quite without time or accent, and often scarcely embracing a determined melody, with a train of complicated and tasteless variations, adding confusion to the original air').

The St Kilda Wedding was the title given to a complex 'lilt' with sixteen 'turns', which seems to have been some kind of sung piobaireachd in its inception. Composed by a native St Kildan called Finlay MacLeod, it was said to be 'very difficult to play' (on what instrument?). It was given its name by an Edinburgh banker named Angus MacLeod, the son of one of the St Kilda ministers – when was this? It was said that an old piper, Christopher MacRae, could play it, but was not able to write it down. There were words to go with it, describing the performance of a skilled cragsman on the island's cliffs. According to tradition, other St Kilda songs seem to have been based on piobaireachd, but no other pipe tunes have survived.

Fanatical ministers later suppressed the musical tradition, one of them declaring that it was easier for a camel to pass through the eye of a needle than for a piper to enter the Kingdom of Heaven (and people believed him).

Apart from the tune *St Kilda Wedding*, the evidence of piping on St Kilda is general and unspecific – but enough to show that before the ministers suppressed it, pipe music was greatly valued there.

Nowadays St Kilda is almost deserted, after a spell of army occupation. It has passed to the National Trust for Scotland, but a handful of MoD personnel still man the rocket-tracking apparatus installed on Hirta. Tony Oldham quotes a verse by Martin Mills, presumably giving the tourist's (or soldier's) view:

> No, there's not a lot to see upon St Kilda,
> Two dozen empty bothies and a wall,
> It's a dreary little dot of desolation,
> One hundred miles due west of bugger all.

Sources

William Donaldson, *The Highland Pipe and Scottish Society*
I.F. Grant, *The MacLeods: The History of a Clan*
Bill Lawson, *Harris in History and Legend*

John MacCulloch, *A Description of the Western Isles*
Col. Jock MacDonald
Duncan MacLean
Alistair MacLeod, Highland Council Genealogist
Canon R.C. MacLeod, *The Book of Dunvegan*
Angus MacPherson
Martin Martin, *A Voyage to St Kilda*
William Matheson, 'Notes on Mary Macleod' *TGSI* XLI
Robert Meldrum, *Reminiscences*
Alick Morrison, 'Contullich Accounts' *TGSI* XLIII
Alick Morrison, 'Early Harris Estate Papers' *TGSI* LI
Alick Morrison, *The MacLeods: Genealogy of a Clan*
Christina Morrison
Alexander Nicolson, *A History of Skye*
Notices of Pipers
Tony Oldham, *The Caves of Scotland*
Barrie Orme, *The Piobaireachd of Simon Fraser*
Piping Times
Barry Shears, *Dance to the Piper*
J.C. Watson, *The Gaelic Songs of Mary MacLeod*

Lewis

Lewis appears in Norse sources as *Ljóth-hús*, a name found also in Norway, apparently meaning 'people's dwellings', but in the case of Lewis, this is almost certainly a corrupt Norse interpretation of a much older name.

The English term 'The Long Island' means both Lewis and Harris, which geographically form a single island.

To reach Lewis, take the car ferry from Ullapool to Stornoway – there is a linking bus service from Inverness, and the crossing of the Minch takes three hours; or go by car ferry from Uig in Skye to Tarbert, Harris (two hours) and drive north to Lewis. Otherwise, fly from Glasgow or Inverness to Stornoway.

Tunes Associated with Lewis

These include:

Alex MacLean of Lurebost, by Duncan Johnstone 4/4 M 4

Angus MacDonald of Stornoway, by Iain MacCrimmon HP 4

The Braes of Brecklett, by William Lawrie 2/4 M 4

The Brevig Reel R 2

Calum a Brasha of Carloway, by William Livingstone sen. 6/8 M 4

Captain Campbell of Drum a voisg, by Donald Galbraith 2/4 M 4

Carlabhagh, arr. Scott MacAulay 3/4 GA 1

Carloway, by Iain MacCrimmon 6/8 M 4

Children of Lewis, by Iain MacCrimmon 6/8 SA 2

Clachnaharry, by Jack Chisholm S 4

Eilean Fraoich, by Neil Angus MacDonald 6/8 SM 2

Evan MacRae's Beard, by Jack Chisholm R 4

Eye Peninsula, by John W. Scott 6/8 J 4

Farewell to RSM M. MacLeod, by M.J. Purdie 6/8 M 4

An Fear Glic (Donald Gillies of Shawbost), by John W. Scott 12/8 SA 2

Glen Galson, by Roddy MacKay 6/8 M 4

The Grays of Tongside, by Andrew Bain R 4

Jimmy MacKenzie, Stornoway, by Andy Venters 3/4 RM 2 – made
    in 1971 for Colour Sergeant James MacKenzie of the 1st (Cadet)
    Battalion QOH, who taught the cadet pipers in Stornoway

John Morrison, by Andy Venters 4/4 M 2

John Morrison, Assynt House, by Peter MacLeod sen. R 6

John Morrison, Assynt House, by Peter MacLeod 6/8 J 4

John Morrison Esquire of Assynt House, by William Ross 2/4 M 4

Lament for John Morrison of Assynt House, by Donald MacLeod P 6

The Lewisoch, by MacCrimmon/Neill 6/8 SA 2

The Lewis Pipe Band, by W. Ross, Soval 2/4 M 4

The Lewis Shepherd, by Iain MacCrimmon 9/8 RM 2

The Lewis Soldier S 2

Murdo MacDonald of Stornoway, by Iain MacCrimmon 6/8 J 4

Murdo Morrison of Lewis's Centenary, by Neil Angus MacDonald
    6/8 SA 2

Norman MacLeod of South Dell, by Norman Gillies 2/4 M 4

Sheshader, by John W. Scott 6/8 J 4

Stornoway 6/8 SA 2

Stornoway Castle, by J. MacKenzie 2/4 M 2

Stornoway Highland Gathering, by 'the Competing Pipers' 2/4 M 4

See also lists (below) of the compositions by Peter MacLeod senior and
junior, Donald MacLeod, Donald MacLean and Iain Morrison, and
works made for them.

Piping in Lewis

Lewis has produced so many of the giants of piping, players, composers and teachers – 'Wee Donald' MacLeod, 'Big Donald' MacLean, the Peters MacLeod (to borrow Andrew MacNeill's name for the father and son), Iain Morrison and a host of others – that it is difficult to credit a letter sent to the Napier Commission in the 1880s. It came from Angus MacPhail, Lewis, and is quoted in *TGSI* XLVII. Angus MacPhail wrote:

> A Lewis elder is the holiest man alive! He is of a class unique and unapproachable, and acts as the moral censor of his village . . . As a result, there is not a bagpipe in the island, and every breath of natural song and every instrument of music are banished.

Donald MacDonald (1978) wrote that by the mid-19th century, the pipe and the fiddle had been replaced by the triomb (Jew's harp) – this was used in Free Church services, to give a starting note for unaccompanied psalms. Not only was the playing of music regarded as frivolous, but traditional instruments were considered part of the foolishness of the unenlightened past, and so to be suppressed.

Arthur Geddes, writing in 1955, said that 'not all the people gave in willingly to the new creed' (an extreme form of Calvinism), and he quoted an instance in Uig where there is a Piper's Cave, 'to which a crofter was wont to resort on dark nights, his pipes in his oxter, when the wind blew *from* the Manse and out to sea!' But Geddes adds 'Much was destroyed that can never be recovered now, and many a fine heart saddened or broken. It was the most intimate expression of their lives that suffered most'. But, he says, song went underground and survived, with the quarter tones of the modal scale intact.

Anyone who has attended the evening ceilidh at the Donald MacLeod Memorial Competition in Stornoway in recent years, and has heard the piping, the singing, the playing of other music, the reciting of poetry, and watched the step-dancing, will appreciate that the strong musical genes of the Lewisach simply cannot be suppressed. The (possibly a little exaggerated?) situation in the 1880s, however, does perhaps explain why all those giants of Lewis piping named above belong to the 20th century, and mostly developed their talents elsewhere, not in Lewis itself but in the army or in Glasgow. There can be little doubt that much piping talent lay in Lewis before the elders took a stranglehold on it, but proof of this is difficult to find, as latent ability leaves no trace. We have to deduce its presence by inference, through genetic transmission.

We do know that Sir James Matheson had his own piper at the castle in Stornoway in the latter half of the 19th century, presumably untouched by the influence of the 'Seceders', and we know the name of Sir James' piper, Thomas MacKay, the grandfather of John Morrison, Assynt House. He bequeathed his superb silver-and-ivory mounted pipe, made by Angus MacKay's brother Donald in 1843, to his grandson. It seems likely that Sir James had bought it and given it to Thomas. Sir James had purchased most of the island of Lewis in 1844, and transferred Thomas from Assynt (see below), probably in the early 1850s.

*   *   *   *   *   *   *   *

What is the oldest reference to piping in Lewis? Is there any tradition of piobaireachd (Ceol Mor) in the Long Island, other than the fine piobaireachd songs which are an important part of the Gaelic culture of the island? Surely the very existence of these songs implies a detailed knowledge of the music in former times. Both Margaret Stewart (from Lewis) and Rona Lightfoot (from South Uist) sing them, and Margaret says she learned one, based on *MacIntosh's Lament*, from her Lewis grandfather. Rona and others sing the Lewis song known as *The Widow's Grief*, which is a version of the Ground of *Maol Donn* (and Rona and Margaret have added vocal variations to it of their own, to good effect). But how far back do these songs go? Are they based on the piobaireachd works, or were the piobaireachd works developed from the songs? How do we tell?

Piping certainly seems to have been part of the shieling tradition which goes back to a time long before the 19th century, and there is oral evidence that ceilidh piping, singing and dancing figured in the shieling life at the summer pastures, up to the 20th century. But can we be sure that this came down from much earlier times?

Just as the arrival of John MacDonald, Inverness, to teach piobaireachd in South Uist, had paradoxically two effects, both to save the music from extinction there and at the same time to obliterate most of the memories of an earlier Uist tradition, so also has the fame of Wee Donald, Big Donald and the MacLeods erected a barrier which seems insuperable. Lewis piping did not start in the 20th century. It must have had earlier roots, even though it is undeniable that the 20th century saw its finest flowering.

The struggle with the Seceders was mirrored in Skye and other parts of the Highlands and Islands, and must have aroused mixed feelings as the religious teaching and the consciences of good men conflicted with their natural instinct and talent for music. In times when there was little other stimulation or entertainment, music and song was important, for full mental and emotional development, and many must have felt starved when deprived of their birthright.

Perhaps it was this very repression which eventually led to that remarkable explosion of Lewis talent in the 20th century. As the grip of the stricter forms of the church weakened, and men of great musical talent went south to make their living, the dormant talents of the next generations burgeoned, all the stronger for having been so long prevented from flowering.

This strict sabbatarian religion is (or was) part of the life of Lewis, and part of what gives Lewis its distinctive character. The looser morals and entertainments of the 21st century will make it ever more 'ordinary', more like the rest of Britain, and, ironically, perhaps, make it unlikely that such a remarkable flowering of piping talent will happen again.

At the beginning of the 20th century, the Lewis Pipe Band was started. The very fact that in 1904 there were 6 pipers and 3 drummers experienced enough to form a band surely suggests that piping had already gained a toehold, even if most of the players were incomers (it must have been rather like the cricket team in Hollywood in the 1930s). The first Pipe Major, CHARLES MACIVER from Laxdale, was a Lewisman, but he had been living in Falkirk, where he had played for some years with the Grange Thistle Pipe Band.

The Library at St Andrews University has a photograph, which appears to be a picture postcard, dating from the early 1900s. This picture was published in Donald MacDonald's book *Lewis: A History of the Island,* in 1978. It is a view along Cromwell Street in Stornoway, and shows several people strolling along the road, including a man in dark fisherman's clothes (dark jersey and trousers and a dark cap): he is playing his pipes as he walks down the street, and close by is another man, similarly dressed, talking to a long-skirted woman and holding pipes in his hands. It is not known who either of these pipers was. The photograph must have been taken around the time that the Lewis Pipe Band was started, and the fact of anyone daring to play a pipe on a public street in broad daylight shows that times were changing in Stornoway.

One of the original six pipers in the band was JOHN MORRISON of Goathill Farm (later known to the piping world as John Morrison of Assynt House: note that Assynt House is not in Assynt, Sutherland, but in Stornoway, Lewis). He was a founder member of the band, and went on to become its Treasurer; he had a long influence on Lewis piping, sparing no effort in its support (see below). Presumably it was his grandfather, Thomas MacKay, who taught him to play. John seems to have been one of the few early Lewis pipers who learnt on his home ground, and remained there.

Several of the original band members were also Highland dancers, and band performances had a tendency to turn into all-round entertainments. In 1905, Ronald MacKenzie, nephew of John Ban MacKenzie, and a former Pipe Major in the Seaforth Highlanders, wrote to John Morrison about the provenance of John's grandfather's pipes, and added 'Glad to hear a good report of your Pipe Band. I wish them every success'. His own band, the Ross-shire Buffs, had 36 pipers at that time.

* * * * * * * *

In his book *The Highland Bagpipe and its Music* (1988), Roderick Cannon observed that not many pipers from the north or the islands attended the national competitions at Falkirk or Edinburgh, in the 1780s. One comment made at that time was on the excellence of the MacKay pipers from the Reay country of northern Sutherland, who played with a uniform standard 'as though trained in a school', but Cannon adds 'Few, if any, came from the Outer Hebrides, but in this case distance may not have been the only factor. Life there was even harder than on the mainland, and there may never have been much of the kind of patronage that encouraged first-class pipers. Certainly there are not many pibrochs associated with those districts.'

He might have added that Lewis seems to have lacked the early Volunteer or Fencible (Militia) regiments which produced, or encouraged, local lads of piping talent. It is surprising, though, that the army did not bring to the national competitions any pipers from the Long Island. Traditionally the regiment associated with Lewis was the Seaforth Highlanders, raised by their landlord, but the methods of recruitment to keep up the numbers were so brutal and violent that there seems to have been little affection for the regiment. Of those forced to enlist, a large proportion did not return, succumbing to either disease or battle (and, later, to the easier life of the south). It was not until after 1859 that a Reserve was established, of men still resident in Lewis, and this probably brought some piping to the fore. Unfortunately it coincided with the rise of strong religious feeling against music, so the talent did not blossom.

Another reason why army influence was weak in Lewis was that many of its young men opted for the sea, joining the Royal Navy or the merchant service, where piping was much less to the fore.

It is known that up until the 19th century, in Barra and South Uist at any rate, the pipe was used to accompany dancing. As the 19th century replaced, or supplemented, reels with polkas and waltzes, and dancing moved indoors, the instruments of accompaniment began to change. Whether this happened in Lewis is uncertain, because of the influence of the church, but an inherited form of the old Hebridean step dancing, still practised in Nova Scotia, is even today much to the fore, performed with enthusiasm on the dance floors of Lewis.

It is lack of recorded information, positive or negative, which prevents an account of Lewis piping before 1900. The patronage mentioned by Roderick Cannon seems to have been lacking in Lewis, where the landlords were often absent and made their homes in other places, visiting their remoter Hebridean lands only intermittently and regarding them merely as bottomless wells of fit soldiery. MacLeod of Harris had his base at Dunvegan in Skye, where his pipers, the MacCrimmons, had a profound effect on piping; MacKenzie of Seaforth had strongholds in Kintail and Easter Ross. Any piping compositions associated with them were not made in the Long Island.

Some of the few recorded Lewis pipers who date from before 1900 were emigrants to the colonies, mostly Nova Scotia. One such was JOHN CARMICHAEL, a piper from Lewis who is listed by Barry Shears as having settled in Tarbotvale, Nova Scotia, around 1848, but nothing more is known of him.

A few more Lewis pipers of the 19th century may be found in the Notices of Pipers, most of them being army players. Whether they were already pipers when they left Lewis we have no way of knowing, but KENNETH MACLEOD (1868–1935) from Stornoway seems to have enlisted as a piper in the Seaforth Highlanders in 1887, so was presumably already reasonably proficient. He won the Distinguished Conduct Medal in South Africa (1899–1902) for his gallantry in battle: he continued to play after receiving several wounds, and stopped only when a bullet smashed his pipes. By 1905, he was Pipe Major of the 2nd Battalion, in India, fighting on the North-West Frontier in 1908, and he retired on pension in 1912, joining the Glasgow Police. On the outbreak of war in 1914, he rejoined as Pipe Major of the 9th Gordons, later transferred to the 51st (young soldiers) Battalion. Described in the Notices of Pipers as 'a man of splendid physique but a moderate piper', he died in Stornoway in 1935. His home was Ladysmith Cottage, Arnol.

The *Oban Times* published an obituary in which the details differ somewhat from those in the Notices: the date of Kenneth MacLeod's death was Christmas Eve 1939, and the date of his enlistment, as a piper in the 1st Seaforth Highlanders, not the Gordons, is given as December 1887, not 1897; when his time with the regiment expired, he left the army and joined the Glasgow Police – but it was not long before he re-joined, this time as a piper with the 2nd Gordon Highlanders at Maryhill Barracks. He was sent to India where he spent the next 17 years. He had a Ghurka knife which he had taken from one of the enemy on the North-West Frontier.

His first battle in the South African War was Elandslaagte in 1899, where he led the pipers at the head of the regiment. Severely wounded in the arm and ribs, he played on until his chanter was smashed between his fingers, but 'he kept his place in front of the pipers until the battle was over'.

The obituary continues: 'He was promoted Queen's Sergeant and awarded the DCM for his bravery. In further recognition of his exploits Colonel Dick Cunningham VC commanding the 2nd Gordon Highlanders presented him with a set of silver-mounted pipes to replace the broken ones. Both these sets of pipes are still in Lewis. Piper Roderick Murray (Lewis Pipe Band) is now [1939] the owner of the beautiful silver mounted set, while Pipe Major MacLeod himself retained as a souvenir the broken set still blood stained from the battle. These pipes might well be permanently preserved'.

It goes on:

> Pipe Major MacLeod went through the Siege of Ladysmith for four months and eight days during which time the garrison received only one biscuit and half a pound of horse flesh per day.
>
> He had the distinction of leading the largest pipe band in the Army with 38 pipers, and he was one of the first Lewismen to receive the medal for long service and good conduct.
>
> At the beginning of the Great War he again volunteered for service, and was employed in Lewis as a recruiter. His service with His Majesty's forces covered a period of 31 years.
>
> Another unusual distinction which he had was that of being the only non-commisioned officer or private in the British Army to receive the Order of the German Eagle. This decoration was conferred by the Kaiser before whom he piped on one occasion at Gibraltar.

The obituary ends by saying that he was 'highly respected', and offering sympathy to his sorrowing widow.

Sources

Roderick Cannon, *The Highland Bagpipe and its Music*
Arthur Geddes, *The Isle of Harris and Lewis*
Rona Lightfoot
Notices of Pipers
Oban Times (quoted in the *Piping Times*)
Barry Shears, *Dance To The Piper*
Margaret Stewart

Thomas MacKay and his Grandson, John Morrison of Assynt House (1877–1975)

Note that Assynt House is in Stornoway, not Assynt, Sutherland, as many suppose – but there are links with Sutherland.

The booklet published in 1989 on the history of the Lewis pipe band, written by JOHN ('LUX') MACLEAN, gives an entertaining account of John Morrison, and some of the following is based on that. I am grateful for permission to use this, also to Neil Campbell McGougan and Malcolm Bangor Jones for additional information.

JOHN MORRISON is a household name among pipers, and not only in Lewis, largely because of the popularity of the tunes composed in his honour, which include:

> *John Morrison Esquire of Assynt House,* by William Ross 2/4 M 4
> *John Morrison, Assynt House,* by Peter MacLeod sen. R 6
> *John Morrison, Assynt House,* by Peter MacLeod 6/8 J 4
> *Lament for John Morrison of Assynt House,* by Donald MacLeod P 6
> *John Morrison,* by Andy Venters 4/4 M 2

This collection of excellent tunes honouring John Morrison is an indication of the esteem and affection in which he was held.

John Morrison came of a piping family in Lewis, his grandfather, Thomas MacKay, being piper to Sir James Matheson of the Lews. John inherited his grandfather's pipe, which had been made in 1843 by Donald MacKay, eldest brother of Angus. Donald was at that time living in London, as piper to the Queen's uncle, the Duke of Sussex.

In a letter to the *Piper and Drummer Bulletin,* written in November 1948, John Morrison said his grandfather 'came to the Isle of Lewis and landed in Stornoway in 1844', the year after the pipe was made. 1844 was the year that James Matheson bought his Lewis estate, but it seems that Thomas, then living in Assynt, Sutherland, was already in Matheson's employ before he arrived in Stornoway, and it is possible that James Matheson sent him in the late 1830s for piping tuition in Easter Ross (James would have been in Lewis as a tenant). Thomas described himself as 'piper' by profession in 1851, when he was still living in Assynt for at least part of the year.

Thomas MacKay was born in Assynt, Sutherland, on the west coast of the Scottish Highlands, and was baptised on 18 May 1816, the son of Hugh MacKay and Jannet MacKenzie, then living at Ballahaskon, in Assynt. It is not certain where Ballahaskon was, nor even if this was the correct name: it could be read in the Old Parish Register as Bollakarkan, or even Sollakarkan, or variants of these. It does not seem to be a placename still used in the present day but it was probably somewhere in the vicinity of Nedd, as Thomas gave his birthplace as 'Nedd, Assynt' in 1851.

There is a Hugh MacKay in the Assynt records: he was listed in the Local Vounteers Roll of 1807 as being able-bodied and aged 27, and again in the list of the Sutherland Volunteers in 1811. He was living at Achmelvich, a few miles north of Lochinver, and may be the Hugh MacKay, described as a 'shepherd' at Ardvar, Stoer, in 1818–19, having previously been a shepherd in the nearby estate of Glenleraig in 1815. Estate employees tended to move round an area, working for a different laird every year or so. On Thomas' death certificate in 1891, his father's occupation is given as 'Shepherd'.

Three MacKay families appear in a parochial Census of 1811, living at Oldany, Stoer, some miles north of Lochinver; one was Hugh, employed in agriculture, in a household of three males and one female, possibly his wife Jannet. Another was the family of Eliza MacKay, whose occupation was 'Non-comprehended', i.e. neither agriculture nor trade. She lived alone, possibly an old woman, possibly the mother of Hugh. The third MacKay family at Oldany was that of 'Mrs Mac-Kay', also 'non-comprehended', with a household of two, herself and a male, perhaps her son. These were the only MacKays recorded in Assynt at that time.

In 1774 the Sutherland estate had made an inventory of its possessions, with a list of inhabitants. The Assynt list includes Oldney (now Oldany), a tack which had belonged to 'Lieutenant John MacKay deceased'; 'Mrs MacKay his widow', with four children and eight servants, heads the list. Also at Oldany in 1774 was William MacKay, with his wife, two children and one servant. In the same inventory, a William MacKay was living at Culag (Lochinver) with his wife and one child, and a Roderick MacKay was in Culin, with his wife and a servant.

A list of heritors and parishioners, compiled in 1746, has MacKays at Phyline (Fillin, Lochinver) and Achnacairn, Stoer, and a roll of those paying Hearth Tax in 1691 has Angus Mcky at Oldinie, the only MacKay in Assynt at that time – but there was 'Murdo Pyper' at Phyline.

We have no way of knowing if any of these early MacKay families in Assynt was related to Hugh and his son Thomas. The Oldany MacKays seem to have been of the gentry in 1774, and it may be that they are red herrings, unconnected to the family of Thomas.

In the Reay country, on the north coast, there is a tradition that Thomas originated there, but his birth is registered in Assynt. Possibly his father Hugh MacKay came from Reay to settle in Assynt. In the early 1800s, the village of Lochinver was built by the Sutherland estate, and tradesmen (builders, carpenters, masons) travelled there for the paid employment on offer there. Many were from the north or east of the county, and some stayed in the Lochinver district when the work was completed.

Thomas appears to have spent most of his early life in Assynt; in the 1841 Census he is listed as livng at Clachtoll, Sutherland, as a lodger in the household of a widow, Christina MacLeod, his occupation being 'Salmon Fisher'. The following year, on 11 February 1842, he was married to Flora MacRae, by the Rev. John Gordon, minister of Assynt, at his Manse. Flora, too, was from Nedd, a few miles to the west of Kylesku, and the couple settled there. MacRaes had lived in Nedd and nearby Glenleraig since the mid-18th century.

The first child of Thomas and Flora had been born a month before the wedding, a boy who was, interestingly, christened James Matheson, clearly after the laird, but two years before Matheson bought the island of Lewis. The marriage notice in the Old Parish Register for Assynt describes Thomas as 'Agentnin (?) of Ardmore' and it seems that he had been living at Ardmore, possibly Ardmore in the neighbouring Parish of Eddrachillis, which had close links with Nedd. There were several marriages between inhabitants of the two places. (Malcolm Bangor Jones kindly supplied this information about Ardmore.)

In the Census of 1851, Thomas MacKay, aged 34, is described as 'Piper', which means he made his living as a piper, it was his profession or occupation. We have to assume that he was already piper to James Matheson (not yet a Sir), and his visit to Lewis in 1844, recorded by his grandson, had been associated with his laird's purchase of Lewis, possibly as part of his duties as James' agent in Assynt – and that James then appointed him as his Assynt piper.

Malcolm Bangor Jones says there were two possible links between

James Matheson and Thomas MacKay before 1844: James had started
a subsidised steamer service between Lochinver and Stornoway, and
Thomas may have been his shipping agent on the Lochinver side; and
James' factor for Lewis, John Scobie, became tenant of Lochinver
sheepfarm in 1840, his family having previously been tenants of Ardvar
sheepfarm from 1812 to the 1840s. Thomas MacKay may have worked
for John Scobie, as his agent on the mainland when Scobie was away
in Lewis. This may tie in with the occupation of Hugh MacKay as a
Shepherd at Ardvar (see above).

If Thomas was indeed an agent for James, we must assume a degree
of literacy; this might indicate a link with the Oldany MacKays, of
whom he may have been a younger son – but of course this is conjecture.

By 1851, living at Nedd, Thomas and Flora (who was now 36) had
four children listed: James 8, Mary 6, Janet 4, Catherine 2, and living
with them was John MacRae, a widower of 79, presumably Flora's
father but described as a 'lodger'; there was also a 'servant', Catherine
MacRae, aged 25, presumed to be Flora's younger sister. By this time
the family seems to have been dividing its time between Assynt and
Stornoway.

Living next door at Nedd in 1851 was Donald MacKay, 52, a 'small
crofter' who had been born in Nedd, and his wife Janet, 52, and
daughter Johanna, 26. It is not clear if Donald was a relative: perhaps
an uncle of Thomas.

There is an interesting drawing or painting, made in 1847, of a social
gathering in Stornoway, to celebrate the laying of the foundation stone
of Stornoway Castle. This picture was found among the papers associated with Thomas MacKay's pipe, along with the letters from Colin
Cameron and Ronald MacKenzie. It is entitled 'Ross Munro' and
beneath the picture, the caption ends '– see p. 42'. The caption reads:
'Freemasons of Fortrose Lodge, and others, who were present at the
laying of the foundation stone of Stornoway Castle, 1847.' 84 people
are depicted, nearly all men, some in Masonic dress with sashes diago-
nally across from their right shoulders.

With the picture is a numbered key, naming each person: no. 13 is
'Thomas MacKay, Piper', who seems to be wearing a plaid (on his left
shoulder) rather than a sash. No. 32 is 'Sir James Matheson, Prop. of
the Lews' and No. 33 is his wife, Lady Matheson, who has a female
companion, a Mrs Watt. It is not clear whether this is indeed a drawing, with colour added later, or a rather crude painting: no. 38 in the
Key is 'Robt. Grant Masson, the Artist', who may have made this
record of the occasion. Below the key, a note says: 'From Annals of

Lodge Fortrose No. 108, Stornoway, 1767–1905. Compiled from the Lodge records by J. Campbell Smith B.Sc. (Printed 1905)'.

There is a discrepancy in the caption to this picture: it refers to 'Sir James Matheson' and 'Lady Matheson', but is dated 1847, and James did not receive his Baronetcy until 1851. Presumably the explanatory caption was added, with hindsight, when the book was published.

Since neither Thomas MacKay nor James Matheson is wearing Masonic dress, and both are standing towards the back, among the general crowd of non-Masons, perhaps we might assume that neither was a Mason. Presumably James had sent for Thomas to come from Assynt for the occasion, and this picture, combined with the 1851 Census, is proof that Thomas did spend time on each side of the Minch for some years before moving permanently to Stornoway.

Thomas is a common name among the Frasers, less so among the MacKays; possibly the mother of Thomas in Assynt, Jannet Mackenzie, had Fraser connections, but there may have been other influences. Between Nedd and Kylesku, on the southern side of Loch a'Chairn Bhain, there is small hill called Ruighean Thomais (the Gaelic *ruigh* may mean a slope or hillside, but in Sutherland it meant a shieling, where animals were taken to graze in the summer to keep them away from the crops. The plural form *ruighean* probably implies several shieling huts). It is not known who this Thomas was, but it is possible that Thomas MacKay was named after someone of local significance.

By 1861, the Thomas MacKay family was living in Stornoway, Lewis. The Census says 'Gairshader, Piper's House' and he is listed among the estate employees of Sir James Matheson. By now Thomas was, it seems, only seven years older than he had been in the previous Census, his wife having advanced nine years.

Five children are given: Marie 16, Jessie (= Janet) 14, Catherine 12, but James had left home (or died); those four were born in Assynt, but since the arrival in Lewis, two more had been added to the family, Hughina 10, doubtless named for Thomas' father, and John 8. This tells us that they had moved to Lewis the same year as the earlier census, in 1851. The family were living in comparative prosperity, their Piper's House having six rooms, luxury for those times.* Thomas' profession is again given as 'Piper'.

---

* In his book *Lewis: A History of the Island* (1983), Donald MacDonald gave us a glimpse of conditions in Stornoway before the arrival of James Matheson: he quotes a report of 1841 which said that the local idea of comfort was to have a house,

In 1864, Thomas MacKay was called upon by his employer, Sir James Matheson, to witness his signature on a document concerning the ownership of Stornoway Harbour. The other witness was Sir James' butler. This probably gives an indication of Thomas' standing in the household – that of a senior and trusted servant, someone who was literate, too.

In 1881, in that same Piper's House, now called Willow Glen, the head of household was still Thomas MacKay, 63, farmer of 5 acres. Both he and his wife were Gaelic speakers. Hughina, then aged 29, was also there. There were two other households of MacKays on the Castle estate: the Coachman was William MacKay 62, born in Lairg, Sutherland; his wife Alexandrina, 56, came from Eddrachillis, Sutherland, which may mean she was from Ardmore. William's father Alexander, 82, was a Sutherland man, too, born in Rogart, and they had a niece Jessie Bowie, 19, living with them – she came from Durness.

Thomas MacKay died at Willow Glen on 7 January 1891, aged 72, the cause of death being Cardiac Disease. His wife Flora had died some years earlier, and the informant for Thomas's death was D.M. Graham, his nephew, living at Mary Bank, Stornoway.

John Morrison, later of Assynt House, seems to have been the son of Thomas's second daughter, Janet, known as Jessie, whose occupation was 'Housekeeper'. She was married, in June 1877, to John Morrison, a gamekeeper on the Gress estate, who came from Alness in Easter Ross. The witnesses to the wedding were James Matheson and 'Sp.

---

self-built, plenty of peat, some grain, between one and five cows, and a few sheep. The houses were small and cheerless, with no chimneys and no windows other than a few holes where the walls met the roof – and there was no glass in these. To have glass in the window-holes was a sign of superiority, and was rare. The houses were one compartment only, housing both people and animals, with no internal partition. It is clear that Thomas MacKay, as Sir James' piper, was fortunate in having the luxury of a farmhouse with some six or seven rooms, and he had five acres of land, of which three were arable. When the wealthy James Matheson bought the island in 1844 he at once began to improve conditions – but he cleared local inhabitants from the site when he laid the foundations of the Castle in 1847. These, however, were the years of the Potato Famine, and he did much to help his tenants survive. By 1849 he had built many new houses, laid on gas and water, provided a school and a jail, and greatly improved the harbour. He received his Baronetcy for his actions in alleviating distress during the famine years. There is a photograph of Sir James in Donald MacDonald's book, Plate 14.

Persival', which suggests that Jessie had been housekeeper at the Castle. Sp. (Spenser?) Persival was probably an in-law of Sir James, whose wife was called Mary Jane Percival. John was the first child of the marriage, born on the 28th March 1878, at their home, Gress Lodge, Stornoway. His younger brother was Angus.

By the 1901 Census, John Morrison was 23, living in the Piper's House (Willow Glen) with his unmarried aunt Hughina MacKay, 48, whose occupation was 'Farmer'. John was then a Clerk in the Lewis Estate Office.

In the letter of 1948, already quoted, John Morrison said he had in his possession an ivory-soled chanter made by John Ban MacKenzie at Taymouth, 'still played upon, though much worn', and played with the drones 'beautifully made by Donald MacKay'. He also had a silver-soled chanter which dated from the same time as his grandfather's pipe.

In 1942, John Morrison had sent his silver-soled chanter (not the John Ban one) to a reputable silversmith in Glasgow, hoping to have the silver work dated; the reply was that it was Early Victorian, dating from 1843, made in London, probably for Fraser – he would have been the London silversmith who presumably put the silver on the pipe, so we may assume the pipe was certainly as old as 1843, possibly a little older. This tallies with what we know of Donald MacKay, who was in London from 1833 until his death in 1850 – and he was well-known as a pipe-maker.

Note that although in 1948, John Morrison knew his silver-soled chanter dated from the 1840s, he did not claim it was made by Donald MacKay, merely referring to the Donald MacKay drones. He might have been justified in assuming the link, but he did not, and we can only applaud his integrity.

We have to wonder how Thomas came to have a John Ban chanter, believed to have been made at Taymouth in the 1840s. Did he buy it direct from John Ban before he left for Lewis in 1851?

Ronald MacKenzie, John Ban's nephew, wrote to John Morrison in 1905 about this silver-soled chanter, telling him that it had once belonged to Angus MacKay himself. It is not clear from the letter whether he thought the entire pipe had been Angus' own, and it is not certain how it came into the possession of Thomas MacKay. It may have been bought for him by Sir James.

In 1906, Colin Cameron, confirming that the pipe was made by Donald MacKay, wrote that Thomas MacKay and Donald Cameron had been 'like two brothers'. It is difficult to see how this could be, as Donald was in Easter Ross and Thomas in Assynt, and Donald was nine years younger. We could assume that before Thomas was married he spent some time in Easter Ross, possibly having piping tuition from Donald Mor MacLennan of Moy, who also taught Donald Cameron and John Ban MacKenzie. This would have been in the 1830s – but there are anomalies in the dating here, as Donald moved to Rosehaugh around 1830, and was there when he married in 1841. He was, however, living in Donald Mor's household in Strathconon when the 1841 Census was taken. This suggests that his position as piper at Rosehaugh was intermittent, possibly only when the laird was in residence.

At that time there was a family of MacKays living near Muir of Ord. Perhaps it is significant that the father was called Thomas, and he gave the name to one of his sons, too. We may suspect that this family was related to that of Thomas from Assynt, and that he stayed with them when he was (we assume) having piping lessons, before he was married.

It seems very likely, though unprovable, that Thomas was one of several pipers taught by Donald Mor, and as fellow-pupils, he and Donald may have struck up a friendship in piping. Balavulich, where the Easter Ross Thomas MacKays lived, lies to the west of Muir of Ord, only a few miles from Donald Mor's home near Scatwell, with a road of sorts, dating back to that time, pretty well direct from one to the other.

Some pupils of Donald Mor were given financial backing by Alexander MacKenzie of Millbank, near Dingwall. He spent a great deal of money on encouraging young pipers, an investment which did not give him a return at the time, but must have been a source of satisfaction when he saw how well his protégés were doing. It may be, however, that Thomas was sent and financed by his laird, James Matheson, and this may be borne out by the fact that Thomas had his first child christened James Matheson in 1842.

John Ban MacKenzie was another of Donald Mor's pupils, and his mother was a MacKay, whose father's name was Thomas – but this Thomas was too old to have been John Morrison's grandfather. These MacKays, and the MacKenzies, lived at Altnabreac, near Contin, not far from Donald of Moy's home, and it is possible that the other Thomas MacKay, piper to Sir James Matheson, was related to them, too. In 1841, 'The widow MacKay' aged 45 was living in Altnabreac with three children, John 17, Margaret 15 and Mary 12. The family was probably related to John Ban's mother, who had links with Raasay. This putative connection with Altnabreac may explain how Thomas from Assynt came to buy (or was given?) the John Ban chanter.

In 1935, John Morrison laid up his pipe, and the chanter made by

John Ban MacKenzie, carefully storing them in their box, with full documentation to prove their origins. They remained in Assynt House until 1975, when they emerged from hibernation, after the death of John Morrison. They were bought and re-conditioned by BOBBY MUNRO, a piper in the Lewis Band. They are now in the possession of NEIL CAMPBELL MCGOUGAN, in Dingwall, who bought them from Bobby Munro's widow.

(I am indebted to Neil Campbell McGougan for permission to use material taken from his documentation of the pipe. He has in his possession the letters from Ronald MacKenzie and Colin Cameron and others, as well as documents showing the provenance of the pipe, and the 1847 Masonic picture.)

John was a founder member of the Lewis Pipe Band in 1904, became its Treasurer, lifelong committee member and devotee, indeed fanatical supporter, of the band.

He was also regarded by many as the personification of Lewis piping. The band booklet describes him as 'a respected member of the community, courteous in his dealings with young and old alike', and he 'always held a passionate interest in all things pertaining to piping. He corresponded regularly with piping enthusiasts and Lewis exiles both in this country and abroad.' His remarkable popularity in Lewis seems to be because of his unbounded enthusiasm for all things Lewisach – and the fact that he was born, lived and worked in Lewis, and never left the island (except when he attended the Northern Meetings in Inverness).

John MacLean said John Morrison was a creature of habit, who had his daily routine. First of all he would take an early morning walk with his dog, and then, later in the morning, embarked on a series of visits which seldom varied.

First, to the Post Office for a short crack with RODDIE MURRAY, a member of the band. Then to the chemist's shop to see WILLIE JOHN TOLMIE, a band committee member. There he might meet up with other band members, and the discussions, sometimes heated, ranged widely over many topics. His next port of call was the cycle shop in Point Street, whose owner, Jimmy MacLean, 'was not a piper, but his keen interest in piping raised him in Johnnie's estimation'. Further along Point Street was the barber's, where both the owner, MURDO 'BOGEY' MACLEOD and his assistant MURDO 'STEVE' MACKENZIE, were involved in the band. 'Bogey' used to strop his razors to a pipe tune which he whistled, varying the speed of his strokes to the tempo of the tune. 'Usually he went through a march, strathspey and reel, finishing the final stropping with a slow march.'

John MacLean continues:

It was in 'Bogey's' shop that much of the band's future engagements
were discussed, and if Johnnie had been displeased with the band's
last performance he wasn't above demonstrating his point with his
own inimitable canntaireachd, helped on with a beat from 'Steve', who
always had a spare set of drum sticks handy in the shop. On one of
these visits a customer asked him what had happened to a well known
local piper who had lost all interest in the band. Johnnie's reply was:
'Oh, he's a lady now, and he's learning to play the violin.'

Johnnie's final call was made at the shoemaker's shop next door,
owned by HECTOR MACDONALD, a committee member of the band.
Hector's command of English could, at times, be erratic, and Johnnie
made full use of this failing by taking up some controversial point of
issue or matters of band discipline on which he knew Hector had strong
feelings.

The daily visits over, Johnnie would then return home to spend some
time with his correspondence.

Johnnie used to tell John MacLean about the night of John's parents'
wedding reception in the Drill Hall. Johnnie was due to play there, and
at that time he lived out at Goathill Farm, then a good half mile outside Stornoway. There had been an exceptionally heavy snowfall that
day, and the drifts at Goathill were deep. 'He left the farm in Highland
dress, but before he had gone very far he found himself up to the waist
in snow. He returned home, put on a pair of trousers, and, with his kilt
slung over his shoulder, set off again, walking on a high ridge of ground
and using the fence posts as a guide to the depth of the snow. He finally
reached the Drill Hall and changed his trousers for the kilt. As he said
himself, 'I couldn't let a band member down'.

One day, John MacLean's father reminded him of an occasion, forty
years earlier, when he had played a selection of tunes for a minister in
Kyle of Lochalsh. Johnnie said 'What a memory you have, Kenny, and
what a gentleman that minister was, beside some of those we have here
today'. As far as he was concerned, a minister interested in piping was
a gentleman, irrespective of his ability in the pulpit.

Another story concerned two ladies, just after the Second World
War, who were enjoying listening to a piper practising in the church
grounds, near Johnnie's house. Later they said they were looking
for Johnnie, as he was the authority who could grant them extended
harvest leave, available to servicemen and those engaged in industry.
Delighted by their pleasure in pipe music, he asked if four weeks' harvest leave would be enough.

He used to act as truant-officer for absent band members, and anyone absent without a good reason 'usually received the sharp side of his tongue'. Once a band member did not turn up for parade because he was leaving for London that morning, to attend a staff function. Johnnie was incensed. 'The mail steamer doesn't leave until 11 o'clock. Fair wind to him, may he never come back!'

One night Johnnie was bemoaning the fact that a very famous piper on the mainland had been buried with only one piper playing at the graveside. In his view, every piper in Scotland should have been there. A friend said 'Never mind, Johnnie, when your time comes, I'll see to it that the whole band plays you to Sandwick', to which Johnnie retorted 'You do that – and on the way back ask them to play Happy We've Been All Together.'

John Morrison died in 1975 – and the Lewis Pipe Band did play him to the grave.

Sources

Assynt Hearth Tax Roll 1691
Assynt Heritors' List 1746
Malcolm Bangor Jones, Dundee
N. Campbell McGougan, Dingwall
John ('Lux') MacLean, *Handbook of the Lewis Pipe Band*
Norman MacRae, *Dingwall's History of a Thousand Years*
Old Parish Register and Census Records, Assynt
Old Parish Register and Census Records, Lewis
Parochial Census, Assynt 1811
Piper and Drummer Bulletin
Sutherland Estate Inventory 1774
Volunteers' Roll, Assynt 1807

20th Century Piping in Lewis

For the rest of the piping traditions of Lewis we must again look to the 20th century – and what riches we find there. It is hard to know where to start, and as many of the Lewis 'greats' were contemporaries, they cannot be arranged in order of time.

Peter MacLeod, Senior and Junior

The works of these two outstanding composers of light music (Ceol Beag), PETER MACLEOD senior and PETER MACLEOD junior, father and son, are often difficult to separate, and compositions may be attributed to the wrong Peter. Lists of their works follow this tribute, and I apologise for any mistaken attributions or omissions. Having sought guidance from different Lewisachs on the authorship of various tunes, I find their evidence conflicts, and I cannot quote some without mortally offending others – so I am not asking for further help unless it is accompanied by irrefutable proof.

In 1999, the *Piping Times* received a letter from Ronald Peter MacLeod, then living in Salisbury (England). He said he was a grandson of Peter junior, whose chanter he had inherited, but it did not come with the talent built in (his own words). His father was Hector, the elder son of Peter and Christina MacLeod, both from Lewis. Christina was a Lewis MacDonald. Ronald said he failed as a piper, but had an interest, and he sent two photographs of his grandfather. He recalled crossing the Clyde on the Erskine ferry (now replaced by a bridge) to visit the old man on Sundays, 'with the compulsory ¼ bottle of Bells (whisky) which fitted rather nicely into the top of his wooden leg, out of Matron's sight!!'. This was when Peter MacLeod senior, his grandfather, was a resident in Erskine Hospital for ex-servicemen, near Bishopton, Renfrewshire.

The life of Peter senior was researched by Angus J. MacLellan, who tells us that Peter R. MacLeod was born in Uig, Isle of Lewis, on 13 December 1878. He was a cousin of the father of 'Wee Donald' MacLeod. He left the island to seek work, and went to Glasgow where he found employment as a shipwright at Connells Shipbuilders in Govan. This career lasted from 1900 to 1927, when he was involved in an accident at the yard, and had to have his right leg amputated. He did not work again until 1941, when at the age of 63 he returned to the shipyards, to contribute to the war effort. He worked there until finally retiring in 1955, at the age of 77.

His home was 7 Exeter Drive in Partick, a district of Glasgow where many Highlanders lived. He was one of several pipers who made their homes in Partick at different times: Archie McNab, Seumas MacNeill, Donald MacPherson and others. Peter MacLeod's home was a meeting-place for pipers from all over, and his sons grew up to the sound of the pipes.

The tunes he made were numerous and excellent (see list, below), and many are still heard in competitions today. Angus J. picked out in particular *Lady Lever Park, Pipe Major Willie MacLean, Dora MacLeod, Major Manson, John Morrison of Assynt House*, and, of course, *The Conundrum*. It has been suggested that the off-beat rhythm of this clever piece is a reflection of the composer's own gait, walking with his wooden leg, but Angus J. refutes this. He says the name was given to it by Peter's eldest sister on hearing it for the first time, and its rhythm is simply an expression of Peter's genius. It was first played in public by his son Peter junior at an SPA meeting, 'probably in 1930', and it had 'a mixed reception'. This first performance probably gave rise to confusion as to which Peter composed it.

At the conference of the Piobaireachd Society in 1983, D.R. MacLennan told a story about the day HECTOR ROSS was piping the Edinburgh University Officer Training Corps through Edinburgh to Waverley Station. Accompanied by a Major on horseback, the company marched from the High Street, to a nice 6/8, but at the North British Hotel, Hector thought 'By God, I'll give them this new tune, they'll love it', so he played *The Conundrum* boldly along Waverley Street, down the ramp and into the station, and stopped.

The Major shouted: 'Ross, what the hell tune was that you were playing?'

'*The Conundrum*, sir.'

'*The Conundrum*? I'll say it was. The only one that was in step was my bloody horse, and he has four legs.'

Some may recall a ceilidh after the Northern Meeting in Inverness in the 1980s, when Gordon Walker, considerably the worse for strong drink after celebrating his success in the Jig competition, was asked, with malice aforethought, to play *The Conundrum*. He could barely stand, but gave a brilliant and immaculate performance of the entire piece, and silenced his tormentors.

Peter MacLeod junior was brought up among pipers in his father's house in Partick. He inherited his father's gift for composition, and today their tunes cannot always be told apart. Peter junior, like so many in the 1930s, fell on hard times in the Depression years, and among jobs he took was work as a steward on the Donaldson line of Atlantic liners. There he met 'Wee Donald' MacLean from Oban, and Duncan MacIntyre from Islay. Soon they were all working on the same ship, and formed small pipe bands to entertain the passengers – and to supplement their wages. Tiree tradition says the players included two from South Uist, one from Barra, one (probably Peter MacLeod) from Lewis, and four from Tiree. They had 'grand piping nights' in their quarters after work. To those days belong two tunes made by Peter MacLeod junior, *Donald MacLean* (RMS *Athenia*) and *Duncan MacIntyre* (RMS *Athenia*), both four-part reels.

While living for a time in Rhodesia (now Zimbabwe), Peter MacLeod junior used to judge piping competitions in both that country and neighbouring South Africa.

The United States Bicentennial Collection of Bagpipe Music, Volume 2, was The Peter MacLeod Memorial Collection, compiled by Peter MacLeod junior, and published in Michigan, USA.

Ascribed to PETER R. MACLEOD senior, in the above collection and elsewhere (possibly mistakenly) are:

Alexander MacLennan, HLI 6/8 J 4
The 7th Battalion Scottish Rifles 2/4 M 4
Captain Charles Hepburn 6/8 M 4
Catterick Camp (1914) 2/4 M 4
Chrissie MacLeod S 2 (Peter senior's wife)
The Conundrum 2/4 M 4
Deen the Nannie 2/4 M 4
Dr E.G. MacKinnon 2/4 M 4
Donald MacLean R 4 and 6/8 J 4. Is this one tune or two? One for
   each of the two Donald MacLeans, 'Wee Donald' of Oban and
   'Big Donald' of Lewis? Both are published in Book 2 of the Edcath
   Collection by Donald Shaw Ramsay.
Donald MacVicar of Partick 2/4 M 4
Duncan McInnes 2/4 M 4
The Eighth Army 6/8 M 4
Exeter Drive 6/8 W 2
Frank Thomson 6/8 M 4
Gaelic Mouth Music 1 S 2
Gaelic Mouth Music 2 (arr.) S 4
Gary Roland Knight 6/8 M 4
Gena MacLeod R 4
Hector MacLeod 2/4 M 4
The Highlanders Institute R 4
Hugh Kennedy MA, BSc 2/4 M 4
Hugh MacPhee 2/4 M 4
Ipswich Camp 6/8 M 4
James MacIver 2/4 M 4
J.M. MacDonald (Bulawayo) R 4
John C. Johnston (Glasgow Police) 2/4 M 4
John M. MacKenzie (SPA Glasgow) 2/4 M 4
John Morrison, Assynt House R 6
John Morrison, Assynt House 6/8 J 4
Kenneth Degree 2/4 M 4

Kenneth J. MacLeod 6/8 M 4
Kenny McGruer 2/4 M 2
Lady Lever Park 2/4 M 4
Leaving Home 2/4 M 4
The Lewis and Harris Gathering 2/4 M 4
Lord Leverhulme 2/4 M 4
Major (David) Manson R 4
Margaret Kennedy R 4
To the Memory of Mrs Peter MacLeod, senior 6/8 SA 2
Morag Ramsay 2/4 M 4
Mrs P.R. MacLeod 6/8 J 4
Mrs Peter MacLeod (senior) 6/8 M 4
Murdo MacLeod 2/4 M 4
Neil Cameron's Jig 6/8 J 2
Pipe Major Donald MacLean 2/4 M 4
Pipe Major Donald MacLeod, 1st HLI 2/4 M 4
Pipe Major George MacDonald 2/4 M 4
Pipe Major Hector MacLean S 4
Pipe Major Iain M. MacLeod 2/4 M 4
Pipe Major Robert Hill (London) 2/4 M 4
Pipe Major Sam Scott 6/8 M 4
Pipe Major Willie MacLean 2/4 M 4
Puck's Glen 6/8 M 4
The Rhodesian Regiment 2/4 M 4
Robert Hepburn of Airdrie 2/4 M 4
Robert Thomson (Silvertone) 6/8 M 4
Roderick MacDonald (Glasgow Police) 2/4 M 4
South Beach, Stornoway 6/8 M 2
Teenie Blue 6/8 SA 3
The Tweed (arr.) 6/8 J 2

Ascribed to PETER MACLEOD JUNIOR (possibly mistakenly) are:

The 6th African Armoured Division 3/4 RM 2
Banana Fingers polka 2
Bertie Gass 6/8 SA 2
The Blue Lagoon 6/8 J 4
Charlie's Welcome (arr.) R 4
Chris Oldroyd 6/8 M 4
The Clan MacLeod
Donald MacLean (RMS Athenia) R 4
Dora MacLeod S 4

The Duke of Perth (arr.) R 4
Duncan MacIntyre (RMS *Athenia*) R 4
Gaelic Mouth Music 3
Master Roderick MacLeod 6/8 M 4
Pat Ewart 2/4 H 3
Peter MacLeod's Farewell 2/4 M 4
Pipe Major John Copeland, HLI 6/8 M 4
Pipe Major John MacDonald 6/8 J 4
Pipe Major Peter MacLeod 6/8 J 4
Pipe Major Robert Reid S 4
Pipe Major William Gray 6/8 J 4
The Sixth MacLeod 6/8 M 4
Stornoway Castle R 4
Traditional Hornpipe 2/4 H 2
Traditional Jig 6/8 J 4
Tsaba-tsaba 6/8 J 4
The Tuning Notes 3/4 RM 4

Sources

Robert Beck
D.R. MacLennan, *Piobaireachd Society Conference Proceedings*
Piping Times

Donald MacLeod (1916–1982)

It would be difficult to exaggerate the impact of 'Wee' DONALD MACLEOD on the piping world, and especially in Lewis where he is still idolised. He was born in Stornoway on the 14th August 1916, the son of DONALD MACLEOD and Donaldina MacDonald. The family lived down at the harbour, close to the pier, 'within twenty yards of the sea'. His father was a good piper, Pipe Major of the Lewis Pipe Band, and a cousin of Peter MacLeod senior, in a family full of musical talent. His brother, ANGUS MACLEOD, known as 'Boxer', was also a skilled player.

In her book of Hebridean memories, Emily MacDonald, niece and hostess of Lord Leverhulme, wrote of a dinner party at the Castle in Stornoway: 'We were piped into dinner by Pipe Major MacLeod in full regimentals, and he remained in the room throughout the meal, playing at intervals. This however precluded all conversation when he was playing. Actually I am very fond of pipe music in the proper place, but I am perfectly certain that that is outside, and not in a room' (quoted by Bill Lawson, 2011). This typically English comment must refer to

Donald MacLeod senior, since Lord Leverhulme bought Lewis in 1917 and withdrew from the Long Island in 1923 – and Donald junior was born in 1916.

It was his father who started him on the pipes, around the age of four. Although much of the piping world refers to him as 'Wee Donald', the young Donald was often called 'Donald Doyle', his by-name by which most Lewisachs knew him. His father had the same by-name, which is a form of the Gaelic Domhnuill. 'Wee Donald' was also called 'Dotts' in Lewis.

Chrissie Morrison (née Chisholm) remembered young Donald from her own young days when she was living in Inverness: Donald, in the 1930s before his army years, used to come over to stay with the Chisholms in Inverness, and compete in junior competitions, along with Chrissie's brothers. In 2000, she said: 'When Donald Doyle first came to stay with us we thought he was hilarious as he was so wee and stuck out his bottom to one side and leaned over when he was playing – but we all sat up when we discovered he was winning all the prizes.'

When he was six, he was taken to the classes held by Willie Ross who regularly visited the islands to give tuition during the summer, sponsored by the Piobaireachd Society. Donald attended for three or four years, and Willie, recognising his talent, taught him to read music. Angus J. MacLellan said Willie used to reward the successful playing of a part from the book by giving him a square of chocolate, adding 'but from the size of him it doesn't look as if he was very successful'. Donald had a phenomenal ability to memorise tunes off the fingers, a great talent which he never lost.

In later life Donald recalled being taken at the age of nine to the Northern Meeting, by John Morrison, Assynt House, who was by then his regular teacher, taking over from his father. It was the boy's first visit to the mainland. In those days the Stornoway ferry went to Kyle of Lochalsh, where it connected with the Inverness train. The ferry left at an unearthly hour in the morning, and that day the crossing was very rough. On reaching Kyle, young Donald spent all the waiting time looking at his first train, the big gleaming engine and three carriages. 'Since then many miles have been travelled, all because of the great Highland bagpipe', he said at his presentation dinner.

Already at the age of twelve he was composing, and made the jig *Rory MacLeod*, really as an exercise, and named it for an elderly relative of his.

When Willie Ross stopped coming in 1924, John MacDonald, Inverness, was making regular visits to Lewis on business (he was a sales rep for a firm of brewers), and John Morrison quickly organised classes for young island pipers. Donald's association with John MacDonald lasted for 25 years. The relationship got off to a bad start, when the irascible John MacDonald put the cocky young Donald in his place, sending him home in tears from his first lesson, vowing never to go back. He did, of course, but he told Angus J. that it was about ten years before he really understood what John wanted, and that 'certain principles could be transferred from one tune to another at the same time realising that each piobaireachd had its own individual characteristic'.

In his teaching John MacDonald always stressed that players should learn all they could from their teacher, but in the end should feel free to express their own feeling, and not merely 'parrot' what they had learned. Of all John's pupils, Donald MacLeod probably took this most to heart – his interpretations were sometimes different in the subtleties of timing from what the master taught, one of his fellow-pupils going so far as to describe his playing as 'syncopated', something of an exaggeration.

In July 2000, Col. David Murray gave us an interesting account of Donald's military career – starting with the observation that he wore his glengarry 'the Highland way, one inch above the right eye and one inch above the right ear'. In 1937, he left home to enlist in the Seaforth Highlanders (formerly the Ross-shire Buffs or the Duke of Albany's). 'At that time each regiment had two regular battalions, one serving at home, the other overseas, usually in India'. Col. Murray explained that each regiment also had Territorial battalions, of which the Seaforth had three: the 4th Ross-shire, the 5th Caithness and Sutherland, and the 6th Morayshire. And each regiment was responsible for enlisting and training its own recruits at its Depot – the Seaforth's depot was at Fort George, on the Moray Firth, and was known as Alcatraz among the Cameron Highlanders, who were cosier in the Cameron Barracks in Inverness.

The Seaforth's Pipe Major at Fort George was D.R. MacLennan, half-brother of G.S. MacLennan. D.R. was very large and appeared intimidating, but keen pipers were devoted to him, and he taught them well. Donald MacLeod's jig *Donald MacLennan's Tuning Phrase* commemorates those early days in the army.

Col. Murray goes on to say that in those days, all recruits from the east coast were posted to the 1st Battalion and sent to China. Those from the west coast went to the 2nd Battalion, usually bound for India, by way of Glasgow. Col. Murray adds 'These numbers are important . . . it is as well to know who were the 72nd who said farewell to Aberdeen.'

When Donald MacLeod arrived at Maryhill Barracks in Glasgow, the Pipe Major was Big Donald MacLean from Balantrushal, in Lewis (see below). On the outbreak of war in 1939, the 2nd Seaforth was sent to France as part of the 5th Highland Division, later transferred to the 152nd Brigade; forced to surrender after a gallant fight at St-Valery-en-Caux, in May 1940, most of the surviving Seaforth Highlanders became prisoners of war.

We get a pre-war glimpse of Donald MacLeod in a reported conversation between Ian Mitchell and Tex Geddes, when Ian called in at the island of Soay, where Tex was living. Ian later published what he had been told, in his book about his sailing cruise, *The Isles of the West* (1999).

It seems that Tex Geddes had been in the 2nd Seaforth at the same time as Donald MacLeod, in the late 1930s. Tex Geddes was a colourful character, given to somewhat lurid narrative, and his account needs a substantial pinch of salt, and some censorship. Speaking of John Flett from Orkney, another Seaforth piper (subject of Donald's march *Flett from Flotta*), Tex, said 'John was bloody nearly seven feet long, and broad as well,' while Donald was so small he 'should never have been allowed into the Seaforth Highlanders. They couldn't get a uniform small enough for him (at five foot three) to send him to the Games. Eventually they cut the pockets off a jacket, and he went out and won everything. He was only about eighteen [he must have been at least 21] so they sent him to Edinburgh Castle to be taught by Willie Ross who was the Highland Brigade piping teacher at the Castle, and Willie sent him back within the week and gave him his Pipe Major's Certificate. He said "I can't teach that boy anything. He's teaching me".' Tex was clearly unaware that Donald had been taught by Willie Ross as a boy in Lewis. This account by Tex Geddes refers to Flett as 'John' or 'Big John' throughout, and others always called him John or Jock, but some reports, such as his obituary in the *Piper Press*, No. 5. March 1998, give his first name as William. In later life he was known as Bill.

Wee Donald and Big John, said Tex, were great pals, and a couple of years later the two of them were going to the Inverness Games ('or some bloody thing like that'), and on the way they were both drunk, on the train. 'And Willie Logan, the Pipe Major, got a hold of them and he put them out of the carriage. He sent them to the guards van. Do you remember the shitpaper you used to have in trains? Like greaseproof paper – well, while they were in the guards van, wee Donald wrote a tune and called it *Flett from Flotta*, and he wrote it out on the train lavatory paper while he was drunk'. (A pupil of Donald gave a different version of this, and so did Donald's daughter – see below.)

Tex Geddes continued: 'I was in the Seaforth myself, not a very good soldier, though – I was five times a sergeant.' He recalled Big John Flett as:

> a bloody good piper in the massed bands when Wee Donald was Pipe Sergeant. But John was a private [Donald's daughter said he was a steward in the Officers' Mess at Fort George], so they shouldn't have been fraternising, but, both being pipers, they always did. One day, afternoon practice was cancelled, so what did they do? They buggered off to the pub and got pissed, the two of them. Both of them drank like fish. Pipers all do. They put a drop of whisky in their bags, and they get the fumes when they're blowing and sucking the bloody bag, Well, this time they came back pissed as bloody newts, and of course the orders had been changed and the practice was on after all, and they had 'gone missing', a serious offence . . . They got ten days in the jail, but we couldn't put them in jail because we needed them to play. After we finished in London – it was 1938 – we had to go to the Empire Exhibition in Glasgow, to troop the colour. When we'd finished with that they still couldn't put them in jail because we had to go to Ballater to be the King's Guard at Balmoral. Then, at last, we went to Stobb's Camp at Hawick, under canvas. 'Right, into bloody jail with you!' But the jail was a bell tent and Tex was the Sergeant in charge of the guard.
>
> The rest of the boys off duty went to get fish suppers and a half bottle of whisky, and threw them in under the tent flap, and then at ten p.m., at Last Post, Tex would go and visit the jail birds, finding them with fish supper, beer and whisky – what a fucking carry on we had getting them sobered up before morning, so that we could inspect them again! An officer said 'God Almighty, I don't know how these men can stand to attention', and if John farted, Donald would do the same, and everyone knew they were pissed as newts, but no one said a bloody word.

When John Flett was eighty, he paid a visit to Scotland from his new home in Australia, and he said the best week he ever spent in the army was that week in the jail, and he mentioned this wild sergeant who was 'wilder than any of us' – presumably Tex Geddes. It is clear that episodes of this kind were regarded as part of Donald's heroic past, when he was young and reckless – and infinitely respected by all, for his supreme talent.

Shorn of its lurid obscenities and obvious exaggerations and inaccuracies, Tex Geddes' account gives us a glimpse of a great piper in the making. It has been included here for that reason alone, and no disrespect to Donald MacLeod is intended. Joe Wilson's stories of Donald

MacLeod and Calum Campbell reflected the same affectionate irreverence, which did not obscure Joe's admiration, and that of Calum, for the Master. Father MacMillan of Barra is said to have once remarked 'It's a funny thing, but I have never yet met a piper who was a saint,' and even Donald's most fervent admirers would not pretend he was teetotal.

It is interesting, and pleasant, to contrast Tex Geddes' account with that of Donald's daughter, Susan, published in the *Piping Times* in August 2012. Asked what her dad was like at home, she remarked on the great affection felt for him in the piping world, adding 'And he was exactly the same at home. He was just a loving husband, father and grandfather. Unconditional love, a ready smile, a great chuckle and very quiet, although he filled the house with his presence.'

She stressed Donald's loyalty to his regiment, the Seaforth, and his affection for Fort George, as well as his modesty – 'he never spoke about any prizes that he won' – and his willingness to do things for other people. She finished her very touching article with a note on her father's beliefs: 'he had a very deep faith. He didn't speak about it much, but at his funeral we sang "Be Thou My Vision, Oh Lord of My Heart", and I think that expresses how dad tried to live his life. He would never ever claim to be perfect; he was a very human being, but he tried to do unto others as he would like to be done unto him.'

In 1939, Donald went to France with the 2nd Battalion, Seaforth Highlanders. At that time he, and all the other pipers in the 2nd Seaforth, were playing Robertson drones and chanters. Captured at St Valery-en-Caux with the rest of his regiment, he escaped the column being marched into Germany by rolling into a deep roadside ditch and lying there until the prisoners and escorts were out of sight. When darkness fell, he crawled out of the ditch and managed to make his way to the French coast. When on the run in France, he was repeatedly challenged by the enemy but always replied in Gaelic, so that the Germans thought he was some Middle European ally. In later life, he usually refused to talk about his experiences, saying merely that when the Germans caught him, they decided he was too small to keep, so threw him back. We can only imagine the courage needed to make this journey on foot, by himself, and admire his resourcefulness. After escaping in May, he was back in Fort George by Christmas 1940.

In 1941 Donald was appointed Pipe Major. Col. Murray says a pipe band had been formed at Fort George, comprising those young pipers and drummers under the age of 20 and therefore too young to be sent overseas. Donald had the task of welding a mix of these youngsters plus men of low medical category into a coherent band, and later had to cope with the introduction of Cameron Highlanders from Inverness. It seems there had always been friction between the two regiments – and, says Col. Murray, even between battalions of the same regiment.

Willie Young, Pipe Major of the Camerons' band, had been hurt in an accident and downgraded medically, so that Donald took over the training of the pipers, while the drummers were under Drum Major Jock MacPherson – who disapproved of Wee Donald, on two grounds: he was too young and he was a Seaforth. Each regiment had its own traditions about the music, both piping and drumming, with endless disagreements. David Murray describes one of these:

> One pipe band duty that came round regularly was playing drafts of soldiers down to the station at Ardersier. On the first occasion the band led out through the Ravelin Gate (at Fort George) playing in good order. Once clear of the Fort, Jock stopped the band for a breather. When it was time for another blow he confidently announced a Cameron tune, *The Inverness Gathering*! Two Four, the Drums! Then would come the executive Rolls! One, Two! The rolls crashed out fortissimo and the drums launched into an Army Manual 2/4 beating. But given the nod from Wee Donald, the pipers kept their pipes under the oxter. No pipes! Enraged, Jock cut the drmmers off, promised Donald 'you're in trouble', and took a majestic huff. While his back was turned, Donald started the pipers off on the *Dornoch Links* and the *High Road to Gairloch*, both Seaforth numbers. But no drums! And so it went on all the way to the station, pipes without drums, followed by drums without pipes. The boys in the band loved it!

Apparently it took all of D.R.'s tact and diplomacy to restore peace and harmony, 'outwardly at any rate'.

In 1942 Donald was posted as Pipe Major to the 7th (Morayshire) Battalion, in which he remained for the rest of the war, and it was with them that he returned to France for the final push. His Division saw the hardest fighting in Northwest Europe during the push towards Germany, and suffered the highest casualties. The 7th Seaforth played its full part in all the Division's battles from Normandy to the Rhine.

Donald's Commanding Oficer, Lt Col. Peter Hunt later wrote of Donald:

> I always tried to prevent him playing his comrades into battle, which he so dearly wished to do, and for which privilege he importuned me constantly. With one exception, however; no orders of mine could prevent him travelling with my Tactical HQ just behind the leading companies in the assault crossing of the River Rhine by 15 Scottish

Division in March 1945, playing throughout a selection of Seaforth marches [and one Cameron] as we chugged across the river in our small boats. To those who were there, it was inspiring and cheering, and materially helped us to win the day.

The regimental record says much the same: 'Although forbidden (for his own safety) by his Commanding Officer to play his comrades into action in the old style, he evaded this instruction in the closing stages of the campaign, and played the battalion across the river during the assault crossing of the Rhine.'

After the war he was Pipe Major of the 9th Battalion, and held a series of Army piping appointments in the North of Scotland, mainly at Fort George, 'and during this period he rose to the heights of the competitive piping scene'. Alasdair Campbell, in his book *Visiting the Bard and Other Stories* (2003), referred to Shakespeare's dislike of the pipes, adding 'Had Shakespeare heard Wee Donald MacLeod on the bagpipes, he'd have changed his opinion of the instrument.' It was at this time that Donald returned to John MacDonald, Inverness, sharing his instruction with Malcolm MacPherson and Donald MacGillivray. He was also a pupil of Willie Ross at the Castle.

He won the Gold Medal at Inverness in 1947, playing *Glengarry's March*, and the Gold Clasp eight times; he won the Gold Medal at Oban in 1955 with *Patrick Og,* and the Senior Open three times. His wins for light music were innumerable, and he is said to have won the Jig competition at Inverness eleven times, but Angus J. MacLellan could trace only ten – and six times out of that ten he won playing his own compositions. Often, it seems, he gave new works an airing at the Northern Meeting ceilidh in the evening.

He told Angus what happened when he composed *The Seagull:* he had made two parts of it and when filling in the entry form for Inverness, he put down *The Seagull,* meaning to compose the next two parts before the Northern Meeting came round. But he had no time, and when the judges asked for that tune, he suddenly realised he had only two parts; so he had to ad lib the second half, and said that was why the third and fourth parts are somewhat repetitive (his own opinion). He said he got on fine the first time through, but was in trouble when it came to playing the repeat.

Another time he had made a tune he liked, so he gave it four different names and entered them all. On the day, the judges asked him which was the best, not having heard of any of them. 'Oh, they're all good' he said. The tune was eventually called *Roddy MacKay.*

The mythology of Donald MacLeod includes a story he used to tell himself, of an occasion 'at some wee games', when the weather was terrible, the cold rain coming in horizontally on a gale-force wind. The judges retired to sit in a car, and when Donald went out to play they said it was 'own choice of strathspey and reel'. He told them he would play *Atholl Cummers* and *Mrs MacPherson of Inveran*, but when he had tuned and turned round, he saw they had wound up the car window to keep out the rain (and in some versions, they had switched on the radio). So he just played the *Inverness Rant* twice through and the *Piper of Drummond* three times, and they gave him first prize. So he said – the judges denied it.

In a discussion at the Piobaireachd Society Conference in 1988, about the playing of a D gracenote on a D taorluath, it was said that Donald used to play the D gracenote, but claimed he played the B gracenote when facing the bench and the D when he had his back to it, because he found it much easier to do the D – but did anyone believe him? ('as sure as God's in Dingwall,' he would say).

Angus said that in 1957 Donald went round the Games and competed in 34 events, winning 32 outright, coming second in one and getting nothing in one. Angus listed some of his many triumphs, saying rightly that they were too many to give in detail.

The *Piping Times* in its obituary of Pipe Major Sandy Spence (January 2011) told how Donald, a friend of the Spence family, once lent his pipe to Sandy, at Birnam Games, for the jig competition. To Donald's surprise, Sandy – who was an excellent jig player – played *Butterfingers*, which was a recent composition of Donald's and had not then been published. And it won Sandy the first prize, with Donald in second place. Being Donald, he congratulated Sandy on his win, and asked how he had learned the tune. Sandy said he had heard someone else playing it, just once, and had picked it up from that single hearing. Far from being offended, Donald thought this was a great feat and offered congratulations. This was typical of his innate modesty and generosity of spirit.

As a tutor in the army, Donald was teaching many pupils, who included Andrew Pitkeathley, Calum Campbell, Finlay MacNeill, Iain MacFadyen, John MacDougall, Charlie O'Brien, Willie Hepburn and other notable players. And as well as his composing, he was making visits abroad, during which he often made more tunes, some of them composed while airborne.

He left the Army in 1963, after 22 years service and with a full pension, to became a partner in Grainger and Campbell, pipe makers in Glasgow. Angus J. said 'You could never go into that shop in Argyle

Street without three or four of us [policemen] being in the back, some playing chanters, some of us fingering police batons. That was what we used them for. And there was wee Dougie Ferguson yapping about, and Archie MacPhail.'

Angus spoke of Roddie MacDonald (Roddy Roidean), who after his retirement from the police, used to spend hours sitting with Donald in the shop, 'chatting away about tunes and personalities of the piping world. It was a tremendous education these days to go in there and listen to the two of them. I'm sure many of the police patrollers in Glasgow must have been amazed in answering the radio to hear the strains of *Donald Duaghal* or *Lament for the Children* in the background. When they asked where we were, the reply was 'the corner of Buchanan Street at Argyle Street' (where the shop was, 1103 Argyle Street).

In 1968, there was a 'general feeling of disquiet' at the low levels of prize money available to professional pipers. Donald MacLeod was one who decided to do something about it, and he organised a competition under the name the 'Highland Pipers Society'. For this 'he called in a few favours from friends, pupils and acquaintances to get the event off the ground'. Members of the Glasgow Highland Club became involved (Donald was their Honorary Pipe Major), and all the leading players of the time took part, except Donald MacPherson, who was away in the south at the time. Probably only Donald MacLeod could have pulled it off, his prestige and popularity being great enough to attract so much backing.

The event was held in Govan Town Hall. The *Piping Times* for December 2003 published the programme – but not the prize money on offer, believed to have been in the region of £500 for a first place, which was even more enormous at that time than it would be now. Donald himself did not compete, but he judged the piobaireachd with D.R. MacLennan, while John MacLellan and Peter Bain judged the MSR, and all four judges sat for the Slow Air and Jig. There were 20 competitors – were they by invitation? We do not know.

The list for the piobaireachd was:

Iain MacFadyen
John D. Burgess
Ronald Lawrie
Duncan MacFadyen
William MacDonald (Benbecula)
John MacFadyen
Seumas MacNeill
Kenneth MacDonald

John MacDougall
Neil MacEachern (Islay)
Angus MacDonald (Scots Guards)
J.B. Robertson
William Connell
Hugh MacCallum
William M. MacDonald (Inverness)
Robert U. Brown
Hector MacFadyen
Roderick MacDonald (Glasgow Police)
Donald Morrison
R.B. Nicol

Flora MacNeill, who seems to have done the secretarial work, also presented the prizes, and Calum Robertson gave the Vote of Thanks.

What an astonishing array of talent, and, as the *Piping Times* editor remarked, 'the remarkable thing is those who *didn't* make the prize list.'

Kenneth MacDonald won the Piobaireachd with *In Praise of Morag*; John MacDougall was second, playing *Lady Margaret MacDonald's Salute*; and Iain MacFadyen third with *MacCrimmon's Sweetheart*.

In the MSR, Angus MacDonald was first, John Burgess second and Iain MacFadyen third. The Slow Air and Jig was won by John Mac-Dougall with Iain MacFadyen second and Hugh MacCallum third.

This seems to have been a one-off event, promoted by Donald in order to enhance the prestige of professional piping.

After his retirement from the Army Donald competed for only three more years, and then devoted his time to recitals, SPA guest nights, his teaching and his composing. Among his many distinguished pupils at this time was John Wilson of the Strathclyde Police. Donald taught pupils three or four nights a week, and Angus J. MacLellan used to go to Donald's house every Tuesday night; he shared the lesson with Andrew Wright, Dougie Ferguson and Iain MacKay, staying from seven o'clock to half-past nine or ten. When the others left, Angus would sometimes stay on and chat with Donald, learning much useful piping information. Angus declared ('but I wouldn't let anybody else say it') that Donald was only a good teacher if you were a good pupil – he would teach anyone, amateur, professional, military or civilian, old or young, just so long as they were truly interested and showed willing. He was not one to flog reluctant offspring through the beginners' stages just to please their parents.

The New Zealand piper Lewis Turrell gave an interesting account of his lessons with Donald, published in an interview with Roddy

MacLeod in the *Piping Notes* in 1998. Lewis had arrived with letters of introduction from Neville MacKay and Donald MacKinnon, which he nervously gave to Donald MacLeod after a recital, and Donald said 'Oh, I've been looking forward to meeting you', making him feel very welcome ('He was such a humble little fella').

The next Monday, lessons began, and Donald asked him to play a tune. He played *Mrs John MacColl*, and the reaction was 'Oh, perfect, just perfect' and Lewis wondered what on earth he meant, until later he realised he was saying the fingering was fine, but there was no music in it, no heart. 'So Donald went to work on me. He would give you a free rein, but would teach you so clearly the boundaries that you mustn't step over and torture your musical line . . . he would lay it out for you, and away you went . . . you knew you had a bit of room for your own interpretation, and Donald let you do that.' Sometimes Lewis would play a tune and Donald would say 'That's very nice, Lewis, but have you considered it this way?' Donald would then play it himself and Lewis had to pick up instinctively the message implicit in the different interpretation.

Lewis said he knew little piobaireachd, so Donald said 'Well, you will have to have six at least', and Lewis promptly got all six to learn, among all the light music. And he won the piobaireachd at Braemar that year (1957) playing *The Earl of Seaforth,* and the Gold Medal at Inverness in 1958, as well as the strathspey and reel, and the jigs. All on the one day. 'I was such a young fella then, and it was all so intense – it was all due to good teaching really'.

Angus J. told how he himself used to memorise his piobaireachd when standing at an intersection in Glasgow on point duty, directing traffic.

> It was a great place for memorising tunes. I used to just stand there and go *hiharin hiahiodin*. On one particular afternoon I was at the junction of Buchanan Street and Argyll Street and there I was, singing away and directing traffic, when Donald MacLeod and his wife Winnie crossed over just beside me. Donald said 'Good morning, Angus' and I never answered. He went to the other side, and Mrs MacLeod said 'I wonder what's wrong with Angus – that's strange.' And wee Donald stood and looked and then he crossed back over the road again. Still I didn't see him, and then he came back again when I was bringing pedestrians across. I'll never forget it. I was standing there going *hiahiodin*, and this wee voice came at my back '*i eveho hio*'.

During his retirement, in the early 1980s, Donald presented a radio series called *Piobaireachd for the Beginner,* which was very well received in the piping world.

He was awarded the MBE in 1978 for services to piping. David Murray tells how, when he and John MacLellan were compiling the Queen's Own Highlanders Standard Settings book of pipe music, they tried to thank Donald for allowing them complete access to all his compositions. Donald would have none of this, and said 'The regiment owes me nothing; I owe the regiment everything'. Col. Murray adds 'That was typical of Donald MacLeod, modest and unassuming to the end'.

When Angus J. was President of the SPA, a dinner was held in the Grosvenor Hotel, Great Western Road, Glasgow, to honour Donald MacLeod. After many tributes, Donald made a deep impression with his reply:

> When I first heard about this presentation dinner, my first reaction
> was to wonder, what on earth for? I've been listening to you all and
> I'm still wondering what on earth for. All I have ever done is share this
> enjoyment with you and many others, the love of the Highland bagpipe,
> its tradition and its music. I am quite convinced that's all I have ever
> done, nothing else . . .' He ended with a memory of Willie Ross at a
> similar dinner, at which Willie was so nervous that he had reduced the
> notes for his speech to confetti before he stood up to address everyone.
> When it came to the point Willie simply said 'Thank you. But you
> shouldn't have done it', and Donald hoped he sounded as sincere as
> Willie did, that night.

Donald died suddenly, at his home, on 29th June 1982, from a heart attack.

He had been obliged to give up his work in Grainger and Campbell in 1980, on medical advice. In 1993, a ceremony was held at Fort George, the depot of the Seaforth Highlanders, to dedicate a bench to Donald's memory. He had served at Fort George for 16 years, and the Piobaireachd Society was honouring him as it had Willie Ross at the Castle, as well as D.R. MacLennan, and John A. MacLellan. At the ceremony, attended by Mrs Winnie MacLeod, Alasdair Gillies played the Ground of Donald's piobaireachd *Roderick MacDonald's Salute*.

The Donald MacLeod Memorial Competition, in Stornoway, was inaugurated in 1994, and has been held annually ever since (see below, Iain Morrison; Neil MacRitchie).

The regimental account of Donald MacLeod says: 'Like all the truly great pipers of the past, 'Wee' Donald wore his honours lightly. He was always ready to help those less supremely gifted than himself. A brilliant and prolific composer, he published six books of Ceol Beag as well as a collection of piobaireachd composed by himself. He gave much helpful advice during the compilation of this book of pipe music'.

He also made a series of teaching tapes, and recorded several cassette tapes of his own playing, including a double album made in New York on the 1960s.

The *Cabar Feidh* summary concludes: 'When he died, General Sir Peter Hunt, Donald's former Commanding Officer in the 7th Seaforth, wrote "I for one will never forget Wee Donald – a loyal comrade in arms and a fine soldier, as well as a wonderful piper".'

Donald MacLeod composed more than 300 light music tunes and at least 25 piobaireachd works. These are in the modern idiom, and do not conform to the old structural conventions of piobaireachd; critics say that some of them are more like slow airs with variations than true piobaireachd. He himself commented: 'I have followed the traditional tonal pattern, which I feel is best. The old masters of piobaireachd composition were not hampered by slavish adherence to regular bar content, nor was I taught that this, in ceol mor, was an asset.' He added: 'In some tunes variations have not completely followed the themal pattern. This has been deliberate.' Whatever the opinion on that, there is no doubt that they are remarkable for their melodic and musical content, and they are among the very few modern piobaireachd compositions that pipers actually play. Well, they are compulsory at the Stornoway competition.

Sometimes he used tunes, airs or ideas taken from other pipers, but unlike some unscrupulous composers, Donald MacLeod always asked for the original author's permission, and discussed his treatment of the tune with him. Most were only too happy, indeed flattered, to have their work used by the great man. One of them said he felt he had dipped his toe in Donald's glory, and thought it might glow in the dark.

In a Gaelic TV programme on the Alba channel, Colin Kennedy remembered how Donald used to carry in his pockets handfuls of slips of paper with tunes of his own composition written on them. These he used almost as currency, said Colin, and gave the example of an occasion in Campbeltown where Donald was giving a recital in one of the town's hotels. The owner of the hotel usually gave him a bottle of whisky as he never asked for a fee, but this time Donald pulled a tune out of his pocket, asked the inn-keeper his name, and wrote it on the top as the title of the tune, before giving it to him – and the bottle became a crate. A small price to pay for immortality.

Colin as a boy was a pupil of 'Big Donald' MacLean from Lewis, and he recalled a lesson in Glasgow when Donald MacLeod came to sit in. He took no part in the lesson, but afterwards he sent Big Donald money to buy Colin a set of pipes. He felt that the boy was both keen enough and talented enough to have earned a pipe of his own. This seems to have been typical of Donald's kindness and generosity, not to mention his wish to encourage young talent. His own pupils spoke of his kindness to them, especially those from overseas. Like John MacDonald and many other leading players, he never charged for lessons.

It is not possible to list all of the compositions of Donald MacLeod, who was possibly the most prolific composer of light music there has ever been. His works, excluding mere settings and arrangements, include:

The Aberdeen City Police Pipe Band 6/8 M 4
Altnaharra 6/8 M 4
Andrew MacNeill 6/8 J 4
Andrew Paul 6/8 J 4
Angus G. MacLeod 6/8 SA 2
Annie Anderson 2/4 M 4
Auchreoch 6/8 J 4
Balmacara 6/8 M 4
Banff to Victoria 6/8 SA 2
The Banks of the Lossie 9/8 RM 2
Benside 6/8 M 4
The Bernera Bridge 6/8 J 4 (there seems to be dispute about this: some
    say Peter MacLeod made it)
Bieldside 2/4 M 4
The Black Isle 9/8 RM 2
The Bobs from Balmoral 6/8 J 4
The Brig o' Feugh 2/4 M 4
The Bugle Call 6/8 J 4 (this tune can also be played on the bugle)
Butterfingers 6/8 J 4
The Butt of Lewis R 4
The Cannister 6/8 J 4 (this was the by-name of a piping 'character' in
    Sutherland)
Captain Colin Campbell S 4
Captain J.M. Sym 2/4 M 4
Catlodge S 4
Charles Anderson 6/8 J 4
Charlie MacEachern of Conesby 2/4 M 4 (some say this is the work of
    Dugald MacLeod of Portree)
Clachnaharry 2/4 M 4
The Cockerel in the Creel R 4
Colonel J.M. Grant 2/4 M 4
Craig-a-Bodich S 3

Cronan (A Lullaby) 6/8 SA 2

Crossing the Minch 2/4 HP 4

Culbokie R 4 (sometimes attributed to G.S.MacLennan)

Dalintober 6/8 M 4 (Iain Duncan wrote in the *Piping Times* that
John MacKenzie had once asked Donald about the name of this
march. Donald told him that one evening, when he was going home
from his work at Grainger & Campbell's, the bus was passing
along Dalintober Street, near the Kingston Docks, and he thought
Dalintober would be a good name for his latest tune. John later
took him to Dalintober, a district of Campbeltown; Donald's comment was that it looked better there than it did in Glasgow)

The Dancing Gypsy 6/8 J 4

David Crosby Miller 4/4 M 2

Doctor John MacAskill 2/4 M 4

Doctor MacInnes's Fancy 2/4 HP 4

Doctor Ross's 50th Welcome to the Argyllshire Gathering 6/8 M 4

Donald Cameron's Powder Horn 6/8 J 4 (composed after Donald
Cameron's grandson had presented him with the powder horn)

Donald MacLellan of Rothesay 2/4 M 4

Donald MacLennan's Tuning Phrase 6/8 J 4 (sometimes confused
with *Donald MacLennan's Exercise,* by G.S.MacLennan)

Drumlithie R 4

The Duck 6/8 J 2 (made in Maryhill Barracks in 1939, for a piper in
the 2nd Battalion Seaforth who stood and walked on the platform
like a duck)

Duncan Johnstone 2/4 HP 4

Duncan Lamont R 4 (made in Edinburgh in 1942. It is also played as
a Strathspey)

Duncan MacColl 2/4 M 4

Echo Lake 6/8 SA 2

Elgin Cathedral (The Lantern of the North) 12/8 SA 2

The Fairy Glen 6/8 M 2

The Falls of Forsy S 4

The Falls of Glomach 6/8 M 4

The Ferryman R 4

The Fiddler S 2

Fiona Ferguson 2/4 HP 4

Fiona MacLeod R 4

The Firth of Lorn S 4

Flett from Flotta 4/4 M 2 (said to have been inspired by a long train
journey in the company of John Flett who was carrying the Seaforth

regimental silver to Claridges, for a regimental dinner. Donald's daughter, Susan, in a letter to the *Piping Times* in 2012, wrote that John had been ordered not to let the silver out of his sight, and that was why he was travelling in the guard's van 'with their practice chanters going all the way' – but see above for a different version, probably fictional. According to the *Piping Times,* John (or Jock) Flett had rescued an injured seagull, and after he had restored it to full health it would come each day for food from John. 'Donald very cleverly weaves into the tune the gull's cry for food and attention'. John served 22 years in the Seaforth, seeing action in North Africa and Italy. In 1967 he emigrated to Australia, where he died in 1998, aged 87. He came from Garson, Flotta, in Orkney).

Francis Rushbrooke Williams S 4

The Garry Sands 6/8 M 4

The Glasgow City Police Pipers 6/8 J 4

The Glasgow Highland Club 2/4 SA 2 (see above)

The Glasgow Police Pipers 6/8 J 2

Glasgow Skye Association Centenary Gathering 2/4 M 4

Glen Mallan 6/8 J 4

Glen Orchy 6/8 J 4

Glenshee S 4

Glentruim S 4

The Hammer on the Anvil 6/8 J 4

The Hen's March 6/8 J 4 (This jig was preceded, some 300 years earlier, by Iain Dall MacKay's piobaireachd work, *The Hen's March O'er the Midden*)

The Heroes of Dunkirk 3/4 M 3

The 51st Highland Division 4/4 M 2 (made in 1941 when the Division was re-formed, after the disaster at St Valery)

The 92nd Highlanders at the Maya Pass 2/4 M 4

The Hills of Kintail 2/4 M 4

The Hills of Kintail 12/8 SA 2

HMS Escalator 2/4 HP 2

Ian Fraser of Foregin 6/8 J 4

Jack Adrift 2/4 HP 4

Jack Aloft 2/4 HP 4

J.L. MacKenzie, Aberdeen S 4

John Garroway R 4

John Morrison MacDonald 2/4 M 4

Kildonan R 4

Kirsty McCracken's Brogues 6/8 J 4

The Kiwi 2/4 HP 2
The Knightswood Ceilidh 2/4 M 4
Lachie's Lullaby 18/8 SA 2
The Laird of Tollcross 2/4 M 4
Leaving Bombay 6/8 M 4
Leaving Lewis 6/8 SA 2
The Lintie R 2 (1944)
Lochluichart R 4
Loch MacLeod 3/4 RM 2
The Long Island 6/8 M 2 (= Lewis and Harris)
MacKay of Strath Halladale 6/8 M 2
MacLeod of Mull 6/8 M 4
Malcolm Ferguson 6/8 SA 4
The Man from Skye 2/4 HP 4
Mary of Dunvegan 4/4 M 3
Master Michael Martin 2/4 M 4
The Maypole 6/8 J 2
The Mill in the Glen 6/8 J 4
Miss Elspeth Stewart 2/4 M 4
Mrs Arthur MacKerron 2/4 SA 2
Mrs Donald MacLeod 6/8 SM 4 (his wife; this was composed in 1946)
Mrs Duncan MacFadyen 2/4 M 4
Mrs MacDonald of Uig 2/4 M 4 (the wife of Dr Allan MacDonald;
    made in 1942)
Neil Angus MacDonald R 4 (see above, Barra)
The Northern Meeting Ceilidh 6/8 J 4
25th of November 1960 6/8 M 4
The Old Women's Dance 6/8 J 4
Pipe Major Donald MacLean of Lewis 6/8 M 4 (made when Wee
    Donald took over from Big Donald as Pipe Major of the Highland
    Brigade Piping School in 1948)
Pipe Major George Allan 2/4 HP 4
Pipe Major J. McWilliams 2/4 M 4
Pipe Major Willie MacLeod 2/4 M 4
The Piper's Polka polka 4
The Primrose Hill 6/8 M 4
The Ramparts R 2 (1942)
The River Creed 6/8 M 4
Roddy MacKay 6/8 J 4
Roderick MacDonald R 4
Rory MacLeod 6/8 J 4

The Ross Battery 6/8 M 4 (1941. The Ross Battery Headquarters was
  in Stornoway)
Rothiemurchus 2/4 M 4
Sally's Party 6/8 J 4
Sandy MacPherson S 4
The Seagull 6/8 J 4
The Shoreline of Lewis 6/8 SA 2
Stac Polly S 4
Stornoway Bay 3/4 RM 2
The Stornoway Hornpipe 2/4 HP 4
The Summer Isles 6/8 SA 2
Susan MacLeod S 4 (his daughter, born at Fort George. This tune was
  made just before her marriage)
Tomnahurich 2/4 SM 2
Urquhart Castle 2/4 M 4
Walter Douglas MBE 2/4 M 4
The Weaver 9/8 J 4
Wee Eilidh Miller 6/8 J 4
Whatever Moreover 6/8 J 4
White Rock 2/4 SA 4

His piobaireachd works include:

Alistair MacLeod Miller's Salute P 5 (for his grandson)
A.S. MacNeill of Oransay's Salute P 5
The Battle of Britain P 7
Cabar Feith Gu Brath P 6 (This was played to great effect by Niall
  Matheson at the graveside at the funeral of Pipe Major Alasdair
  Gillies in Ullapool, in 2011)
The Corrievrechan Lullaby (Cronan Coirebhreacain) P 5 (The Coire
  Bhreacain is a multiple whirlpool lying in the narrow strait between
  the north end of Jura and the island of Scarba. At certain states of
  the tide it is dangerous, and traditionally it is said to sing '*Pos mi
  's posadh mi thu*' (Marry me and I will marry you), that is, once in
  my clutches, I've got you. Donald MacLeod's note adds 'There is an
  old Gaelic song of the same title'
Cronan Phadruig Seumas P 6
The Field of Gold P 6 (inspired by the sun shining on a field of butter-
  cups, 'giving this enchanting acre a look of burnished gold')
The Garden of Roses P 7 (for Donald's wife, whose maiden name was
  Garden and 'by dint of much hard work and care, she has turned a
  veritable desert into a place of beauty')

Lament for Angus MacPherson of Invershin P 8 (Angus was the son of Calum Piobaire, and kept open house for pipers at the Inveran Hotel, near Invershin, Sutherland. Donald's comment: 'During his long association with piping and pipes, his gentlemanly manner endeared him to all')

Lament for Duncan MacFadyen P 5 (this was Duncan senior, father of the piping MacFadyen brothers)

Lament for Islay Flora MacLeod P 6 (the wife of a Pipe Major in Manitoba)

Lament for John MacDonald, Inverness P 6

Lament for John Morrison of Assynt House P 6

Lament for the Bobs of Balmoral P 7 (Robert Nicol and Robert U. Brown, both ghillies at Balmoral, were fellow pupils with Donald, going to John MacDonald, Inverness. 'They spared no effort to teach others what they themselves had learned')

Lament for the Iolaire P 6 (the *Iolaire* was the ship bringing servicemen home to Lewis for New Year 1919. She struck rocks when approaching Stornoway, and hundreds of lives were lost)

Lament for the Rowan Tree P 5 (the rowan tree symbolises the empty ruins of houses abandoned in the clearances of the 19th century)

Neil Angus MacDonald's Salute P 5

Queen Elizabeth the Second's Salute P 4

Roderick MacDonald's Salute P 6 (for Roddy MacDonald, Roddy Roidean, of the Glasgow City Police)

The Rothiemurchus Salute P 8 (dedicated to Col. J.P. Grant of Rothiemurchus, well known as a judge and piping authority)

Salute to a White Primrose P 7 (after a friend gave Donald cuttings of a white-flowered primrose plant)

Salute to the Few P 7 (dedicated to the RAF fighter pilots who won the Battle of Britain in 1940)

Salute to the Glasgow Highland Club P 5 (the club covered 'all ethnic aspects of Scotland' and many of its members were amateur pipers)

The Son's Salute to his Parents P 7

The Sound of the Sea P 6

Arrangements and settings include:

Amazing Grace 6/4 SA 1
Athol Cummers 6/8 J 6
The Badge of Scotland (from John MacKay) 4/4 SM 4
The Banjo Breakdown (parts 3&4) 6/8 J 4
The Battle of Waterloo 4/4 M 2 (an old tune which Donald got from

Stewart Salmond, who may have had it from Angus MacLeod, Dundee)

The Blackberry Bush (parts 3&4) R 4

The Black-haired Maid R 4

The Black Mill R 2

The Blackthorn Stick (parts 3&4) 6/8 J 4

The Bride's Jig (Lord Dunmore's Jig) 6/8 J 4

The Bridge of Perth, or *Brig o' Perth,* (parts 3&4) S 4 (based on an old song about Finlay and his speckled dog who danced back and forth on the bridge)

The Brown-haired Maid (or *Ca' the Ewes)* R 6

Cabar Feidh S 4

Calum Beag (parts 2–4) 2/4 HP 4

The Cameronian Rant S 8

Charlie's Welcome R 8

*Clydeside (*parts 3&4) 2/4 HP 4

The Crofter (parts 3&4) 6/8 J 4

Cuaich Side (parts 3&4) R 4

The Dairymaid (parts 3&4) 6/8 J 4

Dunoon Castle 2/4 M 4

The First of May (parts 2&3) 6/8 J 5

The Gaelic 6/8 J 4

Going Home 2/4 SM 3

The Green Garter 6/8 J 4

The Highland Brigade at Waterloo 6/8 M 4

The 93rd Highlanders Farewell to Edinburgh 2/4 M 4

The Humours of Cork 6/8 J 4

I Laid a Herring in Salt 6/8 J 4

I'll Gang Nae Mair Tae Yon Toon 6/8 J 4 and 2/4 M 4

An Island Lullaby 2/4 SA 2

Johnny Cope 2/4 M 3 (an old setting which Donald learned from his father, who had played it when in the Seaforth, under Pipe Major William Taylor)

John Paterson's Mare 6/8 J 6

John Roy Stewart S 4 (a hero of the '45)

The Keel Row R 4

The Leg of a Duck (parts 3&4) 6/8 J 4

MacKay from Skye R 4

The Maids on the Green 6/8 J 4

The Man of Kettle R 4

The Meeting of the Waters (parts 3&4) 4/4 M 4

My King Has Landed At Moidart 4/4 GA 3
The Nine-Pint Cogie R 4 (with P. Wright)
The Old Dirk 6/8 SA 2
Over to Uist (parts 3&4) 6/8 J 4
The Persevering Lover 6/8 M 4
The Reel of Bogie S 2
The Road to Balquhidder 4/4 M 2
Roddy MacDonald's Fancy R 4
The Rowan Tree 4/4 SM 2
The Sailor's Hornpipe 2/4 HP 2
The 3rd Seaforth Highlanders 2/4 M 2
The Shaggy Grey Buck 6/8 J 8
The Smith of Chilliechassie R 6
The Smith's a Gallant Fireman S 2
The Tailor's Wedding 6/8 J 4
Take Your Gun to the Hill S 2
Tam Glen 6/8 M 2
The Tenpenny Bit 6/8 J 4
The Thief of Lochaber (parts 3&4) 6/8 J 4
Thomson's Dirk R 4
A Traditional Reel R 2
Traditional Reel (parts 3&4) R 4
The Wee Highland Laddie (2nd part) 4/4 M 2

Tunes made for Donald MacLeod:

Donald MacLeod is a 4-part Reel composed by Donald MacLeod
    senior, his father
Donald MacLeod is a Reel in 4 parts made in 1938 by Peter MacLeod
    senior
Donald MacLeod is a 4-part Hornpipe by J.A. Barrie
Memories of 'Wee Donald' is a 4/4 March made by Ian Crichton
Pipe Major Donald MacLeod is a 2/4 March by Jimmie Ritchie
Pipe Major Donald MacLeod's Farewell to Fort George is a 2/4
    March by Alex. M. MacIver
*Pipe Major Donald MacLeod's Farewell to the Queen's Own
    Highlanders* is a 2/4 March by Hugh Fraser
Pipe Major Donald MacLeod's Welcome to Fort Quappelle 1969 is a
    2/4 March by William J. Watt

He published his first collection of bagpipe music in 1954, the second
in 1957, the third in 1962 (with an introduction signed by the Duke of
Argyll), the fourth in 1967; the fifth and sixth were undated.

Additions and corrections to the above lists will be welcomed.

Sources

Angus J. MacLellan, *Proceedings of the Piobaireachd Society Conferences*
Ian Mitchell, *The Isles of the West*
Chrissie Morrison, Uig, Skye
Piping Notes
Piping Times
Queen's Own Highlanders, *The Cabar Feidh Collection*

James Macgregor

A story is told of a Lewis piper, JAMES MACGREGOR, who was a seaman in the days before steam engines, sailing 'before the mast'. On one voyage, the ship was off the Fiji Islands, and the crew was running out of fresh water.The Fijians were known to be hostile, and believed to be cannibals at that time, but the need for water was desperate, so a boat was launched to go ashore to refill their barrels. They were met by a hail of arrows. It just happened (!) that James had his pipes with him, so he started playing a tune and instantly the terrified natives scattered. The barrels were filled, to a musical accompaniment, and the voyage was able to continue.

(Thanks to the *Stornoway Gazette* for permission to use this story.)

'Big Donald' MacLean

Born in Balantrushal, Lewis, in 1908, DONALD MACLEAN served 22 years with the Seaforth Highlanders. He was known in the piping world as 'Big' Donald MacLean, or 'Donald MacLean of Lewis', to distinguish him from 'Wee' Donald MacLean of Oban and Glasgow. David Murray described him as 'a fine player, famous for his robust and solid tone'.

He came of a piping family, with links to many other pipers in Lewis. His great-nephew, Norman MacRitchie, in an interesting article in the *Piping Times* in March 2009, told how at the age of eight he amused his family by marching round with the blackened fire-tongs as his 'drones', and the family cat under his arm for the bag – doubtless playing a raucous tune.

His first teacher was PETER STEWART in Barvas, who gave lessons to him and his brother MURDO on the chanter as they passed his house on their way home from school. Donald left home in1926, to join the Seaforth Highlanders, saying that someone had to make enough to keep the bodachs back home in tobacco – his elder brothers having become a doctor and a teacher, both requiring long training with no wage. At that time, he played with his drones on the right shoulder (or, as it is sometimes put, he walked on the wrong side of his pipes). Some regard this as a sign of left-handedness, but many pipers from the islands played that way and regarded it as more natural. The army would have none of it and ordered him to change to the left shoulder, to avoid upsetting the symmetrical appearance of the Pipe Band on parade (David Murray says it was also to avoid the tassels and ribbons tickling the officers' bald heads when the piper was playing round the table in the Officers' Mess). Donald had to conform, and ever afterwards he played with his drones on the left shoulder – but kept his right hand on top.

He gained his Pipe Major's Certificate in 1931, when a Corporal in the 1st Battalion Seaforth Highlanders, and is said to have become the youngest Pipe Major in the army. Five years later he moved to the 2nd Battalion as Pipe Major. His training included tuition from D.R. MacLennan, Willie Ross and Angus MacPherson. In 1937 he played *The Corn Riggs Are Bonny* at a tattoo staged at Ibrox Park in Glasgow, a choice of tune he may have felt was suited to a lowland venue, though corn riggs are few around Ibrox.

He was renowned for the strength and volume of his pipe. In 1939, just before leaving for France, he was playing a pipe with Robertson drones and a MacRae chanter. Even in later life he played very strong reeds. Donald MacGillivray once had to take over his pipe when Donald was 'a wee bit under the weather', and said he had to lie down for a few minutes afterwards to recover, they were so tough to blow – 'but what volume'.

John D. Burgess used to tell how at one of the Games he found that his bag had become porous so that his reeds were getting damp, and he could not play his pipe; Big Donald MacLean offered him the loan of his – but the reeds were so strong that John could not blow them. Donald then exchanged them all, putting John's own reeds into his pipe, and John then played happily in the competition. He said spectators were marvelling at how easily he managed those strong reeds of Donald's.

On another occasion, Sheriff Grant and Dr Simpson were to judge at the Uist Games, and on the boat going over, they persuaded Big Donald to play. The crossing was rough, and everyone else was sheltering, well wrapped up, but Donald was out on deck, exposed to the elements, and played on and on, oblivious of the weather. The Sheriff said 'That man is wind, water and weather proof'.

He went to France with the 2nd Seaforth in 1939 and was captured at St Valery in 1940, to spend the rest of the war in a POW camp. He lost his practice chanter somewhere en route, but one of his pipers, ALEC CRAIG from Northern Ireland, had managed to keep his, tucked into his socks in his small back-pack, and he was happy to let Donald have it, being his Pipe Major, teacher and mentor. Alec was proud to know that *Major Manson at Clachantrushal* was composed on his chanter. Donald also composed his Retreat March *Heroes of St Valery* while in the camp; presumably the heroes included himself. In June 2002, the *Piping Times* printed on its cover a photograph of Donald MacLean and Donald MacLeod in uniform, with the caption 'Heroes of St Valery'.

After the war he became Pipe Major at the Highland Infantry Training Centre at Redford Barracks, Edinburgh, and later at Fort George, near Inverness. The account of his career in *Cabar Feidh*, the Queen's Own Highlanders Collection, says: 'He was a Seaforth to the core, and when told by his Cameron Company Commander at Redford Barracks that he had just seen a rat in the pipe store, he replied 'And was it wearing a Cameron kilt?'

On his retirement he worked as manager of the piping department of R.G. Lawrie, the Glasgow pipe makers, from 1953 to 1964, 'and his famous right over left fingering stance featured in their advertisements'. While in Glasgow he was Pipe Major of the 5/6th Battalion Highland Light Infantry. He was also President of the SPA for a while.

He won the Gold Medal at Oban in 1951, playing the *MacDonalds' Salute,* and at Inverness in 1953, with *Black Donald's March.* He was a good teacher, who kept Hector MacFadyen in piping when he was on the verge of giving it up to specialise in the 'heavy' events at the Games. It was said that the distinctive playing style of Donald MacLean was discernible in Hector's piobaireachd. Donald played the old version of *Lochaber No More* at the funeral of Willie MacLean, a memorable performance worthy of the old master.

He was also a fine highland dancer, as many pipers were in the old days, and he taught dancing in both Skye and Lewis.

Big Donald MacLean died suddenly, after the Cowal Games, in 1964. His grave is at Barvas, in Lewis.

His compositions include:

The Angler's Lament 4/4 SM 2
Colin MacKenzie of Stornoway 6/8 M 4

Heroes of St Valery 3/4 RM 4
Major Manson at Clachantrushal 2/4 M 4
Major Manson Strides to the Isles 6/8 J 4
Minnie Hynd 6/8 J 4
Mrs Manson's Birthday
Sandy Oliphant R 5

Note also *Pipe Major Donald MacLean of Lewis*, by Donald
  MacLeod 6/8 M 4
and *Pipe Major Donald MacLean of Lewis*, by C. MacLeod
  Williamson 6/8 M 4

Was *Donald MacLean* by Donald Morrison (6/8 J 4) made for Big or
Wee Donald MacLean? Published in Duncan Johnstone's Collection of
Pipe Tunes.

Note that *Donald MacLean* (R or J 4) by Peter R. MacLeod was
named for the other Donald MacLean, 'Wee Donald' of Oban.

Sources

College of Piping
Donald MacGillivray
Norman MacRitchie, *Piping Times*, March 2009
David Murray
Queen's Own Highlanders, *The Cabar Feidh Collection*

Major David Manson

DAVID MANSON (1867–1959) was born in Lewis, but in 1895 he went
out to Halifax, Nova Scotia, as official piper to the North British Society of Halifax. He was a former Pipe Major of the 72nd Highlanders
and of the Shepherds' Pipe Band of Hamilton, and was also a champion
Highland dancer. Scott Williams writes:

> The North British Society had written offering him a six-month
> position at a salary of 30/- [shillings] Sterling a week, with passage
> paid to Halifax. He accepted, and arrived in Halifax aboard the
> steamer *Assyrian* during the summer. A splendid reception was given
> him by the Society at the Halifax Hotel. There was a large attendance
> of members and guests. President Forbes presided over the meeting and
> offered words of welcome in which he described Manson as the best
> piper in his native Ross-shire and one of the top five pipers in all of
> Scotland.

In 1895? A doubtful judgement – John MacDonald, John MacDougall

Gillies, John MacColl, Angus MacRae, Robert Meldrum, Willie MacLean, John MacBean, Danny Campbell, David Mather and Calum Piobaire's sons would surely all rank before Manson. Was this rating perhaps Manson's own?

The following year he was confirmed as official piper, and again in 1897, and his music was said to be 'superb'. He was granted a new tunic and waistcoat, and was paid for reeds he sent for from Scotland. But early in 1897 he resigned, to take up a more lucrative position in Montreal, which caused some resentment in Halifax. He became Pipe Major to the 5th Royal Scots, and later to the Black Watch (Royal Highland Regiment) of Canada, a post he held from 1897 to 1907. After that he was given a commission, the only piper ever to become an officer in Canada, and he abandoned his rank of Pipe Major. He ended up as a Major in the Black Watch of Canada.

In the First World War, however, it is said that he served as Pipe Major of the 13th Battalion of the Canadian Black Watch, and seems to have been Pipe Major of the Royal Scots after John Matheson retired. It is not clear how this sat with his commission.

He was one of the first to wear tartan trews to perform the dance *Sean Triubhais* ('Old Trousers'), which set a fashion in the competitions.

After 50 years in the Canadian army he returned to Scotland (he was back before 1940, so these figures do not quite tally), and was famed as 'the only Pipe Major to have advanced to commanding rank as commander of Canadian pipe bands during World War I'. Norman MacRitchie wrote of an occasion in the Grand Hotel, Charing Cross, in Glasgow, shortly before the start of World War II, when Manson was with Big Donald MacLean. Manson produced a chanter from inside his walking stick, and bade Donald play, while he spent 'a huge wad of five pound notes' on drams all round. This seems to have been a typical Manson gesture, flamboyant and generous.

The reel *Major Manson* was composed for him by Peter MacLeod, and for his wife, *Mrs Manson's Birthday*. Big Donald MacLean made *Major Manson at Clachantrushal* and *Major Manson Strides to the Isles*. *Major Manson at Clachantrushal* is sometimes (but erroneously) called *Major Manson's Farewell to Clachantrushal*; it is said to have been made by Donald when he was a POW in Germany, remembering the day he went with Major Manson to see the Standing Stone at Clachantrushal, near Donald's home village of Balantrushal, on the west coast of Lewis, a few miles north of Barvas. There is an impressive photograph of the stone, which stands some 20 feet high, in Donald MacDonald's book on Lewis (Plate 4).

In 1955, at the age of 88, David had a bad accident, falling down the stairs in his home. He fractured his skull and his wrist. The following year he spent the whole winter in hospital in Montreal. He died in Canada in 1959, aged 92.

Sources

Donald MacDonald, *Lewis: A History of the Island*
Norman MacRitchie
Piping Times
Queen's Own Highlanders, *The Cabar Feidh Collection*
Scott Williams, *Pipers of Nova Scotia*

The Chisholm Family

Mrs Christina (Chrissie) Morrison, latterly living in Uig, Skye, was the daughter of MALCOLM CHISHOLM, a Pipe Major in the 4th Cameron Highlanders. He is sometimes referred to as William Chisholm as his army nickname was 'Bill'. He served in the Sudanese War, and in 1898 played at the Battle of Atbara, using the same pipes he was still playing in 1947, the year he died. On leaving the army he was Pipe Major of the Inverness British Legion Band, and honorary piper to the Gaelic Society of Inverness.

Chrissie described her father as a 'blether, a teller of long, short and tall tales, but he was a good raconteur. Although we found it boring when we were young, we wish now that we had listened more to his stories as he was steeped in the history and the folklore of the Highlands.'

When she first went to the Cameron Barracks during the Second World War, she met some of the 1st Battalion Cameron Highlanders who had been abroad with her eldest brother, Angus. 'When they were posted from India to Khartoum, just before the outbreak of war, one old fellah there approached Angus and brought him round to the back of the Barracks to show him a printed plaque beside a huge nail, which, he told Angus, marked the spot where my Dad tore his kilt, when trying to get back in after "Lights Out", when he was stationed there, circa 1900.'

The Chisholm children were told many stories by their Dad, not necessarily at bedtime. When one of them was afraid to go to the dentist, he told them the Celtic tale of Finn and his tooth of knowledge, making them dwell on the wonder of the story rather than the horror of the dental instruments. He had a typical Hebridean sense of humour, and liked playing tricks on his friends. He enjoyed teaching pipers – so long as they were boys – or at least male. He did have some female pupils but taught them under protest, as he did not really approve of women playing the pipes.

The family came from Back in Lewis, and Chrissie's mother was related to Iain Morrison's mother, her father to Iain's paternal grandfather. Chrissie's cousin in Lewis, Mary Chisholm, married the Canadian piper, Iain MacCrimmon, who became the MacLeod Clan Piper in Dame Flora's day.

Although the Chisholm children were brought up in Inverness, they were taken to Lewis every summer for the whole of the school holidays. Chrissie says she doesn't remember seeing any bagpipes, but every family had a son who played the chanter, so fathers must have been teaching sons. This was between the wars. Her father used to tune his pipes with part of the piobaireachd *Too Long in this Condition*.

Chrissie's husband 'wasn't a piper, but he could play simple tunes like *Corriechoille* and *The Braes of Mar* on the chanter, and said his father taught him'. She had a busy life, bringing up five children, helping her husband in his one-man business, as well as working for a firm of solicitors in Portree and operating the part-time Registrar's post from their home in Uig. As if this was not enough, she was also involved with the Children's Panel (dealing with juvenile offenders), the Girl Guides, the Community Council, and assisting the Skye Week Secretary. Before her marriage, during the war she was called up as a member of the ATS (she was in the women's territorial army), and stationed at the Cameron Barracks in Inverness, where she met many notable army pipers. She was later posted to the War Office.

Malcolm Chisholm had a family of seven piping sons, including ANGUS, CALUM, IAIN, KENNY and JACK CHISHOLM. They were all taught by their father, using both written music and canntaireachd; three of them became Pipe Majors themselves. In the summer they competed as Juniors at the Games, joined by the youthful Donald MacLeod who came over from Lewis to stay with the Chisholms in Inverness, and competed along with the Chisholm boys. At first the Chisholm boys tended to tease Donald, because he was so wee and stuck his bottom out when playing, but he silenced them by beating them in the competitions. Their sister Chrissie said that in those days (between the wars), John MacDonald, Inverness, used to approach the junior prize winners and suggest they should come to him for tuition, but her brothers politely declined, telling him they were happy enough with their father's teaching.

Chrissie said, however, that both Calum and Jack did go for a while to John MacDonald – 'because Mr MacDonald was a constant visitor to the house and Dad thought it might be as well for them to have some lessons – but that was when they were about 14 and had already learnt their basic skills from Dad. We thought Mr MacDonald was a grumpy old man, but we liked Mr Meldrum. The difference was that Mr Meldrum was married with a family, but Mr MacDonald had no family and didn't understand children.'

Today the Chisholms are not household names, even in piping households, because they did not compete much as adults. Chrissie could not recall her father ever competing, and her brothers stopped competing around the age of 18, their piping careers cut short by the war. But the family was steeped in piping tradition, and her father used to judge at competitions. One thing he could not abide, and that was pipers playing tunes which do not fit the scale of the pipe, and in particular he abhorred Scott Skinner's *Cameron Highlanders* being played on the pipe. (Many dislike *Flowers o' the Forest* as a pipe tune, for the same reason.) He and his wife knew Scott Skinner well, and Chrissie's mother used to sing Gaelic songs for him, when she was working for Dr Keith Norman MacDonald, grandson of Niel MacLeod of Gesto.

Chrissie said they had a family scrap-book and in it was a photograph of her brother Jack, aged 14, with Pipe Major Robert Meldrum, and the caption was 'Oldest and Youngest Competitors at Northern Meeting Games'. As long as her brothers were living, they all used to meet up at the Northern Meeting every year – but in 2000, when Chrissie was 81, she wrote 'they are all dead now'. It was Pipe Major Jack Chisholm, who composed *Clachnaharry* (S 4), *Evan MacRae's Beard* (R 4) and *Walking the Floor* (sleepless nights with his firstborn; this tune is popular with Scottish dance bands). *Clachnaharry,* a lively strathspey, appears in the Queen's Own Highlanders Collection (*Cabar Feidh,* 1983), with a note that it was composed after Jack had visited the village of Clachnaharry on the west side of Inverness, and had been followed by a black cat, which he took to be a good omen.

As boys, Chrissie's brothers joined either the Boy Scouts' Pipe Band or the Boys' Brigade Pipe Band, depending on which they thought was better: both provided a good piping training for youngsters. The well-known fiddle player, 'Pibroch' MacKenzie, was also a piper, and he too had been trained in the Boys' Brigade band, along with one of Chrissie's brothers.

With seven brothers the house was seldom quiet, and Chrissie had memories of a day when she was sitting at the kitchen table doing her homework while her mother sat peacefully sewing. The door burst open and four of her brothers marched in, 'round and round the table playing *Lord Lovat's Lament*, with two playing alto'. Chrissie shouted 'I can't stand the noise', and went off to the Room where she banged away on the piano to drown them out – in later years she said she would give anything to hear them playing again.

It is clear that the Chisholm family grew up steeped in piping tradition. She remembered 'listening, enthralled, to the legends behind the music – about the ship coming in to Dunvegan and the crew came ashore with the smallpox, so that MacCrimmon lost seven of his eight sons'. She was moved by the story of the MacKintosh chief dying on the afternoon of his wedding day, when he fell from his horse – 'and my brother Calum used to play me *The Battle of the Birds*, and tell me to listen to the sound of the birds screeching'.

Her youngest brother, like the others, was taught his piping by his father but at 11 he said he would like to play the fiddle; they sent him to the Sarah Walker School of Music, to learn the violin. Then he showed he was different in another way, by joining the Royal Navy instead of the Camerons – most of his brothers were Cameron Highlanders – but by the time the war was over, he had outgrown the wish to break away, and had returned to his first love, the pipes.

One of the brothers, Iain, who served with the Royal Engineers in World War II, was awarded the Belgian Croix-de-Guerre and Palm, but never spoke of this award, and the citation gave no details, so that the family did not really know why Iain had been given it. He was a great friend of Joe Henderson, who was with him in the Royal Engineers. Iain said Joe had taught him a number of Irish Rebel songs, but warned him never to sing them in Glasgow.

Chrissie's brother Kenny was a keen Highland dancer, in the days when girls were banned from the dancing competitions at many of the Games. Kenny as a boy was thrilled when he won first prize at Nairn, beating the reigning champion, MacNiven Cuthbertson.

Another brother, Jack, joined the Edinburgh Police after the war and was in the Police Pipe Band when it was in its prime. Chrissie said he seemed to spend most of his time abroad with the band, 'in Africa and places like that'. Jack left the Police when he had a letter asking him to go over to Washington to form a pipe band. He went across, and then asked his brother Calum to join him and help to get things going. 'They kitted their band out in Chisholm tartan and both played at John Kennedy's inauguration, and the family album had a photo of Kennedy between my two brothers, and his signature on the photo.'

Jack and Calum were both teachers of piping, and when the Chisholms were living in Skye, pupils would call to see them there. Chrissie told how an American called Frank who worked for the FBI wanted her brother Jack to recommend someone to teach his son to play, and Jack recommended Johnny (Seonaidh) Roidean, John MacDonald of the Glasgow Police, who was then living in retirement in South Uist (see above, South Uist).

Frank paid a large sum of money to have a full-length portrait painted of Johnny, and it was Chrissie who drew up the legal deed when Johnny was given custody of the painting for his lifetime: Frank wanted it to be returned to him after Johnny's death. The legal document was meant to ensure that ownership of the painting would be undisputed, and that it would eventually be sent back to Frank, but unfortunately it was destroyed when Johnny's house burned down. It was, however, fully insured. Chrissie had seen to that.

John Allan ('Jackie' to Chrissie), formerly of the Army School of Piping in Edinburgh Castle, said that Calum Chisholm taught him to play the pipes, presumably when they were both living in Inverness. After retiring from the Army School, 'Jackie' taught for some years at an Edinburgh boys' school, where one of his pupils was a great-nephew of Chrissie's who became a good player. Today (2012), Jackie's two young great-nephews are winning prizes for their piobaireachd playing, taught in Easter Ross by Niall Matheson.

Chrissie recalled a retired Pipe Major, James MacDonald, living in the Beauly area – her father and brothers used to buy their reeds from him.

In 2000, Chrissie took her father's and brothers' medals as a donation to the Fort George Museum, and was given several photos of her father with the 4th Camerons' band at the barracks and during his time in the Sudan war.

It is clear that the Chisholm family from Lewis carried a rich piping tradition, and this has come down to later generations. Though they were not as famous as, say, Wee Donald MacLeod or Big Donald MacLean, their contribution to piping was important as an example of the standards maintained in Highland families, especially those with military backgrounds.

Sources

Niall Matheson
Chrissie Morrison, Uig, Skye
Queen's Own Highlanders, *The Cabar Feidh Collection*

Some prominent Lewis players

W.G. ROSS (WILLIE ROSS), Soval Lodge, Stornoway, was one of the original committee members who founded the Lewis Pipe Band in 1904. He was a well known figure in the piping world and a prominent judge, but one of 'the Jolly Boys'. He composed the 2/4 march *The Lewis Pipe Band,* as well as a 2-part strathspey called *J.F. MacKenzie Esquire of Garrynahine, Stornoway.* It was published in the Scots Guards *Standard Settings Collection.*

In a letter written in 1906 to John Morrison, Assynt House, Colin Cameron wrote 'Should you happen to see Willie Ross Soval, I hope he is very well', so clearly he was a friend of the Cameron family at Maryburgh.

DONALD 'SNOWY' MACLEOD is sometimes confused with his great friend DONALD 'LEODY' MACLEOD: both had close associations with the Lewis Pipe Band for many years.

'SNOWY' MACLEOD of Stornoway was Pipe Major of the 2nd Seaforth at the battle of El Alamein (see David Murray, *Piping Times,* December 2002). He appears in a photograph taken in Aldershot in 1939 of the Pipers of the 2nd Battalion Seaforth shortly before they left for France, when his rank was still Piper. The Pipe Major at that time was 'Big' Donald MacLean, and beside him in the picture is L/Cpl Donald MacLeod. One of the twelve pictured was killed in France; all the rest were captured at St Valery, but Donald MacLeod managed to escape.

After the war, 'Snowy' MacLeod returned to Lewis, where he became a stalwart of the Lewis Pipe Band. His friend Donnie ('Leody') told a tale about Snowy when he was Drum Major. To quote Donnie's own words:

> Looking at his photograph reminds me of the time the Band was going to Inverness to meet up with the regiments from Orkney and Inverness.
>
> Quite a few of the boys had a lot to drink on the boat and we poured them onto the train in Kyle. We got to Inverness, and Snowy, along with this fellow called Angie Zulu, was three sheets to the wind. I was sobering them up with loads of coffee as a lot of people were going to be watching the bands, and Snowy, as Drum Major, had to be sensible as he was leading the whole parade to the train station.
>
> I got him in reasonable order but warned him, saying: 'Now, Snowy, once we're out there and ordered to march, hold the flippin'

mace up against your chest – today is not the day for any of your fancy stuff.'

Snowy was a great guy for swinging the mace about, but he agreed with what I told him, and as we marched he was keeping the mace close to his chest – until he signalled a left turn into the station.

Everything was going well, but Snowy got a wee bit cocky and started swinging the mace about in fine style until he brought it down smartly at the station doorway – straight into a grating.

It stuck fast, and Snowy was there struggling to free it as the whole regiment marched past him. We had quite a job trying to straighten out the mace – it was a right comedy.

Snowy's friend DONNIE 'LEODY' MACLEOD was born in 1928, at 1 Kenneth Street, Stornoway, where the British Legion is now. When he was two years old, his father got a job at Avoch, on the Black Isle, where the family lived for four years. Then his company moved him back to Stornoway, to work on the building of the County Hospital. Donnie by that time was speaking with the (very unusual) Gaelic dialect of Avoch, which none of his schoolmates could understand – it is said to be rooted in an old Pictish dialect. He soon adapted to Lewisach, however, with its strong Norse overtones.

He recalled going with his grandfather to watch the Pipe Band, and his own association with it began in 1942. A boy called Andy 'Hirstoch' MacDonald, who worked alongside Donnie's father, was a tenor drummer in the band, and asked if Donnie would like to be his sidekick. Donnie was then 14, and played the fiddle. Within the week he was out on the street with the band, full of pride but finding the drum rather heavy.

On Friday nights the band used to visit different villages in the island, to raise funds. Donnie tells of a trip to the island of (Great) Bernera, on the west side of Lewis, in the days before there was a bridge across. The band had to be ferried over in a rowing boat, equipment and all, and all went well on the way out. They marched in full regalia to the hall at Breaclete, where there was a crowd of people, and a good night ensued, with the concert followed by a dance. After the dance there were a few drams (surely not?), before the boys made their way back down the road in the dark, to meet the ferryman, who had promised to be ready for them at 3 a.m. He had forgotten all about them, however, and was in his bed, and when roused said he couldn't pick them up from the slipway because the tide was running too strong, and the only way it would be possible was if they made their way further along the shore where the channel was wider. What he didn't tell them was that the shore at that point was large boulders covered in wet seaweed.

> We were slipping and sliding all over the place, with our pipes and drums and kit, in the dark – all we had for light was a local man leading us with a wee torch. The shuttle run by boat started again, and after a few choice words to the ferryman, we eventually got back to town at around 7 a.m. Our white spats were not so white any more.

Donnie then did his National Service, before he decided to go to Canada to work as a mechanic. He moved on to become an inspector with an aircraft company, Avro. In Canada he played with the Legion Pipe Band, but in 1954 he returned to Lewis, a sea journey which was memorable for his climbing on a table to dance the Highland Fling, and falling off to break his leg, so that he arrived home in plaster.

Donnie married at this time and was given work as an administrator of the Lovat Scouts group, which also ran a Pipe Band, largely made up of ex-servicemen.

In his article for the *Stornoway Gazette*, Donnie recalled the two barbers in the Lovat Scouts Territorial Pipe Band, Pipe Major Murdo 'Bogey' MacLeod and Murdo 'Steve' MacKenzie, a Drum Sergeant. They often put on an impromptu performance in the shop, one playing the chanter, the other rattling the drumsticks on a table. 'It was good fun', said Donnie, 'like having a mini pipe band playing in front of you'.

Steve liked a good dram, and one Saturday morning he was feeling rough after a heavy session the night before, when who should come in for a shave but the minister. The holy man sat down and Steve sharpened the open razor and soaped up the minister's face. Unfortunately on the first pass of the razor he drew blood from his client, who turned to him and said 'Well, well, Steve, the drink is a terrible thing', to which Steve replied 'Yes indeed, minister, doesn't it make the skin soft'.

In 1978 the Queen came to Lewis to open the new Council building, and Donnie composed a commemorative tune *Comhairle nan Eilean's Welcome to Queen Elizabeth*. He said later: 'I felt great pride and got a real lift from hearing my tune played by the band. I met the Queen, and received a letter informing me that the tune was to be included in her Pipers' Repertoire.'

Donnie composed many tunes over the years, including one that opened the first Mod held in Stornoway, in 1979. He is publishing his collected works in a volume entitled *Original Tunes in Traditional Highland Style*.

Now retired, Donnie gives fiddle lessons in the Laxdale Hall on Monday nights, and is also a repairer of fiddles. When asked if the old adage is true, 'The older the fiddle, the better the tune', Donnie burst out laughing and said 'No, no – I'm standing proof of that – half of me doesn't work, and the other half hurts.' He has, however, an excellent old fiddle made in 1898, and it has a great tone.

Donnie played with the Pipe Band for 42 years, the last 18 as Drum Major, and retired from active duties in 1984 – but has served on the committee ever since, helping to raise the £60,000 needed to clothe and equip the players.

DONALD RUADH MACLEOD was a piper from Arnol – see above, Harris, Alex John MacLeod and John MacKinnon.

KENNETH MACLEOD is a second cousin of 'Wee' Donald, and was born in Lewis, where he played with the Lovat Scouts. Correspondence in the *Piping Times* in December 2012, from Canadian pipers STEPHEN MITCHELL and BILL PETERS, both from Ontario, outlined his career: he was in the class of Territorial Army pipers studying for their Pipe Major's certificates in 1951, under Captain John MacLellan, a class which included NORMAN GILLIES, JOHN RIACH, CALUM MACPHEE, JOE MASSEY, ALEX MACIVOR, ALEC MCCORMICK and CHRIS SUTHERLAND. The *Piping Times* published a photograph of this class in the editions of October and December 2012.

Kenneth later became Pipe Major of the Lovat Scouts, but in 1962 he and his wife Chrissie Ann left Stornoway, to emigrate to Canada, settling in Port Arthur, Ontario (now called Thunder Bay). There he took up the position of Pipe Major of the MacGillivray Pipe Band, and he taught many pupils during his years in Thunder Bay. In 2000, however, he had a fall downstairs, from which he did not make a full recovery, his appetite for piping having been completely lost.

During his teaching career he played Sinclair pipes, originally mounted in ivory, but later they had what Bill Peters describes as 'non-hallmarked runic style silver mounts added to them'. These pipes are now in the possession of Bill, who bought them from Ken's family, after a period of holding them on loan 'to see if the problems I was having with my own were genuine, or if it was just me that needed fixing . . .' He finally bought them, and plays in Grade One amateur solos in Canada, enjoying his former teacher's instrument. The *Piping Times* for December 2012 has pictures of the Sinclair pipe's silver mounts.

Iain Morrison

IAIN MORRISON was born in Back, Lewis, the son of JOHN MORRISON, himself a piper, who composed *Leaving Ireland* (2/4 SM 2) to commemorate the 1st Battalion Queen's Own Highlanders going home from Northern Ireland. John died in 1982. He should not be confused with John Morrison of Assynt House. Iain Morrison's family is related to the South Uist Morrisons, who include Angus, Donald, Louis and Willie (see above).

Iain joined the Lovat Scouts as a boy piper before going to the Queen's Own Highlanders in 1963. After completing the Pipe Major's course at Edinburgh Castle, a pupil of both John MacLellan and Donald MacLeod, he won the Gold Medal at Inverness in 1969, and also won the Strathspey and Reel competition the same year.

In 1975 he became Pipe Major of the 1st Battalion Queen's Own Highlanders, serving in Germany, Scotland, Belize and Northern Ireland. In 1980 he was appointed Pipe Major of the Scottish Divisional School of Music at Aberdeen; that year he won the Senior Piobaireachd at Oban, the Clasp at Inverness, the Gold Medal at the National Mod, and the Glenfiddich Championship at Blair Castle. Around that time he made a recording, and this was played on the radio in 2002: the *Piping Times*' comment was 'Now that is how you play a march, strathspey and reel. No one plays like that now'.

On leaving the army he retired to his home at Back, one of the few of the great pipers of Lewis to return to live in his native island. He became the highly successful schools piping instructor in Lewis. So great was the response to his tuition that an assistant instructor, NICKY GORDON, was appointed. Nicky, too, is a former Pipe Major of the QOH. Today their pupils are making their mark in the piping world, winning prizes in competitions on the mainland.

Iain has been active with the Lewis and Harris Piping Society, and was a leader in the establishment of the Donald MacLeod Memorial Competition in 1994; it is held in early April of every year, when six leading pipers are invited to compete. The Piobaireachd section is restricted to Donald MacLeod compositions, and each player has to include a Donald MacLeod tune in his light music. A feature of the weekend, held in the Seaforth Hotel, Stornoway, is the great ceilidh on the Saturday evening, with a wealth of Gaelic song and dance. In 1999, the ceilidh seems to have been anticipated: Robert Wallace wrote of the light music competition, in the *Piping Times*:

The outstanding moment came when Angus MacColl tipped up his pipe and launched into a few Gaelic airs as a prelude to his MSR. No sooner had he played the first few notes of *M'eudail, m'aighear, 's mo run* (*My love, my joy, my treasure*) when suddenly the audience of a hundred was providing a vocal backing. Hairs which had lain dormant for years rose on the backs of necks as beautifully tuned bagpipe and native Gaelic vocable combined in a choral symphony fit for the leading auditoria in the land. Yet here we were in the function suite of the Seaforth Hotel, Stornoway. Well, that's just the Donald MacLeod for you, and typical of the magic moments you can experience when you cross the Minch early in April.

Angus, of course, knows his audiences and would have realised he would get this response.

Iain suffered serious illness in 2000, but has made a good recovery; subsequent recitals show that he has lost none of the precise fingering, magical 'lift' and musical interpretation which has always marked his playing. He also suffered for a time from Djupetron's Contracture, or Piper's Finger, a disease of the tissues of the hand which causes the fingers to curl up. Fortunately, Iain's was cured by surgery, and did not recur.

He is now a respected judge at many competitions on the mainland. The compositions of Iain Morrison include:

Angela's Wedding 3/4 RM 2 (made in 1977 for the marriage of the Adjutant, Captain Seymour Munro, to Miss Angela Sandeman)
Arthur Gillies HP 4 (1980)
Chiefy's March 6/8 M 4 (made in 1980 for Sergeant Major 'Chiefy' Reid)
Flora MacIsaac 6/8 J 4
The Ghurka Signals' Farewell to Serembam 6/8 M 4 (1968)
Hasten and Come With Me (arr.) 6/8 SA 1
Hielan' Laddie (arr.) R 2
Highland Reel (parts 3&4) R 4
Lt Col. A.A. Fairrie's March 6/8 M 4 (1977)
Lt Col. I. Cross, RHF 6/8 M 4
Lt Col. J.C.O.R. Hopkinson 6/8 M 4 (1974)
Lt Col. R.D. MacLagan CBE MC 3/4 RM 2 (1976)
Major I.M. Fraser's Farewell 6/8 M 4
The Merry Blacksmith (Paddy on the Railroad) (sett.) R 2
The Ness Pipers R 4

Note also

Iain Morrison, Stornoway, by Arthur Gillies HP 4
Pipe Major Iain Morrison, by James Wark, Strathclyde Police 6/8 J 4

More Lewis Pipers

SCOTT MACAULAY was best known to the piping world as the Principal and Director of the College of Piping, Prince Edward Island (PEI), Canada, but he was a Lewisman by blood, and after his untimely death in 2008, he was buried at Dalmore, in Lewis.

Originally taught by Sandy Keith, he won both the Silver Medal and the Jigs at the Northern Meeting in Inverness, and also published a book of pipe music, and made many recordings. In 1990 he established the PEI College of Piping, and developed it into a world centre as his own unremitting hard work and enthusiasm proved infectious. He addressed the Piobaireachd Society at one of their conferences, explaining how he had gone about the founding of his college. It is hoped that he has left it in safe hands.

RSM MURDO MACLEOD from Lewis was the subject of a 6/8 March by M.J. Purdie in 1981. Murdo was in the 51st Highland Volunteers before becoming RSM in the 1st Battalion Queen's Own Highlanders in 1980.

ALEX MACIVER was President of the Lewis and Harris Association in Glasgow, and was tutor to the 214 Boys' Brigade band. He composed *The Hebridean Polka*, a Hornpipe in 4 parts, in 1973.

IAN CRICHTON (1935–2000) of Marybank, Lewis, was an all-round traditional musician who learned to play the pipes as a boy. He also taught himself to play the keyboard accordion, and he composed many tunes for it, which he later transposed into pipe music. He described his music as having 'the heather and the peat, and Gaelic musical idioms, set aside with the musical trickery of the Gael', adding modestly 'Well, you see, it just comes to me naturally'. He made a 4/4 March called *Memories of 'Wee Donald'*.

In the 1990s he published a series of four books of traditional music with the title *Puirt a Eilean Leodhais (Tunes of the Island of Lewis)*, and also 47 tunes specifically for pipers. He composed them in the 'boxie' style, and had the grace-noting added later 'by a piper' when they were transposed into pipe notation.

He died in 2000, after suffering lengthy illness. In the obituary to his friend in the *Piping Times*, Finlay MacRae wrote: 'Every now and again, the broad spectrum of music is enriched by individuals of unique talent. They give their homeland, and indeed our nation, fresh composition, full of surprise and graceful melody. Ian Crichton was such a composer. From his surprisingly spontaneous flow of notes, the traditional music of Scotland, and the Hebrides in particular, was enriched to overflowing.'

A Mounted Pipe Band

In 1996 the *Piping Times* published a photograph of the mounted pipe band of the 1st CMRs (Camerons' Mounted Regiment?). It elicited a letter from DONALD MORRISON, living in the Isle of Lewis. He identified his father ANGUS MORRISON who was the Pipe Major, as well as Lewis pipers MURDO MACLEOD, Tong, and RODDY MACKAY, Galson, also JOHN MACKAY, Tolsta Chaolais (near Callanish, on the west side of Lewis). He said that Murdo was killed in action, and when the first Pipe Major was killed as well, Angus Morrison took over. Roddy Mac-Kay composed the tune *Glen Galson*, published in Donald MacLeod's second book. Donald Morrison said he was still playing the pipes presented to his father by the Colonel of the regiment when they were discharged after the war. Donald MacDonald in his book *Lewis, a History of the Island* has little mention of piping, but he does say that the Pipe Major of the band which led the Highland Division into Tunis at the end of the North Africa Campaign was a Lewisman. Was it Angus Morrison? Or Snowy MacLeod?

Neil MacRitchie (1952–2002)

NEIL MACRITCHIE was not himself a piper, but he immersed himself in piping when his son DON NEIL began lessons with Iain Morrison, proving himself an apt pupil. Neil became Secretary of the Lewis and Harris Piping Society, and was largely responsible for running the Donald MacLeod Memorial Competition. This meant a great deal of work not only to organise the weekend itself but constantly seeking sponsorship and raising funds for the event.

He worked as a layout and design man for the *Stornoway Gazette*, showing his professional skills when he redesigned the Pipe Band magazine for the RSPBA, which at once increased its circulation.

On the day of his funeral, Stornoway came to a standstill in tribute to 'a fine, decent man', who made a big contribution to Lewis piping.

The *Piper Press* in March 1998 had a picture of JOHN KENNEDY from Lewis, playing *Crossing the Minch* on board the Stornoway ferry, on a Piob Beag electronic bagpipe, designed and manufactured in the Highlands by Iolaire Technologies. John comes from a Lewis family who have been pipers for seven generations.

MARGARET STEWART, the fine Gaelic singer from Lewis, Mod Gold Medallist in 1993, has made a name for herself singing Gaelic piobaireachd songs, with and without accompaniment from Allan MacDonald. They have issued a CD, *Fhuair Mi Pog* (1998). Margaret also wrote an article for the *Piping Times* about the relation of piobaireachd music and Gaelic song, from a singer's point of view. She had piping lessons at school, and regrets not having followed them up.

She tells how her grandfather Donald Graham ('Domhnall Piugh') in Upper Coll, Lewis, used to comfort the grandchildren if they had fallen or were upset, by singing to them a song to the tune of *MacIntosh's Lament*. The Gaelic words meant 'They lifted you, they knocked you down, they broke your bones . . .' (*Thog iad thu, leag iad thu, bhris' iad do chnamhan . . .*). The children did not know the tune was *MacIntosh's Lament*: to them, it was the song that 'Shen' sang to them when they needed comfort, and Margaret was grown-up before she identified it. She says 'I had been aware of some of the better known piobaireachd songs, such as *Cro Chinn t-Saile (Return to Kintail)*, *Uamh an Oir (Cave of Gold)*, *Mhnathan a Ghlinne (Women of this Glen,* also known as *Carles Wi' the Breeks)*, etc. but I had absolutely no idea that this lovely little song was related to *MacIntosh's Lament*, probably the oldest piece of ceol mor in the piper's repertoire.'

The discovery was, to her, an eye-opener, and she began to look into the history of the little songs of her childhood, finding, to her delight, that many of them related to the great music of the bagpipe. She believes that the singing of the songs inspired many of the older piobaireachd compositions, and to Margaret, some of the titles, or secondary names, of the works suggest the first lines of songs: she gives as examples *The Big Spree*, known as *Tha'n daorach ort 's fhearr'd thu 'n cadal, You're Drunk, You'd Better Sleep*, and *My Dearest on Earth, Give Me Your Kiss – Thoir Dhomh Do Phog, A Luaidh Mo Chridh*.

In addition she quotes the titles of songs now 'generally accepted as being piobaireachd songs' such as *'S Ann Aig Ceann Traigh Ghruinneart (At the Head of Gruineard Shore)*, *Cul Buidhe, Cul Ban (Blond Hair, Fair Hair)*, and *Caidil a Mhorag, Caidil a Mhorag (Sleep, Morag, Sleep, Morag)*. Whether these were the basis of piobaireachd in the sense of ceol mor, or in the wider Gaelic sense of 'pipe music', might be debated.

It is interesting that Margaret, brought up steeped in the Gaelic tradition of Lewis, says she and others around her had a 'hereditary respect' for ceol mor, but 'disregarded it', because of their lack of understanding of its construction, melody or rhythm. Even to them, the native Gaels in their homeland, it seemed 'strange, inaccessible and rather foreign' – and incompatible with the rest of their Gaelic culture of poetry and song. Only when Margaret studied it was she able to appreciate it fully, and 'fit it in with the rest of my gaelic baggage'. She deplores, however, the modern style of playing which has rejected the rich ornamentation of former days – and seems to have discarded the musical content with it.

Margaret's experience suggests that, in Lewis at least, the tradition of Gaelic song survived the repression of the church better than did the playing of ceol mor – if indeed there was a tradition of ceol mor there. We may infer that there probably was, but there is no tangible proof, not even in the oral tradition. Most of those Lewismen known to have played it can be shown to have learned it outwith their island.

Roddy MacLeod and Niall Matheson

RODDY MACLEOD, Director of Piping at the Piping Centre in Glasgow, is yet another first-class piper whose roots are in Lewis. His line of MacLeods comes from Balallan, twelve miles south-west of Stornoway, on the main road from Stornoway to Harris, in the north side of Loch Erisort. NIALL MATHESON, another fine piobaireachd player, may be related, as his grandmother was a MacLeod from Balallan – which is not a big village. There must be some powerful piobaireachd genes at large in Balallan.

The Lewis Pipe Band

The Lewis Pipe Band was started in 1904, with six pipers and three drummers. It is thought that most of them had been trained by the military outwith Lewis, but certainly one of them, piper (later to become treasurer) and founder member, John Morrison, then of Goat-hill Farm and later of Assynt House, was Lewis born and bred, and learned his piping on the island (see above).

Another stalwart supporter was Willie Ross, Soval, who composed the 2/4 March in four parts, *The Lewis Pipe Band,* not long after the band was first formed.

The original band wore Hunting Stewart tartan and Matheson badges presented by Major Duncan Matheson of Lews Castle. The tunics were bottle green, and each band member paid 6d per week into the funds.

The Constitution of the band stated that no charge would ever be made for their services, and they have kept to this – though donations are always welcome.

In the 1920s and early 1930s, the band practice was always on a Monday night, because that was a half-day for the many band members employed in the herring curing and kippering trade (because there would have been no fishing on the Sabbath).

In 1989, an excellent booklet was published, *The Lewis Pipe Band, A Short History,* written by JOHN MACLEAN ('Johnny Lux'), who unfortunately died when the booklet was still at the printers. After 37 years' service as Secretary of the band, he had been presented with a silver-mounted walking stick – which converted into a practice chanter. He had an encyclopaedic knowledge of the band and its history, and his first-rate booklet is a fitting memorial. It is packed with detail and photographs, including one of John Morrison in 1904, with the first Pipe Major, CHARLES MACIVER (see above).

Charles came from the village of Laxdale, which always had a large number of band players (in the 1920s there were so many that after each parade they would form a 'mini-band' to march home in style, still playing). One of Charles' pupils, ANGUS MACLEOD, emigrated to America and founded a pipe band in Buffalo, New York, calling it the Charles MacIver Memorial Pipe Band.

The booklet lists all the original band members and the committee, all the Pipe Majors through the years, and 90 of the pipers who have played in the band, and 56 drummers. It outlines the development of the band through the years, and gives snippets from the Minutes and accounts (e.g. in 1910, two shillings outlaid 'for a pair of pants for Piper D. Murray for wearing under his kilt'). Initially the money to launch the band was raised by local sponsorship, by holding concerts – and every band member paid in a shilling per fortnight.

The band's place in community life is illustrated by a comment, written by an ornithologist visitor, Robert Atkinson, in 1936. He and his colleague, returning from North Rona, were catching the mailboat from Stornoway on their way home. He wrote of 'the nightly event of the town, departure of the mailboat, the singing and waving and the bagpipes and evidence of whisky'.

Many members of the band were former Seaforths, and one of its patrons was Donald MacLeod himself, whose brother Angus was Pipe Major of the Lewis band, as their father had been before them. Many in Lewis reckoned Angus was every bit as good a piper as Donald.

All institutions in small communities have their problems, and the Lewis band is no exception, but has surmounted them to become 'one of the oldest of its kind' in the country. In the 1960s, it reached a low ebb, with few players and the uniforms in a bad state; but the local

Rotary Club made a determined effort to revive the band, arranging a scheme whereby (almost) all employees in Stornoway paid 6d into the funds every week, voluntarily, and Donnie 'Leody' MacLeod undertook to go round all the businesses of the town on Friday nights, collecting the money. Within 6 months, there was enough to pay for 21 uniforms, four pipes, 3 side and 2 tenor drums, as well as a bass drum, at a total cost of £1,740. The *Stornoway Gazette* points out that the cost of the 21 uniforms was £1,345, which is £338 less than the price of one piper's uniform today.

In recognition of the long service to the band of John Morrison, Assynt House, and the generous donation from his firm, Bain, Morrison and Co, Timber Merchants, the new uniforms were in Ancient Morrison tartan, with the Morrison crest for the cap-badge and plaid brooch.

The band receives no sponsorship money, and has always been supported by local donation. It is also unique in that band members still parade in full No.1 Dress. The Pipe Major's pipes were presented to the band in the late 1960s, and are fully ivory mounted. In 1998, the family of the late Pipe Major, Angus 'Boxer' MacLeod, gave a donation which was used to refurbish the pipes and add silver tuning slides. A silver plaque commemorates the MacLeod piping family: the famous 'Wee Donald' ('Dotts' or 'Donald Doyle' in Lewis), his brother Angus, considered to be just as good a player, and their father, Pipe Major Donald Doyle MacLeod. All three were playing members of the Lewis pipe band.

John Morrison's firm donated the Pipe Major's banner in 1970. Of blue silk, backed with band tartan, it carries the embroidered band crest and the initials J.M.

Two long-time stalwarts of the band gave donations for dirks for the Pipe and Drum Majors and Sergeants: Johnny 'Lux' MacLean and John 'The Chemist' MacDonald, both of whom were Life Members. The landlord of the Lewis Bar, Kenny Sutherland, also contributed towards the cost of these dirks.

The resplendent re-formed band had its first parade on Saturday 25th June 1966; and in July 2004 the band celebrated its centenary, starting with a parade in Stornoway, and following up with performances along with the Isle of Skye pipe band. Later both bands paraded in Tarbert, Harris.

In 2005 the band played at the Hebridean Celtic Festival, and it is hoped to continue this in future festivals.

The present President, Colin Scott MacKenzie, comments that 'it is quite frankly fun to belong to a supremely self-confident local body, run by locals for locals, and members display at all times a fine and very proper conceit of themselves and their art. In short, they don't give a hang for much else than their music and their public'. And quite right too. This independence finds other forms: their Pipe Major, PETER MACKAY, described drilling the band as 'like trying to herd a cat'.

Sources

Lewis Pipe Band booklet
Colin Scott MacKenzie
Piping Times
Stornoway Gazette 'Back in the Day', Issue 5, May–June 2006

Bibliography

[*TGSI* = *Transactions of the Gaelic Society of Inverness*]

BANGOR JONES, Malcolm 1997: *Population Lists of Assynt, 1638–1811.*

BASSIN, Ethel (ed. Derek Bowman) 1977: *The Old Songs of Skye – Frances Tolmie and her Circle.*

BOSWELL, James 1785: *The Journal of a Tour to the Hebrides with Samuel Johnson.*

BRANIGAN, Keith 2012: *Barra: Episodes from an Island's History.*

BUISMAN, Frans and WRIGHT, Andrew (eds) 2001: *The MacArthur– MacGregor Manuscript of Piobaireachd (1820).*

BURNETT, Ray 1986: *Benbecula.*

BUXTON, Ben 1995: *Mingulay: An Island and Its People.*

CAMPBELL, Lord Archibald 1885: *Records of Argyll, Legends, Traditions and Recollections of Argyllshire Highlanders.*

CAMPBELL, Jeannie 2001: *Highland Bagpipe Makers* (2nd edition 2011).

CAMPBELL, John Lorne (ed. and trans.) 1959: *Tales from Barra Told by the Coddy (John MacPherson).*

CAMPBELL, John Lorne 2000: *A Very Civil People: Hebridean Folk, History and Tradition.*

CAMPBELL, Robert Bruce 2000: *The Maccrimmon Pipers of Skye: A Tradition Under Siege.*

CAMPEY, Lucille H. 2004: *After the Hector: The Scottish Pioneers of Nova Scotia and Cape Breton 1773–1852.*

CAMPSIE, Alistair 1980: *The MacCrimmon Legend: the Madness of Angus MacKay.*

CANNON, Roderick 1980: *A Bibliography of Bagpipe Music.*

CANNON, Roderick 1988: *The Highland Bagpipe and its Music.*

CHEAPE, Hugh 1999: 'The MacCrimmon Piping Dynasty and its Origins', in *TGSI* LXII.

CONNOLLY, S.J. (ed.) 1998: *The Oxford Companion to Irish History*.

CRAIG, David 1990: *On the Crofters' Trail*.

CREIGHTON, Helen and MACLEOD, Calum (eds) 1979: *Gaelic Songs of Nova Scotia*.

DICKSON, Joshua 2006: *When Piping Was Strong*.

DICKSON, Joshua (ed.) 2009: *The Highland Bagpipe, Music, History, Tradition*.

DONALDSON, M.E.M. 1935: *Scotland's Suppressed History*.

DONALDSON, William 2000: *The Highland Pipe and Scottish Society 1750–1950*.

EAGLE, Raymond 1991: *Seton Gordon, the Life and Times of a Highland Gentleman*.

1886–77: *Fasti Ecclesiae Scoticanae: the Succession of Ministers in the Parish Churches of Scotland from the Reformation AD 1560 to the Present Time* (13 volumes).

FIONN (WHYTE, Henry) between 1900 and 1907: *Historic, Biographic and Legendary Notes* to tunes in Glen's Collection, 5th edition.

FLOWER, Robin 1947: *The Irish Tradition*.

FOSTER, R.F. (ed.) 1989: *The Oxford Illustrated History of Ireland*.

FRASER, the Rev. James 1905: *The Wardlaw Manuscript, Chronicles of the Frasers, 916–1674* (Scottish Historical Society, ed. William MacKay).

FRASER, Simon – see ORME, Barrie M., below.

GEDDES, Arthur 1955: *The Isle of Harris and Lewis*.

GIBSON, John 1998: *Traditional Gaelic Bagpiping 1745–1945*.

GIBSON, John 2002: *Old and New World Highland Bagpiping*.

GORDON, Seton 1925: *Hebridean Memories* (re-issued 1995).

GORDON, Seton 1950: *Afoot in the Hebrides*.

GRANT, I.F. 1959: *The MacLeods, the History of a Clan*.

GRIMBLE, Ian 1965: *Chief of MacKay*.

HADDOW, Alec 1982: *The History and Structure of Ceol Mor*.

HALFORD-MACLEOD, Ruairidh 1986: 'Everyone who has an intrigue hopes it should not be known: Lord Loudon and Anne Mackintosh, an intrigue of the '45', in *TGSI* LV.

HALFORD-MACLEOD, Ruairidh 2001: 'Donald Ruadh MacCrummen', talk to the Piobaireachd Society Conference.

HIGHLAND PAPERS, volume II, ed. J.R.N. MacPhail 1916.

HILL, J. Michael 1993: *Fire and Sword, Sorley Boy MacDonnell and the Rise of Clan Ian Mor 1538-90.*

HUTCHINSON, Roger 2010: *Father Allan: the Life and Legacy of a Hebridean Priest.*

HUTCHINSON, Roger: article on Donald Archie MacDonald, in the *West Highland Free Press.*

JOHNSON, Samuel 1775: *A Journey to the Western Isles of Scotland.*

KNOX, John 1786 (reprint 1970): *Tour of the Highlands of Scotland and the Hebride Isles, A Report to the British Society for Extending the Fisheries, 1786.*

LAWSON, Alan 1987: *A Country Called Stratherrick* (2nd edition).

LAWSON, Bill 2000: *Croft History in North Uist,* volume 3 in series of Croft Histories.

LAWSON, Bill 2002: *Harris in History and Legend.*

LAWSON, Bill 2011: *Lewis in History and Legend: East Coast.*

LETFORD, Stuart, 2004: *The Little Book of Piping Quotations.*

LOVE, Dane 2007: *Jacobite Stories.*

MACARTHUR MANUSCRIPT: see BUISMAN, Frans.

MACASKILL, Norman, 1990s: *A History of Assynt* (unpublished).

MACCULLOCH, John 1819: *A Description of the Western Isles of Scotland.*

MACCURDY, Edward 1942-50: 'Norman MacLeod – Caraid nan Gael' in *TGSI* XXXIX–XL.

MACDONALD, Rev. A. (ed.) 1894: *The Uist Collection: The Poems and Songs of John MacCodrum, Archibald MacDonald and some of the Minor Uist Bards.*

MACDONALD, Rev. A. and Rev. A. 1896: *The Clan Donald* (3 vols).

MACDONALD, Rev. A. and Rev. A. 1911: *The MacDonald Collection of Gaelic Poetry.*

MACDONALD, D.A. 1974: 'An Dubh Gleannach' in *Tocher* 15.

MACDONALD, Donald 1978: *Lewis, A History of the Island* (reprint 1983).

MACDONALD, Emily 1900s: *Twenty Years of Hebridean Memories.*

MACDONALD, Dr K.N. 1900: *MacDonald Bards from Mediaeval Times.*

MACDONALD, Stuart 1994: *Back to Lochaber.*

MACDONALD, William M. 1993: *The Glencoe Collection* Book I.

MACDONALD, William M. 1999: *The Glencoe Collection* Book II.

MACDOUGALL, Jean 1984: *Highland Postbag, The Correspondence of Four MacDougall Chiefs 1715–1865.*

MCHARDY, Stuart 2005: *The Well of Heads and Other Tales of the Scottish Clans.*

MACINNES, John 1985: 'Gleanings from Raasay Tradition' in *TGSI* LVI.

MACKAY, Angus: Manuscripts, now in the National Library of Scotland, Edinburgh (MSS 3753-4).

MACKAY, Angus A. 1906: *The Book of MacKay.*

MACKENZIE, Alexander 1889: *History of the MacLeods.*

MACKENZIE, Alexander 1894: *History of the MacKenzies.*

MACKENZIE, Alexander 1897: 'Mairi Nighean Alasdair Ruaidh', in *TGSI* XXII.

MACKENZIE, Alexander 1898: *History of the Munros of Fowlis.*

MACKENZIE, John 1877: *Sair Obair nan Bard Gaelach, or the Beauties of Gaelic Poetry.*

MACKINNON, John 1995: *The MacKinnons of Kyle and their Connections.*

MACLEAN, John 1989: *Handbook of the Lewis Pipe Band.*

MACLEAN, J.P. 1889: *History of the Clan MacLean.*

MACLEAN, Somhairle 1974: 'Some Raasay Traditions', in *TGSI* XLIX.

MACLEOD, Dugald C. c.1960: *Isle of Skye Collection of Bagpipe Music.*

MACLEOD, Fred T. 1933: *The MacCrimmons of Skye, Hereditary Pipers to the MacLeods of Dunvegan.*

MACLEOD, John 2010: *None Dare Oppose, the Laird, the Beast and the People of Lewis.*

MACLEOD, Norma 2002: *Raasay, The Island and its People.*

MACLEOD, the Rev. Dr Norman 1899: *Caraid nan Gaidheal.*

MACLEOD, Canon R.C. 1938-9: *The Book of Dunvegan* (2 volumes).

MACLYSAGHT, Edward 1957: *Irish Families.*

MACLYSAGHT, Edward 1964: *The Surnames of Ireland.*

MACPHERSON, Duncan 1964: *Where I Belong.*

MACRAE, Norman (undated) : *Dingwall's History of a Thousand Years.*

MARSHALL, Rosalin 1973: *The Days of Duchess Anne.*

MARTIN, Martin 1697: *A Voyage to St Kilda.*

MARTIN, Martin 1703: *A Description of the Western Isles of Scotland.*

MATHESON, William 1938: *The Songs of John MacCodrum.*

MATHESON, William 1951: 'Notes on Mary MacLeod' in *TGSI* XLI.

MATHESON, William 1970: *An Clarsair Dall, The Blind Harper.*

MATHESON, William 1982: 'Some Notes on North Uist Familes', in *TGSI* LII.

MELDRUM, R. (date unknown): *Reminiscences.*

MIKET, Roger 1998: *Glenelg, Kintail and Lochalsh, Gateway to the Isle of Skye. An Historical Introduction.*

MITCHELL, Ian 1999: *The Isles of the West.*

MITCHELL, Joseph 1883–4: *Reminiscences of My Life in the Highlands (2 volumes).*

MORRISON, Alick 1962: 'The Contullich Papers', in *TGSI* XLIII.

MORRISON, Alick 1966: 'The Contullich Papers 1706–20', in *TGSI* XLIII.

MORRISON, Alick 1967: 'Harris Estate Papers, 1724–1754', in *TGSI* XLIV.

MORRISON, Alick 1974: *The MacLeods: The Genealogy of a Clan* (revised 1988-90).

MORRISON, Alick 1977: 'The Accounts of a Doer', in *TGSI* L.

MORRISON, Alick 1978: 'Early Harris Estate Papers 1679–1703', in *TGSI* LI.

MORRISON, Alick 1979: 'The Feu of Berneray (1767) and the Sale of Harris (1779)', in *TGSI* LI.

MUNRO, R.W. 1962: 'Some Hebridean Hosts: The Men Behind the Travellers' Tales', in *TGSI* XLIII.

NICOLSON, Alexander 1930, revised by Alisdair MacLean 1994: *A History of Skye* (re-issued 2012).

NOTICES OF PIPERS in the *Piping Times* throughout 1968, originally compiled by Captain John MacLennan, with later additions by Archibald Campbell, Ian MacKay-Scobie, D.R. MacLennan and others.

O'BAOILL, Colm 1971: 'Some Irish Harpers in Scotland' in *TGSI* XLVII.

O'DONOVAN, John (ed.) 1856: *Annals of the Kingdom of Ireland by the Four Masters*, volume V.

OLDHAM, Tony 1975: *The Caves of Scotland.*

ORME, Barrie M. 1985: *The Piobaireachd of Simon Fraser with Canntaireachd* (second edition).

OSBORNE, Brian H. 2001: *The Last of the Chiefs: Alasdair Ranaldson MacDonnell of Glengarry 1773–1828.*

PARKER, Derek 2007: *Outback, The Discovery of Australia's Interior.*

PENNANT, Thomas 1774: *A Tour in Scotland and Voyage to the Hebrides.*

POULTER, G.C.B. and FISHER, C.P. 1936: *The MacCrimmon Family 1500–1936.*

POULTER, George C.B. 1936: *The MacCrimmon Family Origin.*

PREBBLE, John 1961: *Culloden.*

PREBBLE, John 1966: *Glencoe.*

PRESBYTERY RECORDS OF INVERNESS AND DINGWALL.

QUEEN'S OWN HIGHLANDERS 1983: *The Cabar Feidh Collection: Pipe Music of the Queen's Own Highlanders.*

REA, Frederick 1964: *A School in South Uist, Reminiscences of a Hebridean Schoolmaster, 1890–1913.*

REGISTER OF THE GREAT SEAL, ed. J.H. Stevenson 1984.

RICHARDSON, Frank and MACNEILL, Seumas 1987: *Piobaireachd and Its Interpretation.*

ROBERTSON, James 2001: *The Mull Diaries of James Robertson 1842-6,* transcribed by J.B. Loudon.

ROSE, D. Murray 1896: *Prince Charlie's Friends or Jacobite Indictments.*

ROSS, Alexander 1877: *Freemasonry in Inverness.*

SANGER, Keith 1992: 'MacCrimmon's Prentise – A Post graduate Student Perhaps' in the *Piping Times* 44/6, March 1992.

SANGER, Keith 2007: 'From the MacArthurs to Pipe Major Willie Gray, Glasgow Police', in the *Piping Times* 49/6, March 2007.

SCOTT, Hew 1885: 'Notices of the Ministers of the Prebytery of Tongue from 1726 to 1763 – from the Diary of the Rev. Murdoch MacDonald of Durness' in *TGSI* XI.

SETON, George 2000: *St Kilda.*

SHAW, Christina Byam (ed.) 1988: *Pigeon Holes of Memory, The Life and Times of Dr John MacKenzie (1803–1886).*

SHAW, Margaret Fay 1955: *Folksong and Folklore of South Uist.*

SHEARS, Barry W. 1986: *The Gathering of the Clans Collection.*

SHEARS, Barry 1995: *The Cape Breton Collection of Bagpipe Music.*

SHEARS, Barry 2008: *Dance to the Piper: The Highland Bagpipe in Nova Scotia.*

SIMPSON, Peter 1996: *The Independent Highland Companies 1603–1760.*

STATISTICAL ACCOUNT FOR ARGYLL, 1795, volume XIV.

STEVENSON, David 1980: *Highland Warrior, Alasdair MacColla and the Civil Wars.*

STEVENSON, David 1988: *The First Freemasons: Scotland's Early Lodges and their Members.*

TEMPERLEY, Alan 1988: *Tales of the North Coast.*

THOMSON, Derick 1974: *An Introduction to Gaelic Poetry.*

THOMPSON, Derick (ed.) 1983: *The Companion to Gaelic Scotland.*

WALKER, John 1980: *Report on the Hebrides of 1764 and 1771* (ed. Margaret M. MacKay).

WATSON, J.C. 1934: *The Gaelic Songs of Mary MacLeod.*

WATSON, W.J. (ed.) 1937: *The Book of the Dean of Lismore* (Scottish Gaelic Texts Society).

WILLIAMS, Scott 2000: *Pipers of Nova Scotia, Biographical Sketches 1773 to 2000.*

Index of People

In this index Mac, Mc and M' are all treated as Mac.

Abbreviations: Aus = Australia, br. = brother, Cam H = Cameron Highlanders, f = father, gf. = grandfather, gs. = grandson, HLI = Highland Light Infantry, jr = junior, m. = mother, NI = Northern Ireland, NS = Nova Scotia, NU = North Uist, NZ = New Zealand, P/M = Pipe Major, QOH = Queen's Own Highlanders, s. = son, sis. = sister, sr = senior, SU = South Uist, Suth = Sutherland, w. = wife

Index of Places

The former Scottish county names are used, rather than the wider regional names.

Index of Tunes, Songs and Poems

Abbreviations: GA = Gaelic Air, HP = Hornpipe, J = Jig, M = March, P = Piobaireachd, R = Reel, RM = Retreat March, S = Strathspey, SA = Slow Air, SM = Slow March

This index does not include the alphabetical lists of works associated with a specific island or islands, or the compositions of a piper. These may be found as follows: